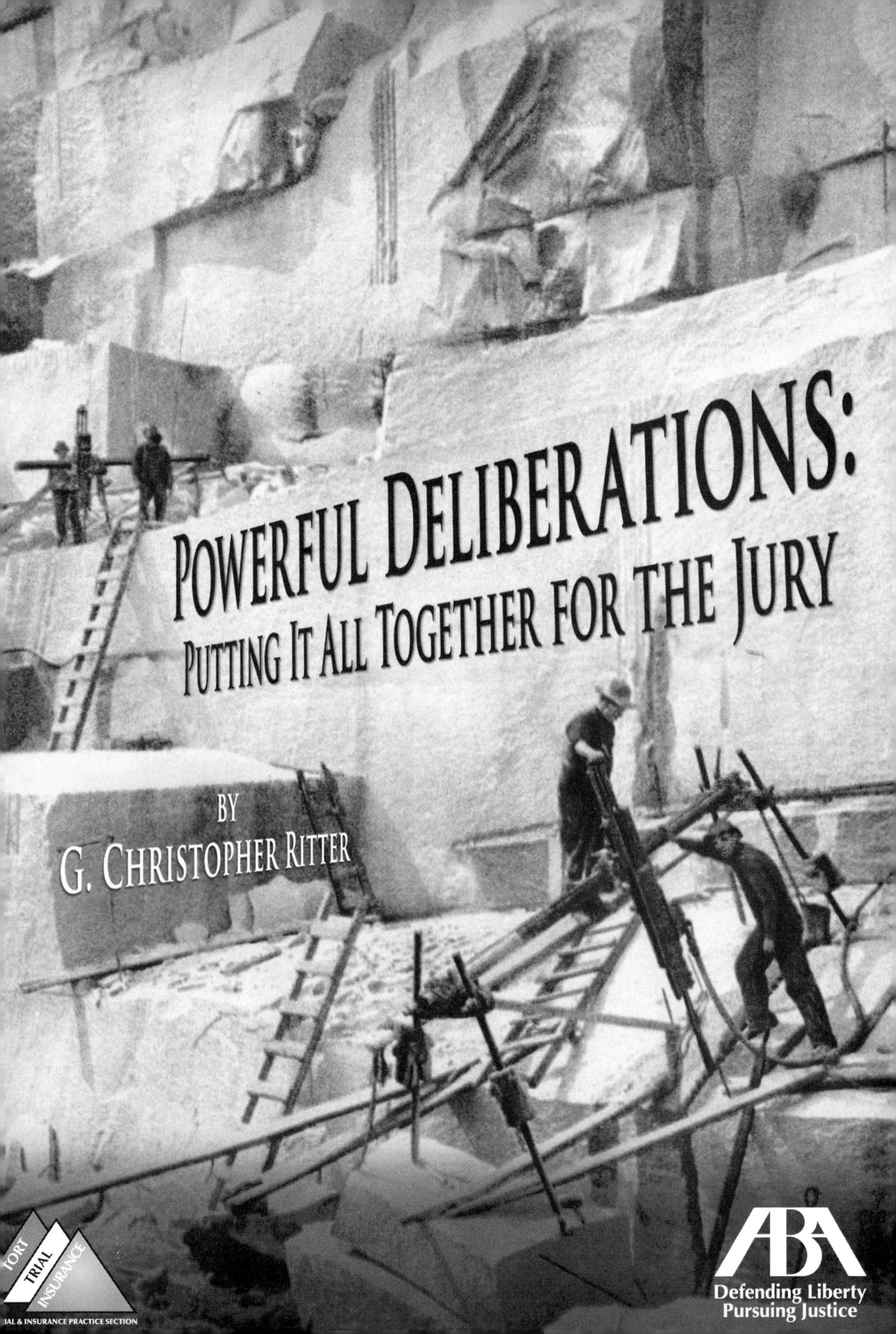

Powerful Deliberations:
Putting It All Together for the Jury

By

G. Christopher Ritter

Tort Trial Insurance
IAL & INSURANCE PRACTICE SECTION

ABA
Defending Liberty
Pursuing Justice

Cover design by ABA Publishing.

Printed in the United States of America

13 12 11 10 09 5 4 3 2 1

Library of Congress Cataloging-in-Publication Data

Ritter, G. Christopher.

Powerful deliberations : putting it all together for the jury / by G. Christopher Ritter.—1st ed.

p. cm.

Includes bibliographical references and index.

ISBN 978-1-60442-378-5

1. Jury—United States. 2. Jurors—United States. 3. Trial practice—United States. I. Title.

KF8972.R58 2009

347.73'752—dc22

2009012504

Discounts are available for books ordered in bulk. Special consideration is given to state bars, CLE programs, and other bar-related organizations. Inquire at Book Publishing, ABA Publishing, American Bar Association, 321 North Clark Street, Chicago, Illinois 60654-7598.

www.ababooks.org

"[R]emember that simplicity is complex . . . but one could have learned this from a glow-worm."

Henry Adams

"Making the simple complicated is commonplace; making the complicated simple, awesomely simple, that's creativity."

Charles Mingus

To my most precious friends, all of whom I am proud to say are also my family: Jill Stevenson Ritter, C. Andrew Ritter, Kelsey S. Ritter, Erich S. Ritter, Dr. E. Gene Ritter, and Connie A. Ritter.

And—

To my partners at The Focal Point LLC, all of whom I am proud to say are also my dear friends: Andrew M. Spingler, Linda W. Spingler, Scott Hilton, and Guy Grogan.

Thanks for everything, including this book!

Contents

List of Illustrations

Chapter 2

Chapter 3

Chapter 5

Acknowledgments

It is hard to write a book. It is even harder to be around someone who spends most of his free time doing so. Fortunately, I am blessed to be surrounded by a group of highly talented and, perhaps even more importantly, exceedingly patient and generous people. To say that this volume would not exist without them is both true and, in many ways, it underscores how much each contributed to this effort.

My wife—Jill Stevenson Ritter—and our three children—Andrew, Kelsey, and Erich—deserve special thanks. I cannot possibly express how incredibly important each is to me and how each inspires me and makes me smile. What more can I say other than: Thanks and I love you all!

About ten years ago, I stopped actively trying cases and teaching law school to join the highly creative and dedicated group of people that is The Focal Point LLC. My partners—Andrew M. Spingler, Linda W. Spingler, Scott Hilton, and Guy Grogan—have undoubtedly had to assume greater professional burdens so I could observe, think, and write. Their willingness to do so is further proof of The Focal Point's ongoing commitment to remaining the country's thought leader in the areas of trial communication strategies and graphics. Thank you all!

I remain amazed at the talent and warm-heartedness of all of my colleagues at The Focal Point, including Yousif Abdelaziz, Marc Aure, Amie Bailey, Sandrine Bourrie, Lou Castro, Richard Cho, Lorraine de Guzman, Dennis Duong, Amy Falcione, Jim Falcione, Seth Friedman, Kathryn Golden, Chris Grimm, Lillian Koponen, Jill Kustner, Jason Lundy, Hem Ching Mai, Maureen McGraw, Susan Meads, Kate McEntee, Shana Rigelhaupt, Paul Roberts, Esther Saidman, Chris Sizemore, Michael Skrzypek, Aaron Stienstra, Mike Vendrell, Carolyn Webster, Pamela Wu, and Jeremy Young. These people make coming to work a pleasure and each contributes to a workplace where there is consistent respect and considerable laughter, even in those frequent moments of crisis in the middle of trials.

A special thanks to Marc Aure, Amie Bailey, Dennis Duong, and Guy Grogan. Dennis and Marc are the artists who worked on this project, and their excellent handiwork is spread throughout this book. Amie coordinated production efforts, and Guy oversaw all of these activities, a task he did with the cool head and steady hand that marks him as the pro that he is. Guy, Amie, Dennis, and Marc, I very much appreciate all of your hard work, talent, and good-natured jokes during our production meetings. You all made the process exceedingly enjoyable.

Esther Saidman, The Focal Point's marketing director, worked tirelessly with Ellen Blattel, Traci Stuart, and Chuck Brown of Blattel Communications in San Francisco in hundreds of different ways. One could not hope for a better team!

Good editors will continually amaze you. As the author, you read and reread your manuscript until you are convinced that it is darn near perfect. Just then, the editors come around and make the manuscript even better, often in ways you never could have done by yourself. I am lucky enough to have had five such editors. I have had the honor and pleasure of working with Richard Paszkiet for the past five years on two different books. As Deputy Director of American Bar Association Publishing, Rick's insight, humor, and dedication to his project/authors are extraordinary. His gentle editorial nudges (at just the right times) were crucial in getting this book not only completed but also done (relatively) on schedule. I have always admired and appreciated Susan Meads's ability as my executive assistant to keep my crazy schedule manageable. As part of writing this book, I was delighted (but not surprised) to discover that she is also a first-rate editor who is not afraid to let me know when a section "needs a lot more work" and when that same section (usually after considerable effort by Susan) "is *now* really good." Other than me, I think Susan has read and reread this manuscript more than any other person alive. Thanks, Susan! I also thank my very first editor, Gene Ritter, who, with the patience of a father and the experience that comes from sixty years of editing everything from newspaper articles to academic journals, has a keen eye for sections that need to be reworked and a very gentle way of letting you know this fact. His comments on this book are, as always, greatly appreciated. Jill Kustner has the sharpest eyes and most intense concentration of anyone I have ever met. She laboriously went through the manuscript, correcting mistakes that others had missed. Jill, your patience is much appreciated and admired. Your colleagues shake their heads in awe of your extraordinary ability. My fifth editor is actually a collection of the four people in my immediate family—Jill Stevenson Ritter, Erich Ritter, Andrew Ritter, and Kelsey Ritter. I can only guess at the number of times I have pulled them aside from whatever else they were doing and said "Listen to this, what do you think?" Their patience and willingness to offer suggestions instead of a slap along the side of my head is greatly appreciated! Erich deserves special thanks. He has had to field a disproportionate number of my questions since both of his older siblings are away at college.

To badly paraphrase Henry Adams, friendships "are born, not made." I consider this to be the case with respect to my friend and wise advisor,

Michael Colacchio, of Clear Impact in Corte Madera, California. Michael, I suspect that it will not be hard for you to recognize that a number of the concepts in this book trace their origins back to discussions we have had, fueled by large quantities of caffeine at Peet's Coffee and Tea and/or plates of Marty's Special at Henry's Hunan. For those readers unfamiliar with Peet's or Henry's Hunan, you have my sympathy.

I have had the pleasure of working with Susan Davis on numerous articles related to topics that found their way into this book. I have great appreciation for Susan's clear thinking and cogent writing style.

Over the past year, I have been working with Seth Friedman and Chris Sizemore of The Focal Point on a project we call "Creative Quality Control"—the purpose of which is to collect supporting material that users can rely on to maximize the impact of their trial graphics. Many of the insights I have gained from that work have worked their way into this volume. Special thanks to Seth for the enjoyable hours we have spent discussing these topics. *Qui docet discit.*

Many thanks to the people at American Bar Association Publishing. If I were to construct a timeline to illustrate all that needs to be done in order to turn a manuscript into an actual book, the timeline would be chock-full of entries listing the hard work and names of all of these people. You all make it look so easy to the rest of us. Thank you for what I know is actually a lot of hard work!

If you think (as I do) that this is a good-looking book, you have to thank (as I do) Jeff Lachina and Annie Beck of Lachina Publishing Services in Cleveland, who, once again, took care of the myriad of technical issues associated with producing the volume you now hold in your hands. Thank you Jeff, Annie, and all of the others at Lachina Publishing Services.

If we are what we eat, then I suspect that we write what we read. One somewhat unexpected inspiration for this book is the historian Henry Adams, and his autobiography, *The Education of Henry Adams.* There is a reason this book won the Pulitzer Prize in 1918 and then, eighty years later, was ranked first by Modern Library in its Top 100 Nonfiction Books of the Twentieth Century. I will be the first to admit that it is not an easy book to read, but it is well worth the effort. Each time I have read it, I have learned something new about human nature and politics—two subjects important to trial lawyers. Recently, I have supplemented my informal studies to include the scholarly (but highly readable and enjoyable) biography of Adams by Professor Edward Chalfant. I strongly encourage any serious student of human nature to read this trilogy: (1) *Both Sides of the Ocean,* (2) *Better in Darkness,* and (3) *Improvement of the World.* As with Henry Adams's works, Professor Chalfant's analysis is insightful and has far-ranging applications. He has graciously allowed me to include several such passages in this book. Edward, thank you for this favor and your always-appreciated correspondence, conversations, and wisdom.

Last, but definitely not least, I need to thank the people who have provided much of the raw material for this book over the years. I am very lucky to work with many of the country's best trial lawyers on a daily basis in pretrial strategy sessions and trial war rooms. While it is impossible to list each of these talented and dedicated professionals individually, I freely acknowledge that the basis of many sections of this book have come from the observations I have made while watching these lawyers think and work. Thanks to all of you, and here is to many more successes together!

Chris Ritter
The Focal Point LLC
Oakland, California
December 13, 2008

About the Author

Chris Ritter is a Member and Chief of Visual Trial Strategy at The Focal Point LLC, a company that develops trial strategies and courtroom presentations for litigators throughout the United States. The company's expertise is in making courtroom presentations more persuasive by making complex cases easier for judges and jurors to understand.

Chris graduated from the University of Chicago Law School and is an active member of The State Bar of California. Prior to joining The Focal Point, he was a partner at a major San Francisco law firm and served as a faculty member at University of California Hastings School of Law.

Considered an expert on trial communication strategy, Chris frequently speaks at seminars and gives workshops across the country. His first book, *Creating Winning Trial Strategies and Graphics,* published by the American Bar Association in 2004, is considered the leading work in the field. He can be reached at gcr@thefocalpoint.com.

Notes

At the outset, it is appropriate to offer a few observations:

- The examples offered in this book all come from real cases. I have carefully confined myself to discussing those matters that were made public in a trial, were published in the press, or have come from some other nonconfidential source. In instances where this was not possible, I either made no mention of confidential information or I changed the facts to make the original case unidentifiable.
- I have kept the number of examples of polished trial graphics to a minimum in this book. For a more complete analysis of this subject, with considerable color examples, please see my earlier book: *Creating Winning Trial Strategies and Graphics*, published by the American Bar Association in 2004.
- The cover of this book includes a photograph from 1906 titled "Channeling a New England Granite Quarry." It appears with the permission of George P. (Pat) and Peggy Perazzo of www.quarriesandbeyond.org.
- Late in the process of writing this book (too late to give it the credit that it deserves), I began reading Christopher Booker's outstanding book, *The Seven Basic Plots: Why We Tell Stories*, first published in 2004 by Continuum. This is a work that deserves greater exposure in the legal profession. I am afraid that many busy trial lawyers will be discouraged from reading this volume simply because of its length. Don't be! Not only is this an important book in the area of literary criticism, but I suspect it will eventually have an important impact on the way that trial lawyers go about assembling the stories they tell their jurors.

Preface

Hanging near my desk is a cartoon by Charles Barsotti (Ill. P-1). I cut the small black and white sketch out of *The New Yorker.* It shows two bartenders standing in front of a crowded bar. While not identical, all of the patrons look alike and they all seem to be nursing similar drinks. One of the bartenders looks rather satisfied with himself and is saying to the other, “In life as well as in politics, identify your base and treat ’em right.”

“In life as well as in politics, identify your base and treat ’em right.”

ILLUSTRATION P-1 This Is Equally Applicable to Jury Trials

I keep this cartoon near me while I work because Mr. Barsotti’s caption could equally have read, “In life as well as in politics *and jury trials,* identify your base and treat ’em right.”

While this advice should seem intuitively correct to every trial lawyer, it deserves a bit of an explanation. By identifying your base and treating ’em right, I am not advocating that you pander to your jury. In fact, I specifically advise against this approach. because most jurors are as capable of spotting insincerity in lawyers as they are in witnesses and politicians. It is second nature for jurors and they can do it from about a mile and a half away. They know you are being paid to be there and it does not take much for them to question (oftentimes unfairly) your sincerity. Do not make matters worse with blatant pandering.

Instead, I am suggesting that your case will undoubtedly benefit—and you will be better able to treat your base right—if you understand what the jurors need and the way things work during deliberations in the jury room. To do so you need to examine: (1) *the resources*—the raw materials that the jurors use to make their decision, and (2) *the process*—how the jurors convert this raw material into an end product, that is, a final verdict.

We bring a group of individuals (historically twelve) together to decide some of our most important societal and personal issues. Typically, jurors *appear* to share little, if anything, in common with one another. But for the fact that the judiciary has summoned them to court and required that they serve together on a jury, these individuals would probably have few reasons to spend any extended time together. Yet remarkably in the vast majority of cases the members of this diverse group not only reach a verdict, but they also—and I always find this amazing—do so either unanimously or by a statutorily mandated supermajority (e.g., nine out of twelve jurors).

Pause for a moment to ponder this last point—twelve previously unconnected common folk almost always agree unanimously or by a supermajority. My family of five, all of whom live under the same roof, cannot agree on which restaurant to go to for dinner or which movie to see, even by a simple majority, let alone unanimously.

This raises two crucial questions. First, how does the jury do it? Second, and perhaps more importantly, what can we as trial lawyers do to increase the chances that the jury will render its verdict in our client's favor? In the broadest sense, this book is devoted to answering these two questions.

The first section of this book, which I have titled "Examining Process," discusses the "why," "what," and "how" of jury deliberations. Specifically, Chapter 1 considers *why* the jury system, though much maligned by its critics, generally works. Is the system perfect? No, but more times than not, the jury gets to the right conclusion. Knowing why something as complex as the jury system works is not merely some academic exercise. Instead, such an understanding will hopefully increase your chances of knowing what really matters to jurors and *why*.

Chapter 2 examines *what* material jurors use to reach their decision. As we will see, this material is primarily of two types. The first comes prewired into the jurors as attitudes, preconceptions, existing knowledge, and so on. Some of this prewiring is common to more than one juror (in fact, some is common to *all* jurors) merely because we all share certain common beliefs.

The second type of material is prepared by the lawyer based on the particulars of the case. This is what I call the "Proto-Story." A Proto-Story is the best possible version of what each side believes happened. Each Proto-Story consists of four subparts—what I call the "Four Inputs":

- The Factual Strand
- The Persuasion Tools
- The Operating Instructions
- The Arguments

Chapter 3 examines *how* the jurors reach a verdict. Specifically, the chapter focuses on:

- How lawyers use the Four Inputs to create two Proto-Stories (one for each party)
- How the jurors combine portions of these Proto-Stories with their own personal attitudes, values, and knowledge to create 12 Secondary Stories (one for each juror)
- How, during deliberations, the jurors initially form at least two coalitions (one for each party), based on the outcome of their Secondary Stories
- How a select group of highly motivated jurors—people I call "Active Jurors"—emerges during deliberations and lobbies, cajoles, argues, and shapes the two coalitions into a single group whose members unanimously (or by a supermajority) agree on the same conclusion (even if the members cannot entirely agree as to why)

No one can win every case. Anyone who tells you they have a way to guarantee winning is either not being truthful or is hoping that you will enter into the same contract allegedly executed "at the crossroads" by the legendary blues guitarist Robert Johnson. Nevertheless, there are tools that you can use to increase your chances of prevailing. Section Two of this book discusses these tools. Specifically, Chapter 4 examines what these tools are and Chapter 5 outlines a Five-Step Process that my colleagues at The Focal Point and I have developed to create these tools for our clients at trial.

Highly qualified social scientists have conducted innumerable studies assessing why and how the jury system works. These valuable studies, which, for the most part, approach their conclusions empirically, are *not* the subject of this book; this book is based on more experiential observations. Both approaches, empirical and experiential, have their advantages; each supplements the other; neither should be ignored nor taken for granted.

More specifically, the experiential material upon which this book is based comes from two sources: (1) the work that my colleagues at The Focal Point and I have done over the past 20 years on more than 1,500 cases in virtually every area of the law, throughout the entire United States, with many of this country's very best trial lawyers; and (2) my work as trial counsel in several hundred other cases since graduating from the University of Chicago Law School in 1981.

Over the years, we at The Focal Point have learned a lot about what works (and some of what does not). It is our hope that this book will allow you to benefit from our experiences so that you have less difficulty during your next trial "identify[ing] your base and treat[ing] 'em right."

SECTION ONE

Examining Process

CHAPTER 1

Why the Jury System Works

A Tragic Case Study

There is an English common law maxim that "Bad facts make for bad law." To this, I would add something of a corollary: "Extreme cases evoke extreme responses."

Consistent with this, I have found that if you want to understand how jurors deliberate, there is no better way to do so than by observing how they respond in extreme cases. Extreme cases trigger extreme responses in jurors (in both mock and actual trials), and these extreme responses often reveal subtleties in the jury process that, while they exist in *all* cases, are not so easily observable in less dramatic and unusual circumstances.

Let me show you what I mean.

I once worked with a team of highly dedicated public defenders on a case involving a 22-year-old mother who drowned her three children, ages six, four, and two. At *precisely* 5:00 PM—the voice she heard in her head had warned her not to be even one minute late—she lovingly undressed her sons and threw each of them into the cold water off one of San Francisco Bay's most picturesque piers.

Only one of the bodies was ever recovered.

According to the mother, the voice she heard—which she knew with absolute and complete moral certainty belonged to God—repeatedly promised that if she threw her children into the bay, each of them would instantly become "part of His [God's] team in heaven" and they would have a much better place to live and grow up than the homeless shelter where they had been staying. The voice further assured her that she need not worry about missing her sons because she was always welcome to visit them in heaven anytime she wanted, merely by taking a San Francisco Muni bus there.

When she finished her appointed task, she made no effort to flee from the scene. Instead, she sat down and waited, convinced that the voice would return to tell her what to do next. Shortly after her arrest, the San Francisco police department tested her for drugs and found none, neither illegal ones nor the prescription medication she should have been taking for her severe schizophrenia.

The police recorded an interview with her a few hours after she was taken into custody. The videotape shows an unfocused and disheveled woman rambling on and on, often unable to concentrate on the questions posed to her. Sometimes she seems almost proud or honored (neither of those words accurately describes exactly what I observed on the tape but, in all candor, I am not sure I can better articulate her affect) that God had chosen her sons to grow up (for I am sure she never thought they had physically died) in such a wonderful place as heaven. Often she seemed confused as to why the police were detaining her—after all, she knew she was following an authority much higher than that which employed the two homicide detectives.

It was clear to anyone who observed her before, during, or after the incident that she truly loved her sons. Nowhere was this more evident than in the letters she sent to heaven pending her murder trial. Sometimes she sent the letters to God and sometimes directly to the boys themselves. She lovingly wrote messages and carefully illustrated them with crayon drawings of flowers, hearts, and rainbows. When she had finished each letter, she asked her lawyers to make sure that the letter was delivered to Heaven by way of one of the many airplanes that she believed routinely flew there.

For me, one of the most tragic aspects of this case was how easily this profoundly schizophrenic woman had fallen through the holes in society's safety net. At least seven times prior to the drownings, she had been involuntarily committed to a mental health facility because she was judged to be a likely threat to herself and others. Despite this, no one in authority ever bothered to take the children away from her and place them into some form of protective custody, nor did anyone seek to have her detained for more than three days for psychiatric treatment.

The focus of the defense's efforts were threefold: (1) to convince a jury not to convict the defendant of first-degree murder (which is how the district attorney charged her), (2) to keep this tragically schizophrenic woman out of a regular prison (which was where the district attorney was intent on sending her), and (3) to make sure that when the judicial process was over, she would be confined to a facility where she would receive the long-term psychiatric treatment she desperately needed.

After a trial that lasted several weeks, she was found to be insane. As of this writing, she remains confined in a center for the mentally ill and is responding well to treatment.

It probably goes without saying that this was an extreme case and, consistent with the corollary with which I started this chapter, it evoked extreme responses—responses from which I learned a lot about how individual jurors make their decisions.

As we prepared for trial, I told a variety of people a short version of the case background. I privately referred to these folks as my "mock mock-jurors." There was nothing scientific about my approach; my only concern was to find people similar to those who I anticipated would eventually be on the real jury.

Almost everyone I spoke with ultimately concluded that the defendant was insane. Frankly, this by itself neither fully surprised nor completely encouraged me. While I always tried to be factually accurate when I described the case, I was part of the defense team and I was convinced that, despite my best efforts to the contrary, at least some of my prejudice and advocacy naturally seeped through whenever I discussed the case with someone, including my mock mock-jurors.

However, there were four things that very much surprised me every time I spoke with one of these mock mock-jurors. First, after hearing the facts and having the opportunity to ask a few questions, virtually everyone I talked to not only came to a "verdict," but could also articulate why and how they had done so. This does not always happen in less extreme cases. Usually, a certain number of people who hear the facts have a hard time deciding who should win, and even those who come to such a conclusion sometimes have problems articulating how and/or why. Not so here; here, everyone seemed to have an opinion and virtually no one had a problem articulating what that opinion was and the basis for it.

Second, I was surprised how people responded to the jury instructions. Everyone I talked with wanted to know what the law was regarding insanity. However, there were two fundamental differences as to (1) when individual mock mock-jurors asked for this information and (2) how they used it once I gave it to them.

One group wanted to have the jury instructions right away; they wanted to know what the law was before they began to examine the evidence. These people treated the jury instructions as "directions." That is, they consulted the law before they acted and let the jury instructions *direct their conclusion*. The law was a road map as to what facts to consider, and these people stuck closely to it. Some of these mock mock-jurors clung to the jury instructions from the outset and leaned heavily on them. It sometimes seemed as if they were using such an approach as a way of buffering themselves from what was clearly a very emotionally charged situation.

The second group did not seem to care as much about the law until *after* they had completed much of their analytical process. In fact, these people tended to use the jury instructions as a way of *confirming the conclusion they had already drawn*. People in this second group reached an initial verdict as to the defendant's insanity with little or no reference to the law. Once they had done so, these mock mock-jurors perceived the instructions as "support" or "evidence" that their preliminary conclusion was the correct one. It was as if once they had initially reached a decision, they stepped back, looked at the jury instructions, and confirmed to themselves, "You see, even the law supports my conclusion."

It reminded me of the way my sons, Andrew and Erich, assemble build-it-yourself furniture purchased from warehouse stores. After working for several hours, they open the instruction book for the first time and use the picture of the finished piece as evidence that what they have already done has been done correctly. And you know what? They are usually right!

The differences between the ways these two groups used jury instructions are extremely important and will be examined again in greater detail when we review how jury instructions influence deliberations and examine Persuasion Tools, which rely heavily on jury instructions.

The third thing that surprised me about my mock mock-jurors was how many different paths they collectively took to get to the same conclusion (i.e., "She is insane."). I encountered at least five different paths or approaches to resolving this issue. For the most part, these paths were relatively distinct; yet no two were entirely contradictory, and I am confident that while advocates for each of the paths might not completely agree with some of the others' reasoning, none would have any problem pushing for a common result—"She is insane." (Ill. 1-1)

The final observation that struck me after talking to the mock mock-jurors was how amazingly transparent their various paths were and, thus, how easy these paths were to observe and follow. Again, I attribute this to the extreme nature of this case.

Let me give you some examples that outline the five different paths that my mock mock-jurors articulated.

The first path was heavily lined with emotion. To the people who followed this path, the drownings were part of a profound human crisis. It was Euripides's *Medea,* but even more tragic because this was a *real* life tragedy with honest-to-goodness dead children and a wholly irrational mother who, after listening to what she truly believed to be God, had caused her own children's deaths. The people who traveled on this first path to their ultimate conclusion (and I admit to being one of them when I was first asked to work on the case) reviewed a chronology of the defendant's life (first pregnant at 15, dropped out of school shortly thereafter, years of voices in her head lecturing to her about "spiritual warfare," tragic event compounding upon tragic event) and concluded their analysis with some kind of statement like, "Of course she is insane, how could any person *feel* otherwise?"

My friend and partner at The Focal Point, Scott Hilton, reached the same conclusion regarding the defendant's insanity, *but he got there by a wholly different route.* He wanted none of the "touchy-feely emotional stuff." It was not that he was unsympathetic; he had two children of similar ages to those the defendant had drowned, and was as disturbed by the story as any of the others who had heard it. But Scott was far more analytical in his approach to answering the question of whether the mother was insane. "Sure, this was a tragic situation," he would argue, "but that is not the question I am being asked to decide. I am being asked to resolve a far more precise issue, whether the defense has established, by a preponderance of the evidence, every element necessary to prove insanity."

Scott's approach was what I call "analysis by checklist." Scott is not a lawyer, but the path he took is a very common way for lawyers to analyze problems. Scott relied on the jury instructions early and repeatedly in his

ILLUSTRATION 1-1 The Jurors Got to the Same Verdict by Different Routes
Jurors often agree on the conclusion, but not necessarily on how they reached it. In the case of the mother who drowned her sons, jurors took at least five paths to arrive at the same conclusion—"She is legally insane."

analytical process. The jury instructions provided him with a checklist of the necessary elements he would need to check off if he were to find the defendant legally insane. You could almost see his brain systematically and logically going through the process, "Give me the checklist of what the law requires in order for a person to be found insane. What are the elements? OK, she meets that one and that one and that one. She meets all of these criteria; ergo I *think* she is clearly insane!"

To someone like me who was moved by emotions, Scott's methodical approach initially seemed unduly impersonal and analytical. Nevertheless, I agreed with (and welcomed) his final conclusion, which was the same as mine—"She is insane." If we had been on the same jury, we would have been advocating for the same side, but for different reasons—and frankly, this difference would have been of little consequence to me and would not have mattered to either of us in the long run, since we both ultimately would have been on the same team and would have been actively pushing for the same conclusion: "She is insane."

There was a third group of mock mock-jurors who wanted to confirm objectively that an insanity plea was not an elaborate hoax or excuse being enacted by the mother. This group wanted to know that the mother's mental illness was legitimate and that there was scientific evidence to support that conclusion. It was as if they wanted to look into her brain and see *objective proof* that something had gone haywire.

At its core, such skepticism is related to the common problem that mental health professionals complain about when they encounter people who do not readily accept the fact that mental illness is as much a "real" medical problem as more familiar and visible physical ailments.

Fortunately, during our preparation for trial, one of the expert witnesses we were working with mentioned in passing that schizophrenia and Parkinson's disease were "related conditions." It turns out that while much remains undiscovered, scientists understand a bit about what causes schizophrenia. The principal culprits are two naturally occurring chemicals found in the brain; one is called acetylcholine and the other is dopamine.

According to our expert witness, these two chemicals are properly balanced in healthy brains. In abnormal brains, the imbalance of these two chemicals causes profound but strangely different symptoms. Too much acetylcholine and a corresponding deficiency in dopamine causes Parkinson's disease, the illness characterized by uncontrollable tremors. The opposite situation, that is, too much dopamine and too little acetylcholine, causes a profoundly different problem—schizophrenia.

The same two naturally occurring chemicals yield two entirely different results, depending on the relative concentrations of each chemical in an individual's brain. As one mock mock-juror pointed out, "Isn't it ironic that we accept without question that people with Parkinson's—people like Michael J. Fox and Mohammad Ali—have a disease, but we see schizophrenia as something less real and somehow not an actual illness." With this knowledge my mock mock-juror navigated a third route—a scientifically based route—through which he, too, *objectively* concluded that the defendant was insane.

As I previously mentioned, I consider one of the most tragic facts in the case to be the multitude of times this schizophrenic mother had been involuntarily hospitalized for her mental illness and the repeated failure of state and local agencies to protect her children from harm. As it turned out, I was not the only one who felt this way. The fact that "they" (as in, the unnamed people who are supposedly in charge of the world) had let this tragedy occur was enough to convince some of my mock mock-jurors to take a fourth route to the conclusion that the defendant was insane. If they could do anything about it, this group of mock mock-jurors was going to make darn sure the defendant would go to a mental health facility and not to a regular prison.

There were at least two interesting elements in what I could glean from the people in this group. First, there was an undercurrent of rebellion in their decision, a kind of feeling that I would characterize as a form of protest that stemmed from the idea that since "they" (again, this nebulous collection of people charged with responsibility) had failed to protect the defendant and her children, these mock mock-jurors were not afraid of taking action on the mother's behalf. Not exactly an example of "jury nullification," but it had that same feel to it.

Second, some of these mock mock-jurors seemed to be motivated more by doing what they thought was "right" than by any detailed analysis of what constituted legal insanity. Let me be perfectly clear on an important point—I am convinced that these folks absolutely believed the defendant was legally insane, but they came to that decision without much detailed analysis of the law. Instead, their process evolved through their innate sense of justice (flavored by anger at and distrust of those who they believed could have prevented this tragedy, but had failed to do so).

I showed a copy of the interrogation tape to my mother who, prior to retiring, had spent many years as a highly skilled pediatric nurse. She had watched an entire generation of children grow up, have children of their own, and bring another set of patients into the doctor's office. Over the years, she had developed a reputation of not only caring a great deal for children, but also of having a very commonsense way of dealing with hysterical parents who were convinced that their precious bundles of joy had contracted the bubonic plague at 2:00 AM (trust me, it always seemed to be 2:00 AM) on what inevitably was either on a Saturday or Sunday.

Prior to watching the interrogation tape, my mother was rather skeptical about my suggestion that the defendant was insane. My mother has a strong belief that people should be responsible for their behavior. She also strongly sympathized with the dead children and instinctively believed that anyone who hurt children should be severely punished—something she was fully willing to do in this case.

About ten minutes into the tape, after silently watching the defendant's erratic behavior, my mother suddenly turned to me and we had the following conversation:

"Is she on [illegal] drugs?" my mother asked.

"No," I replied.

"You sure?" she asked.

"Absolutely!" I replied. "That was the first thing the cops did—tested her for drugs. There weren't any."

"Then, she is clearly insane," said my mother conclusively and without a hint of doubt in her voice.

"How do you know?" I asked, somewhat taken aback with the certainty and relative speed with which she made her decision, particularly because of her prior assertion that anyone who hurt children was evil and deserved the worst possible punishment.

"Common sense!" she replied. "No one who is not on [illegal] drugs behaves that way unless they're insane!"

Common sense, oh yeah . . . common sense—that thing that most of us lost around the third week of law school. *Common sense.* Another mystery solved by my mother using common sense.

I tell you this story about my mother because this form of reasoning was the fifth path that I noticed my mock mock-jurors took to resolve the issue of whether the defendant was insane—these people used what they would characterize as their common sense.

So, at the conclusion of my limited study of potential juror types, I had found five different groups; each had a different reason for doing so, but all agreed on the fact that the defendant was insane.[1] If all of my mock mock-jurors had been brought together in a single room, I have no doubt that they would have easily banded together to support the same conclusion—"She is insane!" I am further convinced that none would have had any problem doing so, despite the fact that they might not agree as to exactly why.

A Tribute to Jurors and Juries

It is an odd system we have. In fact, it sometimes appears that Alexis de Tocqueville got it right when he observed as early as the 1800s that virtually every issue in American life eventually makes its way into court. And, once those issues get there—the intimate, the mundane, the complicated, the terrible, sometimes even the trivial—all of these disputes are resolved by a collection of common folk, evaluating conflicting versions of historical events presented by professionally trained partisan adversaries, in the highly stylized and artificial manner that is the jury trial.

When you describe the process this way, it is easy to see why many of our colleagues from other countries rank the American jury system somewhere between quaintly ridiculous and fatally flawed. It is a system all but abandoned by its creators (the English) in civil cases. It is a system whose primary beneficiaries (i.e., the people who are likely reading this book) often have no trouble criticizing.

None of this changes the fact that it is a system that *generally* works!

It is easy for me to be cynical about a lot of things, but the jury system is not one of them. I have considerable faith in the ability of twelve ordinary people to come to the right decision after pondering the evidence. Do I think that jurors are infallible, that they get it right all the time? Of course not! No system, including one where "well-educated professionals" make such decisions, always gets it right. If you need proof of this, just remind yourself of the last time one of your well-taken motions or objections was denied.

Do I have faith that the jurors get it right the majority of the time, even in relatively complex cases? Yes, I genuinely do—and I have had to admit this

1. I am not suggesting that there were only five such paths. In fact, I suspect that there were more. What is crucial is not the exact number of different paths but that (1) there were a multitude of such paths, (2) the jurors could agree on the conclusion—"She is insane"—even if they could not agree on why or how they got to that decision, and (3) any lawyer who tried to force all of his jurors down a single path (i.e., the one he was most comfortable with) would not likely have been able to prevail with this group.

fact on more than one occasion (privately, of course, but I have had to admit it), when my client has lost his case.

Sadly, I often find that it is the lawyers who frustrate the jurors and prevent them from doing their job. In such instances, I am particularly discouraged by two types of lawyers. The first are those (usually the ones who have lost) who immediately blame the judge and jurors for whatever went wrong in the case and fail to see their own potential shortcomings at the trial.

These are the lawyers who categorically assert that ordinary citizens are incapable of deciding complex issues. They boldly tell anyone who will listen (and there are a lot of people who will) that the jurors "just never got it!" and how these finders of fact could neither remember large portions of the facts nor deal with any of the important subtleties raised by those facts. Ironically, sometimes the jurors these lawyers criticize most are the very ones that they worked so hard to keep on the jury during voir dire.

For these lawyers, saying that the jury "never got it" is sometimes more of an indictment of the lawyers' skills than it is of the jurors' abilities. Does that mean that jurors will always get it? No, but I am suggesting that lawyers owe it to the jury system, the profession, and themselves to try really hard to simplify their case and present it in a well-structured and orderly manner before offering such a blanket condemnation of jurors.

The second group that is often too quick to criticize the jury system is made up of those lawyers who take the concept of a "jury of their peers" to the extreme and insist that the law should provide them with a "jury of their clones." (Ill. 1-2) More specifically, these lawyers generally feel that the way they do things is the same way everyone does or should do things and, as such, these lawyers specifically believe that the way they learn and reason is the way that everyone learns and reasons. These lawyers are then completely flummoxed when their personal style resonates with only a handful of jurors—which is never enough to win the case.

ILLUSTRATION 1-2 A Jury of Your Peers, Not Your Clones
An inexperienced lawyer assumes everyone does things the same way—his way. These lawyers are then completely flummoxed when their personal style resonates with only a handful of jurors.

The problem, of course, is severe myopia, which prevents these lawyers from fully appreciating and successfully using a variety of different Persuasion Tools—tools that these particular lawyers themselves might not have personally used to learn about their case but, nonetheless, tools that will appeal to the broad range of different learning and reasoning styles reflected in the various people on the jury. These are tools that the different jurors will then use in the deliberation room to help persuade their colleagues that the lawyer's position is the right one. As we will see throughout this book, providing these tools to the jury is an important first step in allowing the necessary coalitions of jurors to form.

I did not develop my respect for the jury system because I think jurors carefully study the law, comprehend its nuances, and apply it strictly. Nor do I support the jury system because I think jurors have the analytical skills necessary to peer-review testimony from highly skilled expert witnesses. I champion the jury system for very practical reasons: because I have observed that most jurors believe there is a right answer, they work very hard to find it, and, more often than not (which is the best you can expect from a human-based system), they succeed.

Jurors genuinely believe that the Truth is out there. They also are confident that, with sufficient assistance from one or both sets of the lawyers, they will find it. The ongoing challenge of uncovering the Truth is often what keeps jurors motivated during an otherwise boring trial. In fact, many jurors admit that the most rewarding aspect of jury service is concluding that they did the right thing. Imagine how discouraging it must be to sit through a trial, aware that work is piling up at your office, eating crummy courthouse cafeteria food, and, when it is all over, concluding that you and your fellow jurors have failed to come up with the right answer.

Most jurors take the role very seriously. Of course they complain about jury duty and, admittedly, there is still much to dislike and complain about in the way some courts and lawyers treat jurors. However, most jurors understand that they have a personal stake in ensuring that the system works. As a result, they do an admirable job of applying the law as best they can interpret it to the facts, as best as they are able to understand them.

This is particularly impressive because it is basic human nature to instinctively want to avoid a situation like that which we force them to confront while on jury duty. Most people find it very difficult to make crucial decisions concerning complicated issues about topics of which they initially know very little, decisions that will have a profound impact on the lives of real people. (Just describing it that way gives me a moment of pause.) The fact that jurors have to do this for people they do not know and will likely never see again (as opposed to close family or friends) may make the process a bit easier—but let us not kid ourselves, it is still a very hard process to go through. In fact, I do not believe many people would fault jurors for wanting to run away as quickly as possible from such a responsibility. Fortunately for us, abandoning their posts is not an option and, as such, they are forced to decide difficult issues on our behalf. Even more fortunately for us, they generally get to the right answer.

The Lawyer's Role at Trial—Great Trial Lawyers All Share Certain Characteristics

It is always flattering during post-verdict jury interviews to hear that the jurors liked you and your witnesses the best. Likewise, it is exciting to know that the jury thought you were the more articulate and able of the two advocates. Nevertheless, if you have tried more than a handful of cases, I suspect you know that such flattery often does not matter a whole heck of a lot because you often receive it while you are packing up exhibit boxes after having lost the case.[2]

In reality, the best possible compliment (other than winning)—the one that really matters—is that the jurors found you and your witnesses to be the most helpful.

For those of you (like me) who cringe when you hear the word "helpful" because it has, over the years, been so devalued by insincerity, please bear with me for a few minutes. I am not talking about the feigned helpfulness that seems to surround us in modern life. The great trial lawyers are the ones who help their jurors by providing them with the tools with which to reach the right verdict.

Despite this, it is rare during witness preparation to hear lawyers encouraging witnesses to be "helpful." It is even rarer during the trial to hear lawyers reminding themselves to behave in this same manner. But this is precisely what jurors are looking for and need. In fact, jurors often reward the lawyers and witnesses that they believe are the most helpful in assisting them to uncover the truth.

Jurors want you to provide them with meaningful information without feeling that you are wasting their time. They want to understand what is going on in the case and in the courtroom. This understanding not only helps them decide, but it also keeps them interested, and someone who is interested is much more likely to listen to what it is that you are trying to sell.

Unfortunately, some lawyers are concerned that being helpful will be perceived as either a sign of weakness (as in, "when you are explaining, you aren't winning") or as condescending (as in, "I don't want to be seen as talking down to the jurors").

2. OK, let's admit it. Don't you hate it when this happens after you lost the case: jurors coming up to you after the trial, complimenting you on how great you were but admitting they just could not vote for your client? It has the same sting as "No, I am not interested in a romantic relationship with you, but I hope we can be friends."

I must confess that in many ways I am always initially sympathetic to these concerns. When I ask myself why, I conclude it has as much to do with the word "helpful" itself as it does with anything else. It is so easy when you first hear the word to be overwhelmed by the vision of an anxious Boy Scout promising to "help other people at all times; to keep myself physically strong, mentally awake, and morally straight" or that of a saccharine-sweet hotel desk clerk who smiles at you as he tries to help you by explaining why "*We* have a problem with *our* reservation."

That is not what I mean by helpful!

It should go without saying that nothing done badly, insincerely, or to the extreme will help you, your jury, or your case. Likewise, explanations that are seen as back-peddling are rarely helpful. But genuine and well-thought-out efforts at helping jurors through the difficult process of being part of a jury will likely yield considerable benefits.

There are multiple ways of being helpful during trial. I believe that five are particularly worth discussing here because I will be repeatedly raising them both in this chapter and throughout the balance of this book. These methods include (1) not being afraid to be an advocate who teaches; (2) not behaving like a "mad dog" in court; (3) respecting your jury by limiting your case to what really matters; (4) identifying which key topics need extra explanation and devoting the necessary time to providing it; and (5) taking the time to learn and fully understand your case before you ever appear before the jury. (Ill. 1-3)

You can be helpful by not being afraid to be an advocate who is also an effective teacher

Perhaps the single most important thing you and your witnesses can do to be helpful is to understand what it means to be an effective advocate in the courtroom.

So, what is the proper role of a lawyer at trial? The obvious answer is that the proper role is one of an advocate. OK, but exactly what kind of advocate? My immediate response is always the same—"a good one." My more thoughtful reply is "the best advocates are the ones who take the time to educate their jurors about those issues that really matter." In short, the best advocates know when and how to be *effective* teachers.

Your job at trial is to teach your jurors what they need to know so that they will not only vote in your favor, but so that they will also be willing to advocate on your behalf during deliberations. Never underestimate the necessity to educate the finders of facts. Virtually everything that your jurors will learn about the case will, in one way or another, come through you or your opposing counsel. Even if you do not take the time to educate your jury, I can guarantee that the other side will. If only one side takes the time to explain a difficult or key concept to the jurors, the only image those jurors will have of that concept will be that which was unilaterally presented during trial. When

The Characteristics of Great Trial Lawyers

All great trial lawyers share five characteristics:

- **Great trial lawyers are advocates who teach.**
- **Great trial lawyers do not behave like "mad dogs" in court.**
- **Great trial lawyers limit their case to what really matters.**
- **Great trial lawyers identify and spend their time on the key topics.**
- **Great trial lawyers take the time and make the effort to thoroughly learn their case.**

ILLUSTRATION 1 -3 The Characteristics of Great Trial Lawyers
Despite different surface styles, great trial lawyers generally share five characteristics.

that happens, it is easy to predict which side is more likely to prevail on that point. If neither side makes an effort to teach, you will (in all but the simplest cases) end up with a horribly muddled and angry jury.

Some lawyers have a difficult time understanding the concept of effective teaching; they ask, "Isn't everything we do in the courtroom teaching?" My answer to that is, "No, not necessarily."

There is a difference between knowledge, understanding, and perspective. To be an effective teacher, you need to master and then convey all three of these elements to your jury. (Ill. 1-4)

Developing *knowledge* is a fact-centered process. There may be hundreds of individual facts, but the learning process is essentially memorization (even if the information is only stored in your working memory for the duration of the trial).

Developing *understanding* is an organization-centered process. It is the process that allows you to organize your individual facts into groups, subgroups, categories, and subcategories. While it is possible to have knowledge without understanding, the opposite is not true; that is, it is not possible to have understanding without knowledge.

If I could rank information based on potential power, perspective would be at the top of the scale (or at least very close to it). Developing *perspective* is a connection-centered process; it allows you to draw connections between

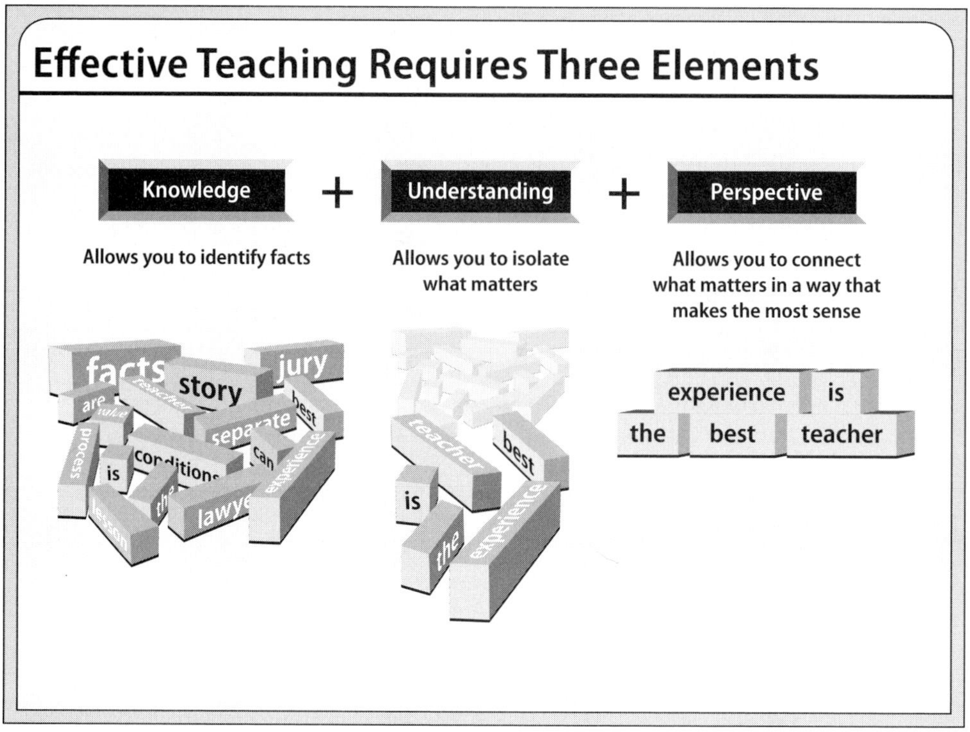

ILLUSTRATION 1-4 Knowledge, Understanding, and Perspective
Knowledge and *understanding* each increase the power of facts arithmetically; *perspective* increases the power of facts geometrically.

certain of the facts or group of facts. Knowledge and understanding each increase the power of individual facts arithmetically. By contrast, *perspective* increases their power geometrically.

Effective teaching, which is what you are trying to accomplish during trial, involves the use of all three of these elements—knowledge, understanding, and perspective—so that you create a series of coherent and persuasive stories and supporting materials, which jurors then use to reach their verdict.

When you teach, do not teach like an arrogant professor whose desire to transmit knowledge has been dulled by years of tenure. Instead, teach like that special teacher we all remember—the kind of teacher that unfortunately comes along all too infrequently in our lives. Teach like the teacher who loves teaching. Such teachers possess many of the same characteristics that are needed to be a successful trial lawyer, including enthusiasm for the subject, a willingness to take the time to explain, respect for students, self-confidence, and the dedication to spend hours upon hours preparing and refining their message.

You should use some of the same teaching techniques that gifted teachers use to capture their students' attention and stimulate their imagination. For example, create a sense of reality around what you teach by providing (but not over-providing) details. Likewise, create visual pictures in your descriptions.

One of the benefits of teaching is that it lets you take advantage of what I call the "recirculating process." As the Romans would say, *qui docet discit,* "he who teaches learns." Throughout the teaching process, you will likely have insights and inspiration that you would not otherwise have. Recirculate this newly learned material back into your teaching. Your presentation will undoubtedly be the better for it. (Ill. 1-5)

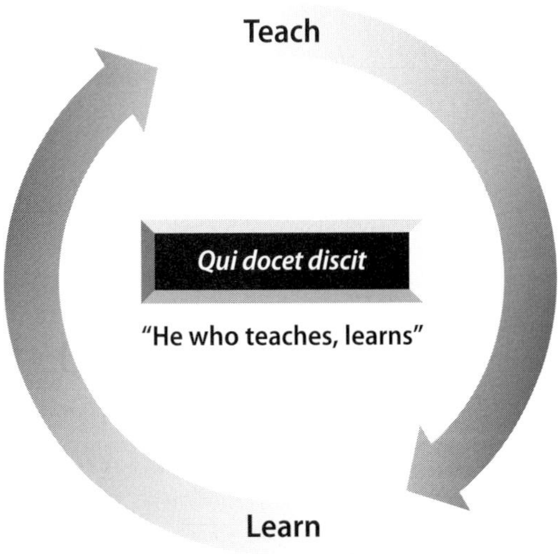

ILLUSTRATION 1-5 ***Qui Docet Discit***
He who teaches, learns. Recirculate what you learn back into what you teach.

There is nothing wimpy about being an advocate who takes the time to be helpful by teaching the jury. After all, the ultimate goal of the advocate is, within the confines of law and ethical restrictions, to win the case for his client. Successful politicking—and that is much of what is going on among jurors during deliberations—always involves three steps: education, persuasion, and consensus building. Of the three, education is the most important since neither persuasion nor consensus building can occur without it. The bottom line is that you should not be afraid to teach; I am confident that your client will benefit greatly from such efforts.

You can be helpful by not behaving like a "mad dog" in court

There is a common perception that "trial is war, and war is hell!" Because of this belief, too many of our courtrooms are filled with lawyers behaving badly, seemingly unaware that such behavior rarely serves them well during a trial.[3] To be fair, I must admit that adversarial activities outside the view of the jury may very well resemble war. In fact, if you really feel the need to do so, this is the safest place to assert your "inner mad-dog, mercenary self." But if you do, remember that sound and fury rarely generate much light, at least for jurors.

At this point, let me be very clear about something: being passionate in your beliefs and being unafraid to display that passion is not the same as behaving like a mad dog. Mad dogs cannot distinguish between well-placed passionate commitment and a widespread angry diatribe. Expert advocates understand that they have a "volume button" and they know when it is appropriate to turn the volume up or down.

3. I would go so far as to argue that it rarely benefits them anywhere, but I know it does not do so in front of the jury.

For me, this point was driven home when I heard the jurors' insights concerning a particularly partisan advocate I worked with several years ago on a case. This particular lawyer liked to play the tough guy. He shouted. He trumpeted. He sneered at witnesses. He gave new meaning to the words "cross-examination." In short, for him the term "civil litigation" was an oxymoron.

It was quite a performance, but not a particularly successful one. In fact, when we interviewed the jurors after the trial, they unanimously gave him negative feedback. As one juror noted:

> He reminded us [the jury] of Yosemite Sam, the cartoon character that is always running around wild, swearing, and randomly shooting his pistols up into the air. Sometimes his [the lawyer's] ranting and raving was fun to watch, but we never really took him seriously or trusted very much of what he said. No one ever learned much from Yosemite Sam!

Certain trial attorneys seem to think that acting like a mad dog in the courtroom is a good strategy. But the truth is, being overly antagonistic can do more damage than good to you, your client, and your case. Mad dogs are rarely as effective as they believe they are.[4]

In fact, a take-no-prisoners stance is often very *ineffective* in the courtroom for at least five reasons. (Ill. 1-6) First, being a mad dog makes you look inexperienced. By and large, most of the mad-dog attorneys that I have seen have not been in the courtroom enough times—and they are not yet confident enough—to see that masterful litigators are more like teachers and storytellers than professional wrestlers.

Such attorneys confuse "conflict" (on which all trials are based) with the adversarial process. That is, they miss the point that the purpose of a trial is to *resolve* the conflict, not make it worse by acting like a bully in the courtroom. Likewise, they fail to understand that, in order to resolve a conflict in your favor, you need to *teach* the jurors about your case, *persuade* them as to the veracity of your client's perspective, and *engage* them by using good storytelling techniques, such as analogies, metaphors, and good graphics.

Second, being a mad dog turns off the jury. While a quick dust-up in the courtroom gets your jurors' attention, constantly getting in witnesses' faces, dressing down opposing counsel, or making tortured facial expressions can make you seem like a mad man (or dog)—and therefore not to be trusted. Most jurors question whether such a delicate object as the truth is likely to be found in the hands of a mean-as-a-snake trial lawyer.

Third, being a mad dog keeps you from telling your story. Although the media sometimes glamorizes the image of a frothing-at-the-mouth attorney (. . . *And Justice for All* with Al Pacino certainly springs to mind), the focus in

4. I want to thank Jim Stiff, who heads Trial Analysts, Inc., a litigation consulting firm in Dallas and College Station, Texas, for some of his thoughts on this topic.

Avoid Being a Mad Dog in Court

Being a mad dog in court is ineffective because:

- **It makes you look inexperienced.**
- **It eventually turns off the jurors.**
- **It prevents you from being able to tell your story effectively.**
- **You too often telegraph your punch.**
- **People don't like mad dogs (or mad people).**

ILLUSTRATION 1-6 Avoid Being a Mad Dog in Court

your trial should be on the right way to tell your client's story, not on adapting an angry persona as a strategy to winning your case.

Much of the art of storytelling in the courtroom involves patience, being attuned to your jurors, and being able to modulate your demeanor to match your material; all of which is hard to pull off if you are in the midst of one angry outburst after another. When I taught trial practice, I always reminded my law students, "It is a lot harder to turn down the volume than it is to turn it up." What I meant by this was that you can get loud and confrontational in an instant, but once you do, it takes a lot of effort to get yourself and everyone who has been affected by your outburst to calm down.

I am not advocating that you never turn up the volume; instead, I am merely advising that you do it when you really need to, at a point that makes sense, and that you understand that there are always consequences in doing so.

Prior to law school, I was a teaching assistant for a professor of American constitutional law and history. Because of the large number of prelaw students in the class, the professor always cautioned us that we needed to be very careful of certain students. He warned us not to worry too much about the boisterous ones, because you could spot what they were up to a mile away. Instead, he suggested we worry about the polite ones, because "you never see it coming from them, so these students always get away with murder!" For me, this sentiment—beware of the polite ones because they always seem to get away with murder—summarizes the fourth reason not to behave like a mad dog in court. Politeness often pays unexpected dividends because your opposing counsel may never see "it" coming. Mad dogs always telegraph their punches and then seem surprised that you saw it coming.

William Herndon, who was Abraham Lincoln's old adversary and eventual law partner, had an observation to this effect about Lincoln. Herndon described how Lincoln would politely defer to his opposing counsel and was nothing but polite and accommodating, but:

> [A]bout the time he [Lincoln] had practiced this [polite behavior] three-fourths through the case, if his adversary did not understand him, he [the adversary] would wake up in a few minutes learning that he had feared the Greeks too late and find himself beaten. . . . Any man who took Lincoln for a simple-minded man would very soon wake up with his back in a ditch.

If you need images of lawyers to inspire you, in addition to Lincoln, think of Atticus Finch in *To Kill a Mockingbird.* The old-fashioned gentleman lawyer—smart, tough, kind, skilled—is still a potent force in the courtroom today although, unfortunately, his ranks are shrinking with the years.

Fifth and finally, being a mad dog can make you look like a . . . well, like a mad dog, and very few people like mad dogs. Assume for a moment that you are about to cross-examine a witness who is well-liked by your jury. If you take too much of a bullying stance—if you get downright aggressive—your jurors will decide you are mean and they will not focus on how inconsistent, untrue, or unreliable the witness's testimony may be. If the jury feels sorry for the witness or thinks she is a really good person, they are likely to defend her in their own minds against you.

This is not to say that you should never get heated, animated, or adversarial in the court room. That would not be effective either. But the number of situations in which it is appropriate to act the "mad dog" is relatively low. If you catch a witness in a lie, for instance, taking a more aggressive stance is certainly warranted. And if a witness is being nonresponsive, evasive, or is actually obstructing the legal process, it may be time to turn up the volume, as that will draw the jurors' attention to the witness and the problems that she is creating. A little scrap in the courtroom can catch the jurors' attention, but if it happens too frequently, the jury will stop paying attention and you will likely end up in worse condition than your opponent.

You Can Be Helpful by Limiting Your Case to What Really Matters

The third way to be helpful is to limit your case to those claims, facts, and arguments that really matter. This is not just good advice; it is fundamental and it makes complete common sense.

The truth is, we waste a lot of our time wasting the jurors' time. We do so by forcing them to sit through badly edited and poorly structured trials and, in the process, we bore them to a point beyond numbness. What is particularly unfortunate about this is that these are the very people we are trying to impress!

The easiest way to simplify your case is to eliminate anything that does not advance your position or is inconsistent with your basic Case Theory or Case Themes.[5] This is important for three reasons. First, great facts often appear less magnificent when they are surrounded by meaningless muck. Get rid of what does not matter so the jury can better discern what does.

Second, this form of simplification allows you to increase your credibility by eliminating inconsistent positions. Arguments made in the alternative are not favored by jurors. Such arguments are viewed with suspicion, even more so when the person advocating the inconsistency is a trial lawyer. Let's admit it—most jurors are suspicious of us. This is particularly the case because in the juror's eyes, rightly or wrongly, lawyers are believed to be entirely capable of talking out of both sides of their mouths. Any inconsistency will be duly noted and almost certainly discussed (and probably discussed adversely) by the jurors during deliberations.

One of the rarest resources in the courtroom is time. Judges will give you only so much of it before insisting that you move on. Jurors will devote only so much time to your case before they begin ignoring you, then actively resenting you and your client. This is the third reason for simplifying your case—you really have very little time to waste; be helpful by using it wisely.

Over time, the ability of any juror to understand a topic is a function of two variables: comprehension and interest. There is a direct, positive relationship between comprehension and time; as a general rule, the more time you spend on a subject, the greater the jury's comprehension of that subject. On the other hand, there is an inverse or negative relationship between interest and time; the longer you spend on a subject, the less interested the jury will become. Taken together, this means that the more time you spend on a subject, the more the jurors will learn, but the harder it will be for them to do so because boredom (which is the opposite of interest) will begin setting in at an ever-increasing rate. You must be constantly aware of this and err on the side of well-conceived brevity.

By all reports, Abraham Lincoln was a master at keeping things simple and not wasting either his time or, more importantly, the jurors' with things that ultimately did not matter. In fact, Lincoln once advised young lawyers, "In law, it is good policy to never plead what you need not, lest you obligate yourself to prove what you cannot."

You could do far worse than emulating Abraham Lincoln at your next trial.

---

5. This process of taking away everything that does not matter is what I call "simplification by subtraction." While it is extremely effective, it is not the only way of simplifying your case. For three other effective methods—simplification by addition, simplification by division, and simplification by multiplication—see Ritter, G. Christopher, *Creating Winning Trial Strategies and Graphics,* American Bar Association, 2004.

You can be helpful by identifying and devoting the necessary time to the key topics that require extra explanation

At first glance, the fourth suggested way of being helpful may appear to contradict the third. In every case, there are key concepts that not only require, but also deserve, extra time in front of the jurors. You must identify what these issues are, study them until they make sense to you, and then be prepared to take the time that is reasonably necessary to explain these important concepts to the jury in a way that its members can understand and later use during deliberations.

Much of what jurors learn, they learn for the first time at trial. As we will discuss in greater detail later in this chapter, learning something new cannot take place unless the student (in this instance, the juror) can first compare what she is trying to learn to something with which she is already familiar. That is why identifying and teaching these essential concepts are so important—this material provides the necessary "toeholds" from which jurors can begin to understand and, as such, it often serves as the foundation for the entire learning process at the trial.[6] Until the jurors have at least this toehold of preexisting understanding, they cannot begin to learn. (Ill. 1-7)

Once you identify which topics deserve this extra effort, the teacher in you must determine the general level at which a majority of the jurors can begin to relate to at least some discrete subpart of the topic. This common level of understanding provides the entryway; it is the point where you begin the education process.

This process often requires that you use an analogy or some other basic teaching device that allows the jurors to compare a crucial element of the new complex topic to something with which they are already familiar. After you have established this connection (and *only after* you have established this connection), you can begin to show the jurors how they can take small steps toward understanding the key concept in greater detail.

How hard can this process be? The answer is that it is sometimes harder than one would initially imagine. Usually, this is the case for two diametrically opposed reasons—some lawyers/witnesses have difficulty identifying *any* key subjects they feel need clarifying, while others identify and want to teach the jury about *too many* such topics.

Both problems often arise from the same source: the trial lawyer and/or her witnesses (particularly expert witnesses) know too much about the subject matter and, as such, no longer have a good intuitive sense about which topics are unduly complex and/or how best to teach others about these subjects.

I suspect you have encountered this problem before in both of its manifestations: (1) the lawyer or witness for whom the subject matter is second nature to the extent that nothing about it seems complex or requires further

6. I thank Michael Colacchio of Clear Impact LLC in Corte Madera, California, for helping me to clarify my thinking on this topic.

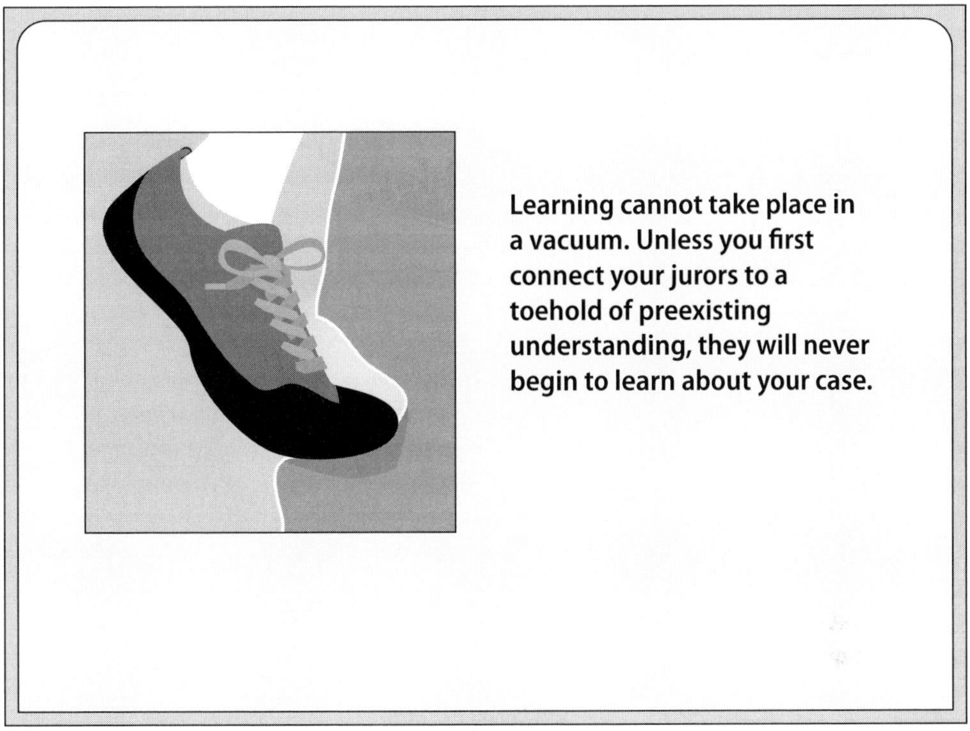

ILLUSTRATION 1-7 Toeholds
You cannot begin to learn unless you can relate what is new to something that is already familiar. This connection is often established through analogies, stories, or other learning devices.

explanation in her eyes and (2) the lawyer or witness who loves the topic so much that she wants to teach everything she can about it to her audience, convinced that everyone shares her interest and passion.

As an example of those in the former category, I remember once asking an economist to make his presentation more understandable or "juror-friendly." He responded by providing a series of regression formulas and something that made repeated references to standard deviations and "varying confidence intervals." When I went back a second time and suggested that we still needed to further simplify his presentation, the expert looked at me with surprise and expressed his sincere concern that if he made it any simpler, he would be perceived as talking down to the jurors. I guess that proves that "down" is a relative concept. It also confirms my belief that many experts (particularly those who have never testified in court) do not remember what it is like to not understand.

People in the latter category, that is, the lawyers and expert witnesses who wish to teach too much, think that everything about the topic deserves a high level of special appreciation and, consequently, they usually have a hard time accurately identifying the key issues that merit extra attention. Such affection for the subject matter often manifests itself in a desire to "overshare." Unfortunately, most jurors do not share the same level of enthusiasm for detail and often find such witnesses boring.

With help, both sets of these lawyers/witnesses can figure out how to minimize their respective problems, but it requires effort and conscious thought as to which issues a juror needs to understand in order to make sense of the subject. The easiest way to solve the problem of identifying these special topics is to rely on a Critical Listener who, upon hearing the details of the case (or the "story"), can alert you to the "black holes" (areas where the listener has absolutely no understanding) and the "mountains of mush" (areas where there is too much detail).[7]

YOU CAN BE HELPFUL BY TAKING THE NECESSARY TIME TO LEARN AND BY MAKING THE NECESSARY EFFORT TO THOROUGHLY UNDERSTAND YOUR OWN CASE

A fifth thing that you can do to be helpful to your jury is to take the time and make the necessary effort to learn—really learn—your case. You cannot do this overnight. The necessary "mental composting" process that we will describe throughout this book takes considerable effort and (equally, if not more importantly) it takes substantial time.

As you prepare your case for trial, you need to do three things, which I list in no particular order. (Ill. 1-8) You need to spend considerable time in deep, deliberative, and conscious thought, systematically examining what really matters about your case. This is "information hunting and gathering." While much of this can be delegated to others, there is no substitute for taking the time and making the effort to do the most crucial parts yourself.

A second thing you must do is to allow yourself periods of stillness where, to the outside world, it appears as if nothing is happening. Looks can be deceiving because in these quiet moments, something very important is happening: Your subconscious is humming along, processing what you previously dealt with in your conscious mind. I call this Passive Mental Mining. We have all experienced the effect of giving ideas the freedom and space to percolate—these are the ideas that come to you on a long walk or while you are driving your car.[8] As Professor Edward Chalfant so accurately observed, it is often "indispensable . . . to get away from a difficult subject at intervals, as means of getting close to it in the long run."[9] I can contribute nothing more to this important observation, other than to wholeheartedly endorse it.

A third thing you must do is to make an effort, usually in a group setting, to consciously pull ideas from your subconscious that help explain (in already

7. We will discuss the role of Critical Listener in greater detail later in the book. Specifically, see Chapter 5.

8. The initial concept for this book, for example, came to me while I was pulling weeds in my front yard. While my wife claims this inspiration was nothing more than an excuse that allowed me to stop weeding and go back inside to sit at my computer, this does not change the fact that the idea came about as part of my "downtime" from more intellectually grueling work.

9. Chalfant, Edward, *Both Sides of the Ocean: A Biography of Henry Adams, His First Life, 1838–1862,* Archon Books, 1982, 11.

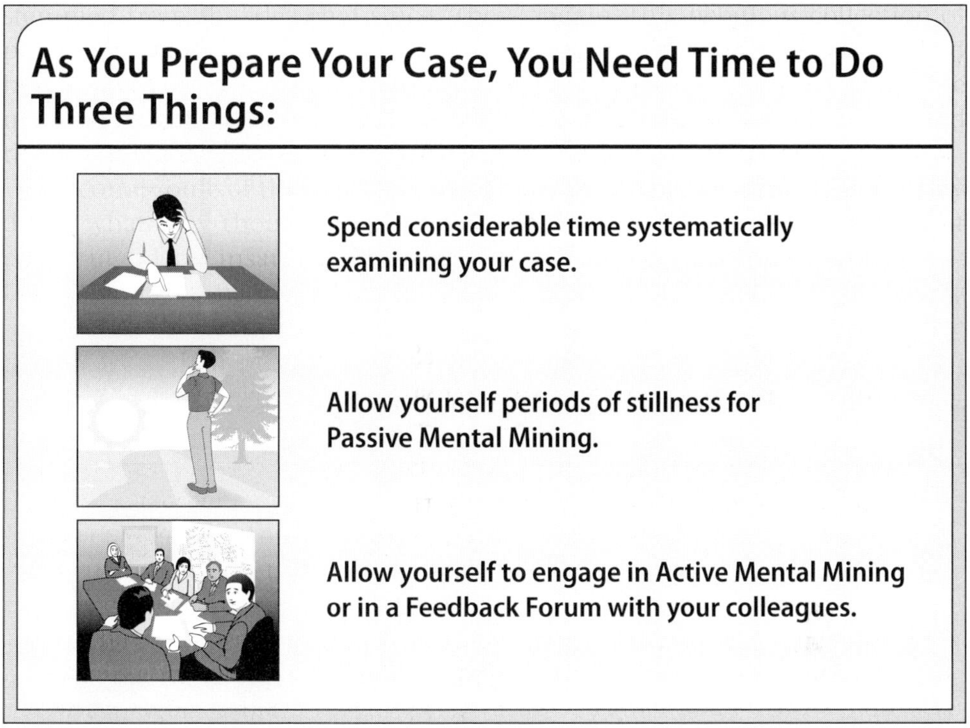

ILLUSTRATION 1-8 Mental Composting Takes Time
You need time for deep deliberate thought, periods of stillness, and opportunities for Active Mental Mining with your colleagues.

familiar terms) the essence of your dispute and/or that help explain the key concepts of the case. We call this Active Mental Mining. We then sometimes follow this up with another exercise, called a Feedback Forum, where we test the ideas derived from Mental Mining on a sample of laypersons. We will discuss Feedback Forums and Mental Mining in greater detail in Chapters 4 and 5.

What is the desired end product? What is it that you hope to accomplish from pursuing this level of effort? The ultimate goal, of course, is to win your case. More specifically, you are seeking three results that will enhance your chances of obtaining this goal. First, you hope to develop what I described earlier in this chapter as perhaps the most powerful form of knowledge—perspective. That is, you hope to begin to see the connections between facts or groups of facts that might not be apparent at first glance. Second, you hope to increase your ability to communicate new concepts and to do so in ways that make sense to the average person. The third desired result is an increased level of confidence in your ability to tell your client's story in a way that makes sense and convinces the jury.

This is powerful stuff and, put simply, it takes effort to develop—effort that can only occur in an unhurried fashion over time. Give yourself this luxury of time—start early!

Why the Jury System Works

Most jurors take their jobs very seriously. While they may not always be happy giving up their time to resolve questions in areas where they have no prior experience, for people they have never met before, jurors are generally an optimistic bunch. They believe that the truth is out there, and most jurors are confident they will find it if they are given the right help from one or both sets of lawyers. They see the process as an important challenge and, as we will discuss in greater detail, they often reward the lawyers and witnesses who they feel help them through it.

Most jurors work hard to find what they believe to be the correct answer. This is particularly admirable when you consider how emotionally difficult it is for the ordinary citizen to serve on a jury. Jurors suddenly and unexpectedly find themselves pushed to the forefront and charged with the enormous societal responsibility of "having to decide." At the same time, most jurors are unfamiliar with everything we trial lawyers take for granted and with which we are comfortable in the courtroom. Except in the vaguest sense, jurors do not know trial procedure. They do not know the substantive law with which they are being required to decide an important question that they know will have a profound effect on the life of someone who oftentimes has been sitting within a few yards of them throughout the trial.

Nevertheless, jurors do an admirable job of getting it right. Are they infallible? Of course not. But, more often than not (and I am not sure you can expect much more than this from a human-based judgment system) the jurors generally get to the right verdict, even if the internal reasoning process that they use to get there can leave some outside observers stupefied and others terrified.

So, why does this system work? For a more technical or scientific explanation, you would do well to go elsewhere because my answer is almost embarrassingly simple and experientially based. (Ill. 1-9)

In my opinion, the jury system works for eight primary reasons:

- Most cases are defined by a common core of recurring elements that jurors find familiar.
- All of the participants share much in common with each other, around which you can build consensus.
- We use stories to educate our jurors.
- We repeat the story three times in three different ways, thereby allowing us to use a variety of Persuasion Tools.
- We require the essential characters to tell their stories in first-person narratives to the jury.
- There are opportunities at key points in the trial for the lawyer to talk directly to the jurors.
- Jurors have "collective intuition."
- Jurors have "collective wisdom."

Before going into each reason in detail, let me momentarily digress and explain why I believe that this information is important and not offered

Why the Jury System Works

- **Most cases are defined by a common core of recurring elements that jurors find familiar.**
- **All of the participants share much in common with each other, around which you can build consensus.**
- **We use stories to educate our jurors.**
- **We repeat the story three times in three different ways, thereby allowing us to use a variety of Persuasion Tools.**
- **We require the central characters to tell their stories in first-person narratives to the jury.**
- **There are opportunities at key points in the trial for the lawyer to talk directly to the jurors.**
- **Jurors have "collective intuition."**
- **Jurors have "collective wisdom."**

ILLUSTRATION 1-9 The Jury System Works for Eight Reasons

merely as some form of interesting trivia or civics lesson. Specifically, if you are going to master a system, it is crucial that you know why and how it works. This knowledge allows you to work in a way that is consistent with the system and not at cross-purposes with it.

For example, knowing that one of the reasons the jury system works is because a trial is essentially a story repeated three times, allows you to adjust your presentation accordingly. Likewise, knowing that each time we tell the story, we do so in a slightly different manner, allows the astute lawyer to use different types of Persuasion Tools each time he retells the story. Different learning tools appeal to the different learning styles and motivating factors that are likely represented on the jury. In short, knowing why things work will hopefully help to increase your level of mindfulness about what you are doing and will make it easier to prevail.

Reason One: The Jury System Works Because Most Cases Are Defined by a Common Core of Recurring Elements That Jurors Find Familiar

"Outside-In" Versus "Inside-Out"

In the broadest sense, trial lawyers are usually one of two types. The first tell you that their case "is incredibly complicated and will be nearly impossible for anyone, let alone a jury, to understand." The second group would describe

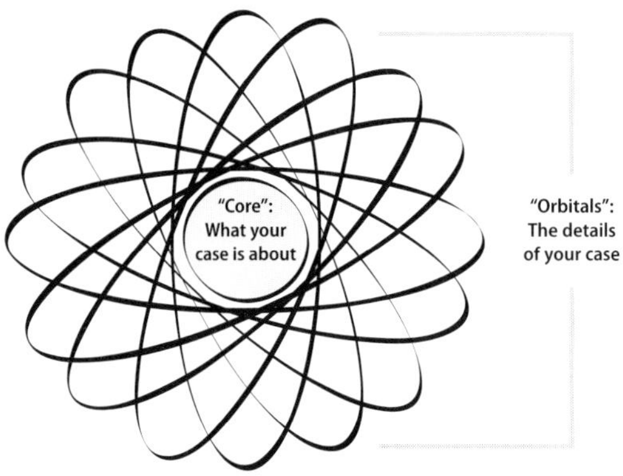

ILLUSTRATION 1-10 If Your Case Were a Single Atom
There would be two parts: the "Core," which is what your case is about, and the "Orbitals," which are all of the details.

the same case as having "a lot of details, but at its core it is not really all that complicated."

What is the fundamental difference between these two types of lawyers? It is not that one is pessimistic and the other optimistic. It is not that one group is somehow smarter or more articulate than the other. Instead, what distinguishes these two is *where* they begin their analysis and *what* they consider most important when developing their case before trial and explaining their case to the jury.

To better understand this, for a moment imagine your entire case shrunken down to the size of a single atom. As you probably remember from chemistry class, atoms generally consist of two parts: (1) the nucleus, which is at the center, and is compact and dense and (2) the orbitals, consisting of electrons that swirl around the nucleus in ever-expanding outward layered patterns. (Ill. 1-10)

In this analogy, the nucleus of your case contains those elements that, quite literally, are at the core of what you need to persuade the jury. These include the Case Themes; the Case Theory and information concerning what motivated the key parties to do whatever it was that they have allegedly done. (Ill. 1-11)

Around the core are a series of ever-expanding and increasingly complex orbitals. These circling electrons represent the details of the dispute, which are numerous and varied. You can imagine a complicated case as a complex atom with scores of electrons in multiple layers in strange shapes, all expand-

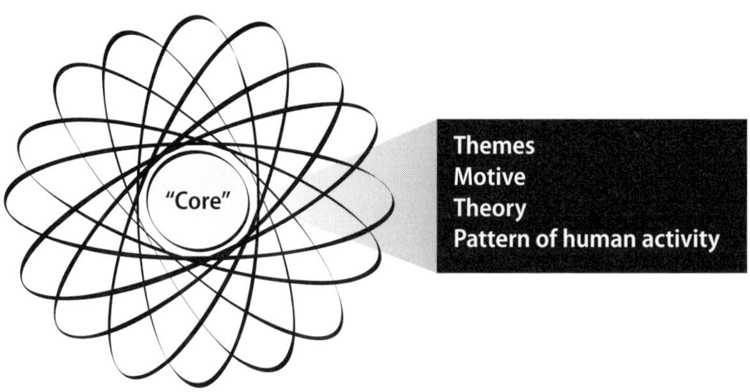

ILLUSTRATION 1-11 The Core
The jurors care most about the core of your case; fortunately, it is often the easiest part for them to understand.

ing outward from the core and, relatively speaking, taking up far more space than the nucleus.

At this point, let us return to the two different types of trial lawyers I described at the outset of this section.

When asked to describe their case, the lawyers in the first group, that is, the ones who bemoan the incredible complexity of their case (or in this analogy, their atom) come to this conclusion because they begin their analysis by focusing on the outermost portions of the orbitals and work their way toward what really matters at the central nucleus. Said slightly differently, those lawyers in the first group primarily analyze and explain their case from the "outside-in." They see the case as layer upon layer of detailed complexity that they (and eventually the jury) must struggle through before they can understand the case. (Ill. 1-12)

ILLUSTRATION 1-12 Lawyers Often Work From the "Outside-In"
This inductive process mistakenly assumes that you must understand **all** of the details of a case before you can know what it is really about.

Consistent with this approach, lawyers tend to like to select facts and then pile them one on top of the other. Unfortunately, this thickening eventually results in considerable instability and explains why many lawyers develop cases that are far too convoluted.

In its broadest sense, this is an *inductive* form of learning or reasoning that is, the lawyer starts the process with specific, individual facts and then, based on what he finds there, eventually moves to general principles.

Often, these "outside-in" lawyers become so obsessed with details that they miss the essence of their case. If they miss it, you know the jurors who

ILLUSTRATION 1-13 Jurors Generally Work From the "Inside-Out"
Jurors reason deductively. They start by focusing on what the case is really about and then work outward through the details.

eventually hear the case do not stand much of a chance of ever figuring out what the dispute is really about.

By contrast, the second group of lawyers (those who see their case as not being overly complex—and I should note that these tend to be the more experienced trial lawyers) see their case from the "inside-out." They begin their analysis inside the core of the dispute, figuring out "what the case is really about," and working their way outward into the specific detailed facts. This is essentially a *deductive* process.[10] (Ill. 1-13)

Technically, neither of these routes (outside-in nor inside-out) is right and the other wrong. In practice, one is usually far more efficient and effective than the other. With unlimited resources, time, and energy, both paths will give you the material that you need to first understand and then eventually try your case. But, in the real world—where the client's resources are limited, judges do not permit trials to go on forever, and jurors rapidly lose patience when they feel their time is being wasted—the inside-out approach is usually far more effective and efficient.[11]

This is the case for three reasons: (1) The inside-out process more closely parallels how jurors themselves will eventually analyze and reach their verdict; (2) it is easier to get there if you know where you are going; and (3) it rests on a key, but often overlooked, truism of the jury trial process—that at its core, a case is unlikely to be either entirely unique or unduly complicated.

The "Inside-Out" Approach Most Closely Parallels How Jurors Themselves Will Eventually Analyze the Case and Reach Their Verdict

Jurors typically make decisions by initially identifying a few fundamental principles that they consider to be at the core of the case, and only then do

10. There is never going to be a case that requires an entirely inductive or entirely deductive approach. In the real world, there may be a bit of inductive reasoning in the deductive process and some deductive reasoning in the inductive process. Nevertheless, the fact that neither approach can be used to the exclusion of the other does not change the fact that the outside-in approach is predominantly an inductive process and the inside-out approach is predominantly a deductive one.

11. For those who favor the outside-in approach, I offer some consolation from Henry Adams, who claimed that the "great artist" works inductively, that is, "from multiplicity to unity," while a "small one [artist] had to reverse the method and work back from unity to multiplicity."

they move on to supplement these basic principles with specific facts. Generally, these jurors make a relatively quick decision as to who should win and then search for support for these conclusions. Given this fact, it is crucial that you provide them with the necessary information and a reason to form a favorable conclusion very early on in your case, even as early as in the opening statement.

As such, working one's way from the inside of a case outward is consistent with—and clearly parallels—the most common form of analysis used and wanted by the jurors themselves.

Human beings are generally uncomfortable dealing with the complex and unfamiliar. Given our druthers, many of us would rather simply turn away and not deal with this type of situation. Unfortunately for jurors (and fortunately for us), this is not an option for them since they have been formally charged by the judge with examining, confronting, and resolving a situation, even though it often deals with unfamiliar and complex matters.

Learning cannot take place in an experiential vacuum. Regardless of whether you are a student studying calculus or a juror struggling to understand a case, you must begin the learning process by first finding and then relying on something that is familiar to you. Once you have this "toehold" of understanding, you can then proceed by small steps into new material and eventually master it.

Jurors most often find these toeholds by latching onto basic Case Themes, Party Motives, and other common factors that are at the center of the case. Why do they do this? It is simple; they are already familiar with these basic bits of information from their everyday, ordinary lives. Once they have connected with something that is familiar and relevant to the dispute, jurors can then (and only then) move slowly outward through the facts, gathering the material they deem necessary to make sense of the overall case. In other words, their analysis commonly proceeds deductively, or from the inside-out, beginning with a general familiar frame of reference and adding detailed facts to it.

Of course, jurors care about the details. I do not want to somehow lead you to mistakenly think that they do not. But jurors are not obsessed with the details. They care about the facts only so far as the facts allow them to feel confident that they have made the correct decision at the time the verdict is reached. To this extent, jurors are generally practical in their approach. They know that there is no way they will hear, let alone remember, every single detail of the case. Time will not permit this and, frankly, jurors want and need to get back to living their own lives. Consequently, what jurors tend to do is to first view the case as a whole, determine what it is about at its core, and then process the facts in a manner consistent with this perception.

It Is Easier to Get There if You Know Where You're Going

There is a second advantage for those who work their way from the inside-out, namely that it is ultimately easier and takes less time because they already know where they are going.

As support for this, let me tell you about a very interesting phenomenon that a client of mine observed when he took his young children to a "family style" restaurant for dinner.[12] When the restaurant's hostess seated the family at their table, she gave each child crayons and a placemat on which various puzzles had been printed. The puzzles included a variety of different mazes. Each maze was built around a central square that was marked "Finish." There were at least four different entrances to the maze, each leading to one of four rather complicated paths, only one of which eventually ended in the central square; the other three came to dead ends. The hope was that these placemats would keep the children entertained and provide the parents with at least a few minutes of silence while they waited for the food to arrive.

Unfortunately, the puzzles failed to work as planned for my client. Within a minute, his children had not only solved each of the mazes but had done so each time on what appeared to be their first attempt. My client was amazed and asked his children how they were able to solve the problem so quickly and so perfectly.

In response, his children let him in on their secret. Instead of starting on the outside of the maze and randomly beginning at one of the four entrances (remember, three of the four starting points ultimately lead to dead ends), the children started in the middle of the maze at the finish mark and worked their way backward to the entrance, thereby guaranteeing that they remained on the correct path the entire time. (Ill. 1-14)

ILLUSTRATION 1-14 It's Easier to Get There if You Know Where You're Going

12. My thanks to Darryl Woo, a partner at Fenwick & West in San Francisco, California, for relaying this story to me.

Smart kids; we can learn from them. Concentrating your efforts early on at the center of the case—the place where you can best determine what the case is really about—has the advantage of later helping you be more selective as you analyze the details in the outer layers of facts. Hopefully, with this knowledge you will not have to work your way through every single layer of material, and you will be able to concentrate on the areas and facts that really matter. As my father told me once when I was a kid: "It is easier to get there if you know where you're going."

The Inside-Out Approach Rests on the Fact That, at Their Cores, Most Cases Are Neither Entirely Unique nor Unduly Complicated

One of the reasons the inside-out approach is so effective is because it rests on an important truism, which you should never forget—at their core, most cases are neither entirely unique nor as unduly complicated as we lawyers mistakenly make them seem.

Almost every case, regardless of type, has certain common elements that are readily understood by virtually every juror. In fact, without these recurring elements and common understandings, the jury system—that is, a system where a group of laypeople decide on a verdict—would have absolutely no chance of working.

When I offer this observation, many lawyers vehemently disagree with me. "How can you say this?" they ask; "My case involves more than a million documents and twenty-five causes of action. It has taken my team and me over a year to understand all of these details."

In response, I try to emphasize that in some ways, these lawyers are proving my point for me. Sure, the particulars or the details change from case to case and a mastery of these particulars is important, but I stand by my original assertion. *At their cores*—which is the place that really counts, the crucial place where most jurors *begin* their analysis and often form their crucial first opinions about who should prevail.

Most cases involve recurring themes, motives, behaviors, and/or patterns of human activity. Of course, the specific reactions of individual jurors will vary, but this does not change the fact that the core of a case is likely to be familiar to them, and the typical juror will develop (or at least begin to develop) his conclusion about the case based on this familiarity.

While jurors may not know the details of why mitochondria are so important, or exactly what derivative stock sales are, or how the government procurement process works, or how drywall responds to moisture, they *do know* what it is to work hard and then be betrayed; or how, despite all of their genuine best efforts, bad things occasionally happen that cannot be prevented; or how arrogance is often ugly and rarely cares about its victims. These are the kinds of building blocks that are at the cores of most cases. This is where jurors are likely to begin their analysis and where you should begin when you present your case to the jury.

My point is that, while jurors might be learning the details of a particular dispute for the first time at trial, the foundation or latticework upon which both the lawyer (who is explaining the case) and the juror (who is learning about the case) organize and analyze the details is often familiar.

These essential elements revolve around a limited number of the basic themes, motives, and elements of human nature. They recur and are familiar to us simply because we are living human beings.[13] As Willa Cather accurately analogizes in *O Pioneers!,* "[T]here are only two or three human stories, and they go on repeating themselves as fiercely as if they had never happened before; like the larks in this country, that have been singing the same five notes over for thousands of years." [14]

Let me pause for a moment and stress an important point. Nothing of what I have just written should be seen as trivializing how hard it is to organize and successfully try a case (or, with deference to Ms. Cather, to write an acclaimed novel). One should never confuse something being simple with something being easy. Henry Adams got it right when he cautioned us not to lose sight of the "extreme complexity of extreme simplicity."

As the great jazz composer, bassist, band leader, and occasional pianist Charles Mingus once observed (in a quotation I have posted next to my computer), "Making the simple complicated is commonplace; making the complicated simple, awesomely simple, that's creativity." The bottom line is that it is precisely this level of creativity that separates great trial lawyers from merely ordinary ones.

To me, the notion that all cases contain basic core issues and that these core issues repeat themselves and are generally familiar to most jurors makes complete sense because we all (lawyers, witnesses, judges, and jurors) share the same basic internal wiring. This wiring works (and, in fact, it can only work) because the basic challenges we face are human-driven and finite, not infinite.[15] If our challenges were infinite, we would live in something approaching true chaos where predictability, comprehension, and empathy would be impossible. And let us not lose sight of the fact that the jury system is possible only because of predictability, comprehension, and empathy.

This notion of a series of familiar and repetitive Core Values is a reality that works to our benefit as trial lawyers because of the way people learn. In order to learn, the student (in this instance, the juror) must start with some-

13. For an in-depth analysis of this and related points, see Booker, Christopher, *The Seven Basic Plots—Why We Tell Stories*, Continuum, 2004.

14. James Boswell notes that Samuel Johnson came to the same conclusion and had planned to study this phenomenon, but apparently left it as an uncompleted project at the time of his death in 1784.

15. Alternatively, by putting the infinite variations of our challenges into a finite number of categories (or "buckets"), we create a fictional image of these challenges as being finite. Either way, every reasonable person (including all of your jurors) perceives these challenges as being finite in order not to be overwhelmed. You should act consistently with this perception by initially giving them the information they need most—that information at the core or the "inside" of your case.

thing that is already understood and concrete. Learning something new is an incremental process. By definition, it must start with a toehold that is already familiar or known to us, and then it can expand outward in baby steps into the unknown. Each outward baby step provides us with another discernable bit of information necessary to learn the next step, and so on. (Ill. 1-15)

The jury system could not even begin to work if everything it entails, including the core issues, were completely alien to jurors. In fact, the process works only because all cases contain a core of common knowledge and understanding upon which the typical juror can begin to learn the specific details of the case. In short, the familiar and repetitive core serves as the essential nucleus around which the new and potentially confusing facts can be assembled, analyzed, and layered (there is that atom analogy again).

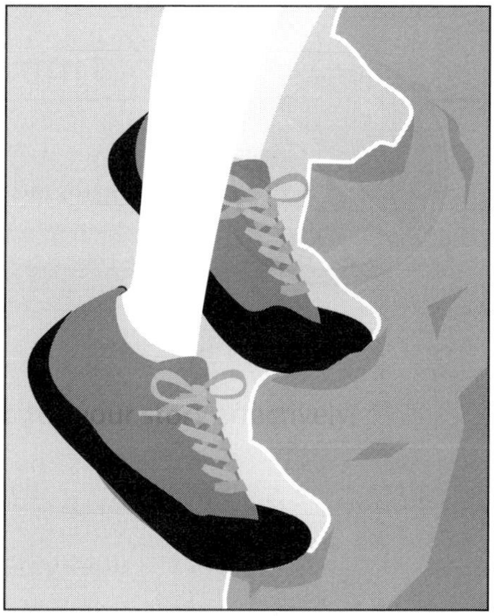

First you need a toehold; then you can move in baby steps.

ILLUSTRATION 1-15 Learning Is an Incremental Process

Even though a case may consist of hundreds or thousands of facts, names, and documents, the great trial lawyers do not *see* their cases as a collection of hundreds or thousands of facts, names, and documents. More importantly, the great trial lawyers do not *present* their cases as a collection of hundreds or thousands of facts, names, and documents. Instead, they *see* and *present* the details of their case by relating these aspects of the dispute to a central core or theme, one already familiar to the jurors.

Why do they do this?

Because (to look back to where we started) great trial lawyers instinctively understand three things: (1) At their core, all cases share basic values that occur over and over again. (2) Trial lawyers can and must use these recurring themes in order to start the process of educating the jurors. (3) They can most effectively do so by building their cases upon stories with elements already familiar to the jurors.

How All This Affects the Way You Get Ready to Try Your Next Case

So, what are the practical applications of all of this? I think there are at least five. (Ill. 1-16)

First, trial lawyers need to determine early on what their case is really about and focus their energies there. I suspect that, as a general rule, trial lawyers spend excessive energy on issues that are, at best, collateral to what really

Implications of Working From the Inside-Out

- **You must determine early on what your case is really about and focus your energies there.**
- **You need to find ways to bring underlying structure to your case early on.**
- **You need to identify the core of the case, build outward from that core, and periodically test to see if this approach appeals to jurors.**
- **Once you determine what matters, you must be fearless in eliminating what is extraneous.**
- **You must constantly find ways to tell the jury, "This is what the case is about."**

ILLUSTRATION 1-16 Implications of Working From the Inside-Out

matters. How else can one explain a laundry list of causes of action, mounds of transcripts that sit unopened after the deposition ends, and thousands of documents marked as potential exhibits that remain in black binders at the back of the courtroom throughout the trial?

Second, lawyers need to begin early on to find ways to bring underlying structure to their cases and, more specifically, to find how they can best present their cases to jurors. This involves a constant effort to stay focused on what is really important and then to only spend time on what really matters.

Third, lawyers need to identify the core of the case and build outward from that core. As they do this, they need to periodically find ways of testing to see if their approach makes sense and appeals to potential jurors. This testing needs to occur well before discovery closes, when there's still enough time before trial to constructively use the resulting information. As we will discuss later, two of the most effective ways to do this is to engage in Mental Mining and to conduct a (formal or informal) Feedback Forum.

Fourth, once they determine what really matters, trial lawyers must be fearless in their willingness to cut out what is extraneous. For many lawyers, this is a lot harder than it sounds and, as such, we will be spending considerable time discussing this later in the book.

Fifth, lawyers should find ways (consistent with the rules of evidence and procedure) to let jurors know from the very beginning of the trial what the case is about at its core. This requires structuring every interaction the lawyer has with the jury, implicitly or explicitly, from voir dire through closing argument, around the opportunity to repeat and reinforce the message.

Reason Two: The Jury System Works Because All of the Participants Share Much in Common, Around Which You Can Build Consensus

When you look at the twelve jurors who will decide your case, it is easy for you, your client, and your witnesses (especially your expert witnesses) to conclude that the concept of a jury of our peers, is just that—a concept, with no basis in reality. In other words, when you initially look at your jury you may be tempted to conclude that these folks share very little in common with each other, let alone with the lawyers, parties, and witnesses. Except for the Notice to Appear for Jury Service, I doubt that these twelve people would have an opportunity to interact for any length of time. In fact, I only know of two places that are routinely as diverse as the jury assembly room: the waiting room at a metropolitan hospital and the bleacher seats at a major league baseball game.

A lawyer colleague of mine, for instance, once observed that the members of her jury appeared to share nothing in common except the "same area code and an inability to come up with an excuse to get struck for cause." After surveying a different jury, another colleague noted that the only time he had seen a more diverse group was in the cantina scene in the original *Star Wars* movie.

Such comments are amusing, but over the years I have learned that they are not particularly constructive and can be incredibly misleading and unproductive.

Yes, individual jurors are very distinct (e.g., your jury may include an impoverished twenty-five-year-old white man and a wealthy sixty-three-year-old black woman; a distinguished scientist with a Ph.D. and a high school drop-out; a stay-at-home mother and a woman who is the vice presideant of a bank). But the truth is, those people sitting in the jury box have more in common than at first might seem apparent. Understanding this fact will not only help you better understand why the jury system works, but it will make it easier for you to find ways to *educate* your jurors.

By now, you have undoubtedly realized that I use the word "educate" quite deliberately. As I note repeatedly, over many years of watching cases unfold in the courtroom, I have consistently seen that the best attorneys want their jurors to *learn* the facts at hand and respect their jurors for wanting to do a good job. Such educators are not lesser advocates—or any less adversarial. They just know that the fastest way to a juror's heart is through her mind—and the fastest way *inside* a juror's mind is via the ideas and values we all hold in common—and yes, we all share many ideas and values in common.

It is only a slight overstatement to claim that such wisdom and values are universally shared within a community. Obviously, there will be differences among juries—after all, a jury is made up of twelve *individuals*.

Nevertheless, there is enough overlap in this understanding so that a dozen randomly selected people, screened during voir dire to filter out the most obvious and obnoxious biases, can sufficiently understand and agree with each other and to form coalitions and develop consensus—two elements necessary for a jury verdict.

What You and Your Jurors Share in Common

Psychoanalytic pioneer Carl Jung talked about the "collective unconscious"—the idea that each person's psyche is part of a "reservoir of the experiences of our species" that has been passed across generations and societies. Jung theorized that our unconscious minds contain images, patterns, and themes (better known as "archetypes") that we all understand, simply by virtue of being human.

Some of the best-known archetypes include the Hero, the Outcast, the Star-Crossed Lovers, and the Femme Fatale, as well as the Quest, the Initiation, and the Loss of Innocence. If you tap into these archetypes—by portraying a betrayed investor as having lost her innocence, for instance, or a crusading activist as a hero—you tap into the deep emotions within each and every one of your jurors.

But archetypes are not always as "high brow" as those mentioned in the prior paragraph. *I Love Lucy* episodes, sketches from Monty Python, cartoons from Gary Larson's strip *The Far Side*—all work (I know this because I have used them) and they work because they, too, are part of Jung's "reservoir" of common experiences that resonate with all mankind. In fact, much of humor, literature, movies, and other forms of communication leave an impression upon us only because of our innate familiarity with the archetypes.

In addition to the collective "unconsciousness," it is important to be aware of the collective *consciousness* of a group of people—that is, the fact that your jurors, though cut from very different cultural and economic cloths, probably come to the courtroom with certain ideas and abilities, including:

- An ability to relate to analogies as a way of beginning to understand unfamiliar concepts
- Ideas and beliefs that the whole community feels and shares
- Metaphors, similes, stories, verbal expressions, and witticisms that participants understand intuitively
- Shared assumptions and presumptions, both favorable and unfavorable

These kinds of common connections are what make the jurors' collective decision-making process possible—and what make it possible for you, as a trial lawyer, to communicate with, educate, and persuade those jurors about your side of the case.

In the jazz standard "Lullaby of Birdland," Ella Fitzgerald sings, "Never in my wordland could there be ways to reveal in a phrase how I feel." I love this song, not only because Ella sings it, but also because it reminds me that all of us, particularly we lawyers, live in Wordland, a world where we often

"Never in my wordland could there be ways to reveal in a phrase how I feel."

–Ella Fitzgerald, Lullaby of Birdland

ILLUSTRATION 1-17 Ella Got It Right; Listen to Her

rely too heavily on words and forget that some of the most effective ways to communicate are much more subtle and indirect, and involve shared values or experiences as manifested in images, instead of words. (Ill. 1-17)

These shared experiences and images allow us to go beyond the limitations of the literal into the much more nuanced forms of the figurative. This is a form of communication that goes beyond relying on words and instead relies on emotion, instinct, and shared cultural memory to explain concepts. (Ill. 1-18)

To better appreciate this, it is helpful to imagine human activity along a spectrum. At the far left end of the spectrum are concepts that are often hard to describe because they involve considerable subtlety. At this end, the ordinary literal tools of "Wordland"—which is the realm in which most lawyers are comfortable operating—are not sufficiently delicate to convey the required nuance. At the other end of the spectrum are concepts that are often hard to describe because they are so vast. Here the common practice of explaining the situation by offering one or two examples does not adequately capture the magnitude of the situation.

Words tend to work best in the middle of this spectrum. At either end, the preferred approach is often indirect rather than straightforward and head-on. At the ends, you will often find both the person telling the story and the person learning from it relying on analogies, metaphors, or other less direct forms of communication.

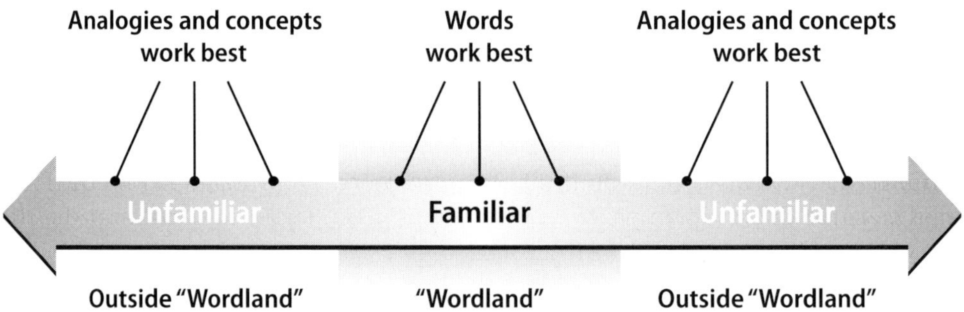

ILLUSTRATION 1-18 Inside Wordland Versus Outside Wordland
Words tend to work best in areas where we are already familiar; analogies and visual devices work best in areas with which we are less familiar.

The fact that these more subtle tools deliver their messages indirectly does not make them any less powerful. In fact, sometimes this is the only way to convey a message. Alan Watts, a scholar of Eastern religion, once used astronomy to explain this point. He noted that there are certain star clusters that, when you view them at night with the unaided eye, are easier to see using peripheral vision, rather than staring at them directly. He likened analogies to this peripheral vision, and chided those (many of whom may be lawyers) who insisted that the only acceptable approach was the most direct method.

Susan Cooper, the author of several fantasy books for young adults, has commented that analogies and metaphors allow the audience to "think bigger" and that greater truths can more easily be learned indirectly as opposed to directly. This is in part because the audience is first made comfortable by the analogies and is eased into the more complex process of finding the truth. It is also the case because, as a Zen Buddhist will tell you, some wisdom is beyond wisdom.

Let us take a closer look at the shared ideas and abilities your jurors bring to the courtroom.

The Ability to Relate to Analogies as a Way of Beginning To Understand Unfamiliar Concepts

Jurors (like all people) start learning unfamiliar material by connecting it to material (e.g., facts, concepts, or emotions) with which they are already familiar. That is, once jurors know what the new stuff is *like,* they feel confident enough to go to the next level of learning more. That is why analogies are so powerful and allow you to communicate with your jurors. If you want to explain a money-laundering scheme, for instance, explain that it is like washing dirty fingerprints off a towel (there's a reason it is called "laundering," after all). Or if you want to explain how DNA replicates, compare the initial step in the process to a zipper unzipping. The examples are endless.

Shared Ideas and Beliefs

Yes, your jurors may come from different cultures or social classes. But there is a pretty good chance they all believe that exploiting children is wrong; altruism is good; raping, pillaging, and plundering cannot be tolerated (at least not in their neighborhood); and caring for the elderly is important. Other beliefs that most people share are that people who work hard should be rewarded, that bad things can happen to good people, and that no one should be allowed to "get away with murder." As basic ideals held by large groups of people, you can use them to appeal to your jurors' shared sense of decency and to what is right or wrong, acceptable or unacceptable.

Metaphors, Similes, Stories, Verbal Expressions, and Witticisms That Participants Understand Intuitively

Stories, metaphors, and expressions provide shortcuts to understanding for the jurors because the references are loaded with long-held cultural meaning and values. Most of us know, for instance, that "David and Goliath" is a story of a small youth who defeats a larger, more experienced warrior. Using this story is an easy way to get jurors to understand what it is like for an independent retailer to battle a "big box" store.

Similarly, you could use "Hansel and Gretel approaching the candy cottage" to describe homeowners lured by too-good-to-be-true mortgage offers. Or use "stuck between a rock and a hard place" to describe the situation a drug dealer finds himself in when offered immunity to snitch on higher-ups, "from the frying pan to the fire" to help jurors visualize what it must be like for that same dealer to go back into his community after a plea bargain, or "like scaling Mount Everest," when the dealer makes heroic attempts to go straight.

Whatever the narrative device, your efforts to impress information upon your jurors using adages, stereotypes, metaphors, and similes will provide your audience with instant, gut-level feelings from which they can then build understanding. Often these gut-level feelings could never be explained except by using one of these commonly shared and understood shortcuts. Or, if the concept could be explained, it could only be done after prolonged efforts, and remember, time is scarce in the courtroom.

Here is another example: At the beginning of this section, I used the images of a major league baseball bleacher section and a *Star Wars* scene to help you understand my point about jury diversity. I did this intentionally because I know three things about these everyday images and expressions. First, they are likely to be more effective and more interesting than statistical information drawn from academic studies of juries, and the impression they create is likely to be just as accurate. Second, I know that most readers will know exactly what I am referring to. If I had been talking to twelve jurors, at least a couple of them, acting as my surrogate advocates, would know the reference and be able to explain the image to the rest of the group. Finally, I know that such words will produce images that are far more powerful than mere words in a juror's brain and will do it much more efficiently.

As a society, we use shortcuts like this all of the time. For example, political candidates refer to their opponent as a "Grinch" instead of saying that he is a "nasty, small-minded, mean, vindictive person." Those characteristics are compressed and assumed by the word "Grinch" because we as a culture share this concept. If you appreciated that shortcut, think how appreciative your jurors will be when you use similar shortcuts to help them understand a complex topic with which they have little familiarity—the stuff, that is, of many jury trials.

Shared Assumptions and Presumptions

While we do not want to traffic in most forms of prejudice, there are certain preconceived ideas that jurors tap into with great effect. Fortunately, the law has worked to eliminate the worst and most blatant prejudices—for example, those that discriminate based on ethnicity, gender, and religion. Nevertheless, many people believe that insurance companies are primarily out to make money and, therefore, cannot be trusted. Similarly, many people believe that government workers are uncaring bureaucrats, or that certain companies always deal fairly while other companies do not.

Sometimes these perceptions hold merit; other times this is not the case. But the fact is, these presumptions exist and present advantages and disadvantages to lawyers, depending on which side they are advocating.

How All of This Helps the Jury System Function

OK, so neither lawyers nor jurors are blank slates. There are a lot of applicable concepts already firmly entrenched in your mind and in the collective mind of the jurors. But what does this have to do with how and why the jury system works?

In a very real sense, the collective unconsciousness and consciousness, which we all share, act as a common currency that make learning, teaching, understanding, persuading, and ultimately building coalitions possible. Specifically, these shared concepts keep the jury system functioning by (1) helping you learn your case before coming to court, (2) helping you teach your case to the jury during trial, (3) helping the jurors understand your case, (4) helping to persuade certain jurors to become willing advocates on your behalf during deliberations, and (5) helping provide the tools that your jurors can use to persuade the others that your position is the correct one and, as such, that you are entitled to your desired verdict.

Whether unconscious or conscious, a metaphor or a simile, or any of the other shared tools described above, these cultural understandings that you and your witnesses share with your jurors provide the framework upon which every single case, no matter how factually complex, is ultimately resolved. They help jurors understand the "necessary stuff" that we must eventually attach to this framework in order to prove our case. Acknowledging and respecting this allows you to be a better advocate for your client and a much better teacher for your jurors, who, in turn, will hopefully advocate on behalf of your client and form the coalition necessary for a verdict. By leveraging the qualities we all share, you are more likely to get that kind of unity—the kind that you need to win your case.

Reason Three: The Jury System Works Because We Use Stories to Educate Our Jurors

The third reason that the jury system works is because of how we educate our jurors. Each side does this using a story. Granted, the bulk of the story can be somewhat disjointed, its internal cohesion repeatedly disrupted by questions, objections, and delayed answers. Nonetheless, it is still a story and, as we shall see, any disadvantages arising from this disjointed presentation style are offset by the fact that we tell the story three times, each time in a slightly different way and with a slightly different focus.

Over the last several thousand years, we have learned how to use stories to educate ourselves, educate others, and find common ground with which to relate to and communicate with strangers. Not coincidentally, all three of these accomplishments are necessary for a successful jury trial.

As a practical matter, using stories is a much more effective way to educate than simply listing relevant (but otherwise unconnected) facts. Lone facts are highly unstable and reactive compounds. They will either quickly disappear (i.e., are forgotten) or they will reach a state of equilibrium by clumping together and forming "fact chains," which will eventually combine to create a story.

So, why should a trial lawyer care about presenting individual facts if all they will do is either disappear or join other facts in a juror-created story? The short answer is that, as with all unstable compounds, it is often difficult to predict exactly what will happen with these isolated facts. Facts that you want to stick around may disappear; those that you wish would disappear may become permanently associated with you and your client's case. Additionally, you may not like the way that the jurors reassemble or link individual facts. While there is no way to guarantee that this will not happen, the facts become considerably more stable when they are revealed to the jury in context, that is, when they are told as part of a story.

A story is far easier to remember and use than a series of randomly collected facts. I can remember words in a song for decades, but I struggle to retain the definition of a single vocabulary word on my Word-Builder daily calendar. This is not because a song has more words. If more words were, by themselves, sufficient to improve memory, learning a long list of vocabulary words would be a piece of cake—and it is not. The process of remembering a song is made far easier by what connects the individual words.

I am more likely to lose a single key than I am to lose a collection of keys assembled on a chain. This is not just because there are more keys on the chain; it is also because of the thing that connects the individual keys—the chain itself. The same is true of a story. Facts communicated by way of a story tend to stick. They do not stick because there are a large number of random facts. They stick because the facts are *not* random; that is, the lawyer has very carefully chosen, in a logical manner, those elements necessary to create a successful story.

I want to pause to emphasize this last point: Facts do not stick merely because there are a lot of them! This point is obvious in theory, but easily forgotten in practice. How else do you explain the six-hour opening statement, weeks of expert testimony, and direct examinations, which, when transcribed, rival *Anna Karenina* in length, complexity, and the desire of the audience for a speeding train?

Pulling the jury together to hear the story of what happened subjects this diverse group to a common or shared experience. It is much the same effect as one observes when people discuss a movie or play they have just seen or a book they have all read. There will likely be a multitude of diverse opinions, but these opinions and the ensuing discussion have a common focus—the shared process of having experienced the story.

This shared experience increases the chance that the participants (lawyers, judge, witnesses, and jurors) are able to draw upon shared cultural experiences, which most often manifest themselves in the forms of adages, analogies, metaphors, and other indirect ways of communicating complicated information. In short, stories allow us to go beyond the limitations of the literal into the much more nuanced forms of the figurative. This is a form of communication that goes beyond relying on words and instead relies on emotion, instinct, and shared cultural memory to explain concepts. You are outside of "Wordland" and able to communicate what Ella was feeling.

Reason Four: The Jury System Works Because, at Trial, We Repeat the Story Three Times in Slightly Different Ways, Thereby Allowing Us to Use a Variety of Persuasion Tools

Even though we use stories to educate our jurors, a trial does not provide the most ideal conditions for doing so. The story we tell at trial is often disjointed. Sometimes it is told in the first person, sometimes in the third. Its internal cohesion is repeatedly disrupted by questions, objections, and delayed answers, and the order in which we offer evidence is affected by the availability of witnesses. Nonetheless, it is still a story and, as we will see, any disadvantage arising from this disjointed presentation style is more than offset by the fact that we tell the most important parts of the story three times, each time with a slightly different narrative style and emphasis. These subtle changes each time the story is told allow the lawyer to use a variety of teaching tools, which appeal to the different learning styles and Core Values on the jury. (Ill. 1-19)

The first time we tell the story is in opening statement through a third-person overview delivered directly by the lawyer to the jurors. Next, we tell the story during our case in chief, using direct and cross-examination testi-

	Life of Case		
	Opening	Case in chief	Closing
Storyteller	Lawyer	Witness	Lawyer
How story is told	Third Person Non-Argumentative	First Person Non-Argumentative	Third Person Argumentative

ILLUSTRATION 1-19 We Tell Our Story Three Times, in Three Different Ways

mony to present a series of first-person narratives from those with the most direct and detailed knowledge of the event—the percipient witnesses themselves. We conclude with the lawyer telling the story once again—this time by speaking directly to the jury in a third-person narrative but with virtually none of the restrictions the law imposes during opening statement.

Telling the story to the jury this way has at least two clear advantages. The most obvious advantage is the possibility of "constructive repetition."[16]

This approach is consistent with what teachers have told you in every public speaking class you have ever taken: "Tell them what you're going to tell them, tell them, and then tell them what you've told them."

Not surprisingly, this advice lines up perfectly with how we tell the jury our story in three parts at trial. Specifically, in opening statement we tell the jurors what we are going to tell them. During the case in chief, we tell our jurors what it is that we are there to tell them. Finally, during the closing argument, we tell them what we have told them.

There is a second and, to my mind, even more important benefit in our telling the story to the jury in three parts. Each time we tell the story, the rules of procedure, evidence, and common sense force us to tell it a bit differently and with a slightly different emphasis. These differences make it possible for the lawyer to provide a variety of customized Persuasion Tools designed to appeal to the different learning styles of the individual jurors.

To illustrate this point, let us go back for a moment to the case study that I used to start this chapter, the tragic case of the schizophrenic mother who drowned her three sons. I described how I encountered five different types of decision makers during the informal survey of my mock mock-jurors: (1) those who responded emotionally, (2) those who skipped emotion and resolved the dispute using checklists based on the jury instructions, (3) those who were

16. I want to draw a very important distinction between (1) "constructive repetition," which (as its name implies) is a powerful tool to stress what is truly important, and (2) "mindless repetition," which serves the function of, of—well, it serves absolutely no worthwhile function.

impressed by and relied on the science, (4) those rebels who were angry that "they" (as in a faceless government) had not stepped in earlier to prevent the tragedy, and (5) those who primarily relied on common sense to decide.

These jurors relied on different factors, from different parts of the case, to make up their minds. For example, those who were impressed by and relied on science were heavily influenced by the direct testimony of the expert witnesses. For them, the trial lawyer illustrated how having too much of one chemical led to Parkinson's disease, while having too much of the other caused schizophrenia. The "checklisters" (remember, these were the folks who wanted to know what elements were required to prove insanity, then looked to see if each had been established) used the jury instructions as their personal checklist and methodically evaluated the evidence accordingly. The common-sense followers (at least, those like my mother) would have relied on the playing of the interrogation tapes shown during direct testimony.

Experienced trial lawyers accept the fact that the jury will see the case in a variety of different ways; some of the jurors will see it the way the lawyer sees it; others will see it differently. This does not mean that those who see it differently will reach a different opinion (unless you give them no other opportunity); it just means they will reason and will potentially get to the same result by way of a different route.

As a result, the experienced trial lawyer is smart enough to provide a variety of different learning tools to the jury. To say that he will provide something for everyone is too broad, but he will provide material sufficient for a variety of people, who are influenced by a variety of factors, and who will then have the necessary raw data and Persuasion Tools to reach the end point desired by that lawyer.

In anticipation of a future discussion, let me stress that I am *not* suggesting that you "cover all the bases" by haphazardly inundating the jurors with multiple sets of inconsistent material. Nor am I advocating that you espouse multiple or alternative positions. All of the tools—and the paths they create—must be consistent with your central theory and themes.

Reason Five: The Jury System Works Because We Require the Essential Characters to Tell Their Stories in First-Person Narratives to the Jury

The fifth reason jurors generally get it right is that, as part of telling the story, we make the primary characters come into court, face the jury, and relate what they believe happened in an essentially first-person narrative. Very few things that these witnesses say or do when they tell their stories escape the scrutiny of the twelve pairs of eyes, twelve different backgrounds, and twelve different personalities on the jury. It is the kind of scrutiny every father wishes he could apply to his daughter's first prom date. It is the kind of scrutiny that every first prom date is afraid his girlfriend's father is applying to him.

Having the actual person there to give a first-party narrative provides considerable information to the jurors that could not be presented in any other way. The storyteller is subject to close inspection. Witnesses can be asked directly about bias and the jurors can watch how they respond. Jurors are able to observe body language and look for other subtle clues that are completely absent in any third-party narrative.

As trial lawyers, I think we sometimes forget how much our trial system cues off this notion of the first-person narrative. For example, all of the rules of competency are designed to protect this form of testimony. We require that witnesses have personally "absorbed" the events through their own senses and then, after having done so, be sufficiently competent to personally relay what it is that they heard, saw, felt, tasted, and/or smelled. Witnesses must have personal knowledge in order to testify. We test veracity by making the actual person come to the stand. Likewise, our hearsay rules are designed to make sure that there is a proper and personal link between witnesses and the "statements" that they are asked to testify about in court. The use of leading questions is limited. Here again, we want to be able to evaluate what the witness has to say, not the monosyllabic grunts that usually follow leading questions. Additionally, one of the reasons that cross-examination is so powerful and is considered to be the cornerstone of our adversarial system is that it allows the lawyer to question the person who offers a first-person narrative, again all so the jury can examine what this person has to say.

Reason Six: The Jury System Works Because There Are Opportunities at Key Points in the Trial for the Lawyer to Talk Directly to the Jurors

A powerful technique common to many great stories is the ability of the narrator to directly address his audience. You can trace the use of this tool back to sections of Homer's *The Iliad* and *The Odyssey,* to the choruses in Greek tragedies, through the asides and soliloquies in Shakespeare, to the voice-overs in modern film.

At trial, lawyers have three "sanctioned" opportunities to address the jury directly.[17] These opportunities occur during (1) voir dire (to the extent permitted by specific courts), (2) opening statement, and (3) closing argument. Directly addressing the jury contributes to the jury's success not because it is

17. There are at least two other opportunities that are less "sanctioned" by the court: (1) leading questions, in which the lawyer puts her own words into the mouth of the witness—a technique approved by a court only in limited circumstances (e.g., in cross-examination, when the court determines the witness as having substantial problems expressing himself, and in preliminary matters) and (2) "speaking" objections by which the lawyer presents a long explanation in the jurors' presence as to why he is objecting to the admission of particular evidence—a technique rarely permitted for very long by the court. It should go without saying that it is improper to rely on speaking objections as a deliberate strategy for directly addressing the jurors.

a substitute for the storytelling process, but because it is an effective way of ensuring that subtle nuances are highlighted and specifically addressed by the lawyer. It is almost a way for the lawyer to turn directly to the jurors and say, "Hey, did you get that? Did you get the point of what I said or did?"

Arguably, speaking directly to the jurors in order to uncover and explain subtlety is most crucial in closing argument, when the trial lawyer is allowed, with very few restrictions, to remind the jury of the testimony they heard oftentimes weeks before, to explain how the facts intertwine with the law, and to make explicit the arguments he has been making implicitly throughout the trial. It is the lawyer's opportunity to become the personification of that phrase you often see at the end of crucial quotations in legal briefs—"Emphasis added."

Reason Seven: The Jury System Works Because Jurors Have "Collective Intuition"

Jurors generally get it right because of what I call Collective Intuition . . . horse sense . . . common sense . . . you pick the descriptor. It is this unpretentious, highly impressive, intangible factor that surprises and often humbles even the most experienced trial lawyer. After struggling for years to come up with an apt term for this phenomenon, I can think of no better way of describing it than "Collective Intuition." As the American novelist Nathaniel Hawthorne so accurately noted in his masterpiece, *The Scarlet Letter:*

> When an uninstructed multitude attempts to see with its eyes, it is exceedingly apt to be deceived. When, however, it forms its judgment, as it usually does, on intuitions of its great and warm heart, the conclusions thus attained are often so profound and so unerring, as to possess the character of truths supernaturally revealed.

Counsel should never underestimate this powerful force with which the jurors uncover "The Truth" and then favor one side over the other. As we will discuss throughout this book, there are a variety of ways that you can appeal to this Collective Intuition and, hopefully, channel it in a way that benefits your client.

As noted above, this Collective Intuition can sometimes startle lawyers, who are both impressed and depressed by the ability of the collective jury to spot issues and problems ignored or not previously seen by the lawyer. The lawyers have lived with the case for years; how is it that the jury that has only known of it for a fraction of this time sees something that the lawyer has not?

I think that the answer to this question has to do with a principle closely related to Collective Intuition—namely, the concept I call the "Insight from a Distance." While knowledge of a case (by this I mean knowing the facts and details) will continue to grow in direct proportion to the time you put into it, insight (by this I mean perspective and understanding) will not. At some point, the law of diminishing returns comes into play and the detailed knowledge of facts pushes out increased perspective and understanding. If you construct your case correctly, by not burdening the jurors with excessive detail, they will hopefully not experience this effect. Instead, they will retain Insight from a Distance and still be able to develop their own sense of perspective about the case.

Reason Eight: The Jury System Works Because Jurors Have "Collective Wisdom"

The jury as a whole is often much more intelligent than the collection of its individual parts. As James Surowiecki noted in his 2004 book, *The Wisdom of Crowds: Why the Many Are Smarter Than the Few and How Collective Wisdom Shapes Business, Economies, Societies, and Nations,* groups often come to better decisions than the decisions that could have been made by any single member of the larger group.

While *The Wisdom of Crowds* focuses on groups other than juries, many of its observations are equally applicable to what goes on during deliberations. Surowiecki has observed that "collective wisdom" is particularly effective where the group has four specific characteristics:

- The group must start with a *diversity of opinion,* with each member having his or her own perspective and interpretation of the underlying facts.
- There must be a *degree of independence* in the decision-making process such that each member can reach an opinion without necessarily being affected by others in the group.
- There must be *decentralization of informational sources,* that is, the members must be able to draw on a wide area of local knowledge.
- There must be some form of *aggregation,* that is, some formal method of turning the individual opinions into a collective decision.

For the most part, all four of these conditions exist in a jury. We pull together a relatively diverse group of individuals to serve as jurors. These jurors bring with them diverse informational sources based on their own individual lives and experiences. The court expressly orders that none of them communicate among themselves until after the case is done—at which time the vast majority of the jurors have independently formulated their own conclusions of what happened and who should prevail. The requirement that the jurors reach a unanimous decision in order for there to be a verdict forces the jurors through an aggregation process, which will be discussed in greater detail in Chapter 3.

CHAPTER 2

The "Four Inputs"

Chapter Introduction

When I am asked what it is that trial lawyers do, I often fall back on the simplest and best explanation I have ever heard. It came from the 12-year-old son of a lawyer friend of mine who concluded that what trial lawyers *really* do is go into court and "make their [client's] version the TRUTH."

Out of the mouths of babes. . . .

I love two things about this description (besides its naïve accuracy). First, it is an elegant reminder of what philosophers describe as the "consensus theory of truth." This theory provides that the truth is whatever a specified group concludes it to be.

At first glance, some people are offended by this suggestion and believe that it somehow belittles something as noble as the truth. After all, at its most trivial, the consensus theory of truth echoes what a high school student once told me, "Fashion is what the cool people tell me it is." At its most pernicious, the theory potentially leads to considerable mischief (or worse) and confirms that the victors are the ones who get to write history—accurately or otherwise.

Nevertheless, in a very practical sense and with a reluctant bow to necessity, we accept this theory and apply it to our trials. For trial lawyers, the specified group is obviously the jury, and its consensus, which is ultimately reflected in that group's verdict, is about as close as we get to "the TRUTH."

The second thing I like about the job description is that it reminds me that we are engaged in a process through which we hope to shape a particular outcome, although we have only limited control. If you have any hope of consistently succeeding in this process and making your client's version "the TRUTH," you must appreciate two things: (1) the resources (or inputs) that go into the process and (2) the mechanics by which these resources are transformed into a final product. This chapter deals with the resources; Chapter 3 deals with the mechanics. (Ill. 2-1)

Throughout a trial, jurors are constantly receiving and processing massive amounts of information, which eventually serve as the basis for their verdict. At various points, the judge pauses to remind them that they can rely on only a fraction of this material when making their decision. We label this subset of

ILLUSTRATION 2-1 Jurors Receive and Process More Than Just Evidence
Jurors receive massive amounts of information, including not only what we officially label "evidence" but also material prewired into the jurors and the Proto-Stories prepared by the lawyers specifically for the case.

material "evidence." Officially, this "evidence" consists of the "viva voce" testimony of witnesses and such other material as is marked, authenticated, and admitted by the court into the official record. Technically, this is the raw data upon which the jury bases its decision. Realistically, this is *not* what happens, or at least, this is *not all* of what happens.

Despite what a neatly typed and bound trial transcript and subsequent record on appeal may suggest, what jurors actually rely on when they decide a case is not limited to the "evidence." In addition, the jury relies on two broad sources of material, one internal and one external.

The internal material is what comes prewired into the jurors by way of attitudes, preconceptions, existing knowledge, and so on. Some of this prewiring is unique to a *single* juror as part of what makes that person unique. However, much of this material is common to more than one juror (in fact, some of it will be common to *all* jurors) simply because they are human and, as such, often share common attitudes and knowledge.

The second source is the external material prepared by the lawyer based on the particulars of the case. The most important type of this material is what I call the "Proto-Story." For purposes of this introduction, let us define the Proto-Story as the party's best version of why it should prevail. It is how each side would respond if you challenged: "Go ahead. Give me your best shot!"

Simply put, the best lawyers are usually the ones with the best Proto-Stories. This chapter focuses on the elements of a good Proto-Story as well as how one goes about selecting these elements and combining them with other facts for the jury.

The Proto-Story

Throughout the trial, each side presents its Proto-Story to the jury.[1] The Proto-Story is the gestalt or "organized whole" of what you believe you need to persuade your jurors. The Proto-Story is made up of what I call the Four Inputs: (1) the Factual Strand, (2) the Persuasion Tools, (3) the Operating Instructions, and (4) the Arguments. (Ill. 2-2)

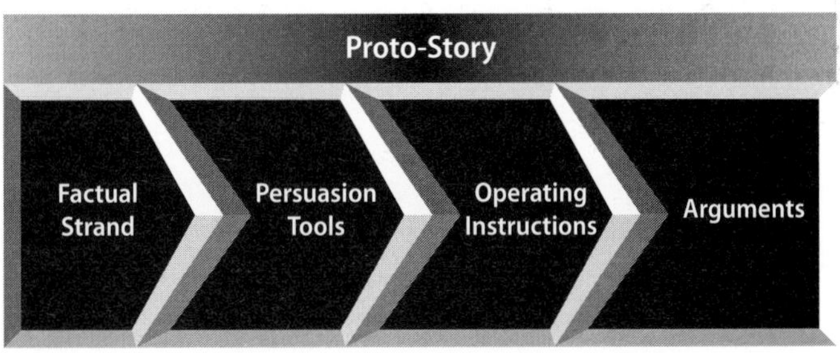

ILLUSTRATION 2-2 The Proto-Story Consists of the Four Inputs

THE FACTUAL STRAND: AN OVERVIEW

When my daughter Kelsey was little, the "hypsies" (part hippy, part gypsy) along Telegraph Avenue in Berkeley would "wrap" sections of her hair. For a

1. As this sentence suggests, since each side has its own Proto-Story, there are at least two Proto-Stories in every trial. Obviously, this number increases with the number of parties. For purposes of simplicity, every case described in this book has two parties and, thus, two Proto-Stories.

small donation, they would interweave ribbons and colorful string into a section of her long hair and then thread different-shaped beads onto the resulting strands. As a six-year-old, my daughter was always delighted with the result. In my mind's eye, when I picture the collection of material that I call the Factual Strand, it resembles one of my daughter's colorful hair wraps.

The Factual Strand consists of two parts: the Central Cord and the Included Facts. (Ill. 2-3)

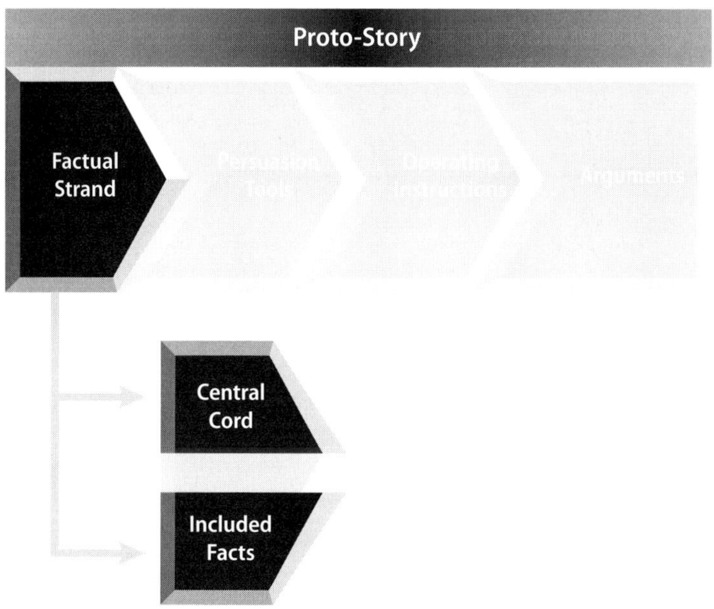

ILLUSTRATION 2-3 The Factual Strand
The Factual Strand consists of the Central Cord and the Included Facts.

The Central Cord is made up of three subparts. In the center of the Cord lies the Case Theory. I imagine multiple threads of colorful Case Themes and Explanation of Motive interwoven or braided through this core. (Ill. 2-4)

We will spend considerable time in this chapter examining these three subparts of the Central Cord, but for now you can think of the Case Theory as the "what" of the case, that is, as an outline or condensed version of the story line or an explanation of *what* happened. As we will discuss below in greater detail, each side should have only one such explanation. Your Case Themes explain three "whys"—*why* events described in your Case Theory happened, *why* the jury should care, and *why* the jury should rule in your client's favor. Your Explanation of Motive explains a fourth "why"—*why* key people behaved the way they did.

Strung onto this Central Cord are the "Included Facts," which I visualize as a series of differing beads. (Ill. 2-5) The differences in the beads (i.e., their varying sizes, shapes, and colors) help illustrate that not all facts are of equal value, weight, or significance. Most facts are contested; others are undisputed.

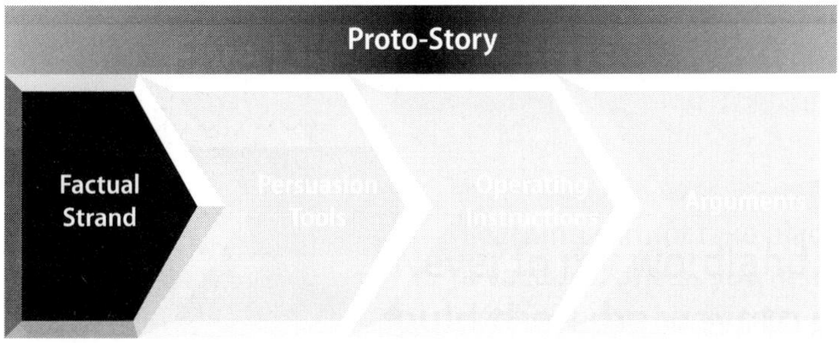

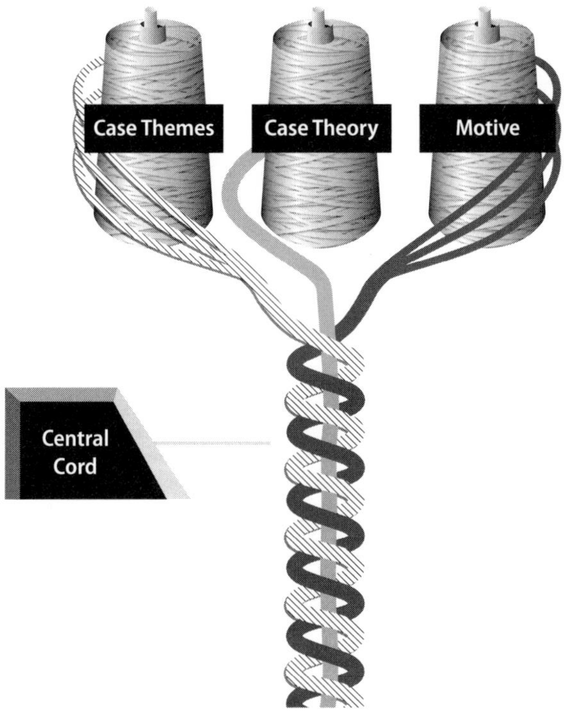

ILLUSTRATION 2-4 The Central Cord
The Central Cord is made up of a single Case Theory around which one or more Themes or Explanations of Motive are wrapped.

Some come from wholly unbiased sources; others come from unreliable people such as "snitches" who hope to shorten their own prison terms by increasing someone else's. Many facts will be easy to prove; others will be battled over all the way through deliberations. As we shall see, these differences need to be taken into account when assembling your Proto-Story.

What is important about the Factual Strand is not only the individual components and the way they interact, but also how the successful trial lawyer selects these parts and physically assembles them. For now, I will concentrate on describing the key components and identifying the role each plays (individually and in concert with one another); later we will discuss how to select and assemble this material in an effective manner.

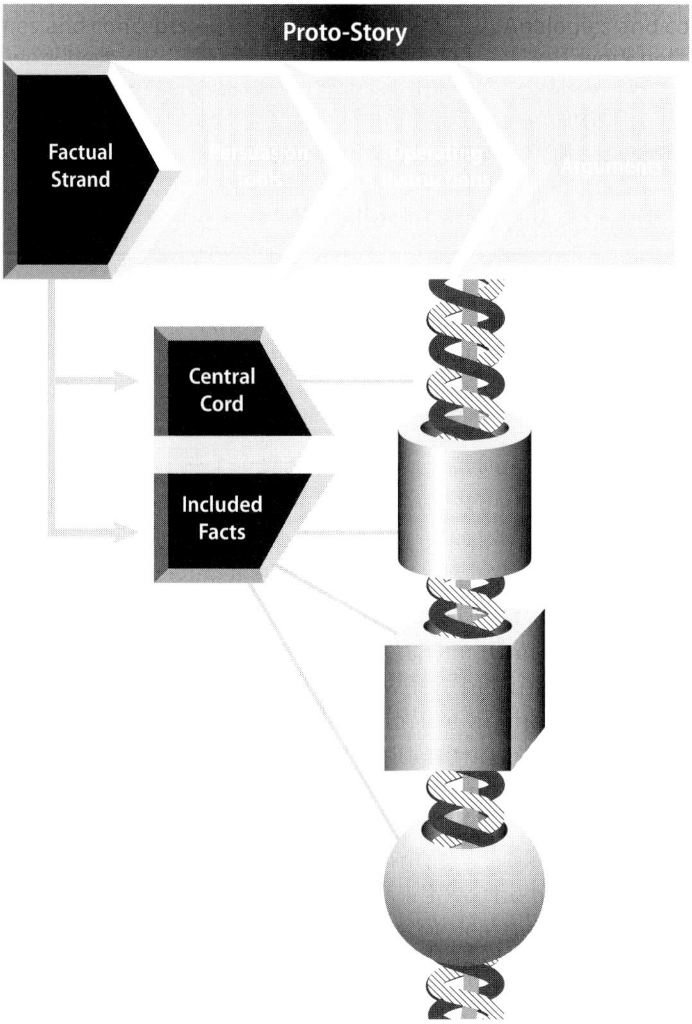

ILLUSTRATION 2-5 The Included Facts
The Included Facts are "strung" onto the Central Cord.

THE CENTRAL CORD

Your Case Theory

Case Theory Defined

Your Case Theory is the legally relevant story line with which you hope to convince the jury that your version of "the TRUTH" is accurate and that your side should win. It is your "hypothesis" of what you believe happened, almost always tempered a bit by the limitations of what you know you can actually prove, and then stretched here and chopped there to fit the Procrustean bed that is your Legal Theory.

Your Case Theory is the unifying concept underlying the foundation upon which you present all other elements of your case. It provides the necessary internal logic that helps convince the jury that your version of what happened is the one that they should trust and believe. Said differently, your Case Theory is the single best version (based on what the court is likely to allow as admissible evidence) of what you claim happened leading up to the litigation.

A Case Theory consists of two subparts or interwoven strands: (1) the Factual Theory and (2) the Legal Theories. (Ill. 2-6) The skillful lawyer fashions Case Theory from specific facts unique to his case and from general Legal Theories established over centuries by the common law and statutes.

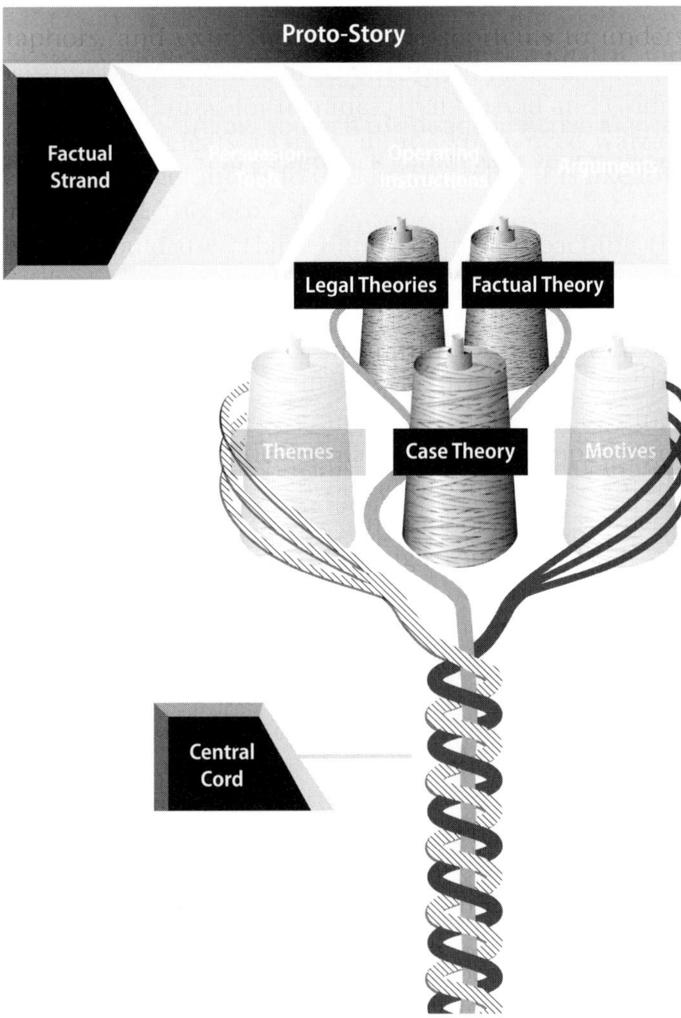

ILLUSTRATION 2-6 The Case Theory Is Fashioned From the Legal Theories and the Factual Theory

Your case's Factual Theory and your case's facts are *not* the same thing. The Factual Theory is a high-level narrative or outline that exists because of the facts, but it is a summary and, as with all summaries, it stands at some distance from the facts themselves. If we imagine facts to be individual pieces of a mosaic, the Factual Theory is the overall pattern. It is what we see from a distance—and can see only from a distance—when perspective momentarily trumps detail.

Intertwined with the Factual Theory are the case's Legal Theories. The sources for this material include pattern jury instructions, defining statutes, regulations, and the common law. As noted above, Legal Theories are not unique to your set of factual circumstances. Legal Theories are merely impersonal attempts by society to broadly classify recurring patterns of human behavior into legally definable wrongs or defenses and, once classified, to prescribe how to deal with them in a consistent manner.

Based on this description, you can probably understand why, when I think of Legal Theories, I inevitably think of taxonomists—those scientists who, after staring at trays and trays of creatures, classify them according to the specimen's characteristics. "This one is an *Agelaius phoeniceus*. . . . And this one? This one is a. . . ."

Indeed, the relationship between the Factual Theory and the Legal Theories is circular. The Legal Theories define what facts are relevant and converts what might otherwise appear to be unconnected facts into a viable cause of action or affirmative defense. In turn, the Factual Theory defines what evidence you need to assemble for a particular cause of action or defense. A Factual Theory exists because of the presence of certain facts. At the same time, these facts are relevant only because of a particular Legal Theories.

My point is that in many ways, the distinction between Legal Theory and Factual Theory is artificial, much like the distinction between the Taoist version of yin and yang. (Ill. 2-7) One does not fully exist without the other; each defines the other; neither is completely meaningful without the other.

Said slightly differently, an overall Case Theory that lacked the necessary substrand of Legal Theories would not survive a demurrer because it would fail to include a legal claim upon which relief could be granted. An overall Case Theory without the necessary substrand of Factual Theory would never

ILLUSTRATION 2-7 Legal Theory and Factual Theory Define Each Other
The distinction between Legal Theory and Factual Theory is somewhat artificial, much like the difference between the Taoist version of yin and yang.

survive summary judgment because you would lack the necessary facts to prove your Legal Theories.

The trick lies in knowing how to integrate the facts and the law in a way that leads the jury in the direction that both you and your client desire. When you construct it properly, the Case Theory will be helpful in a variety of ways for you and for the jury. For example, the Case Theory helps you formulate your plan of attack or defense and, as such, helps you choose what evidence you need, which witnesses to call, and the order for presenting this material to the jury. For the jurors, the Legal Theories should provide a comfortable vantage point or platform from which they can view the evidence and law, and come to the conclusion that you are right.

Characteristics of a Good Case Theory

A good Case Theory has twelve key characteristics. (Ill. 2-8) Not all twelve must be present for a Case Theory to be successful, but clearly, the more of them you have, the more likely your overall approach will be accepted by the jurors.

Characteristic One: A Good Case Theory Has Internal Logic

First, and perhaps most importantly, a good Case Theory has internal logic. This requires that the facts you use support, not contradict, each other. One of the easiest ways to accomplish this is to avoid the lawyerly habit of "arguing in the alternative." Suggesting that your client was nowhere near the murder site, but that when he killed the victim he acted in self-defense, is just plain stupid. At best, jurors see such arguments as confusing. More likely, they see this approach as disingenuous.

So, what is the natural extension to the rule that tells you to avoid arguing in the alternative? The answer is straightforward: In jury trials, you should have one (and only one) overall Case Theory. This means you should pick a single, consistent version of the facts and stick to it. Having more than one Case Theory effectively guarantees that you will be arguing in the alternative.

An observant reader might have noticed what *appears* to be a contradiction: I strongly urge you to have a single *Case* Theory, but mention the possibility of pursuing multiple *Legal* Theories. Allow me to explain why this is not contradictory.

Your Case Theory is your overall version of what happened—you should have only one of these. As discussed earlier, your Case Theory is made up of two parts: (1) your Factual Theory and (2) one or more Legal Theories. A single version of what happened (your overall Case Theory) may meet the requirements of multiple Legal Theories. To repeat an earlier mythological reference, with a bit of minor stretching and hacking, your single Case Theory may fit comfortably (if such a thing is possible) in variations of a Procrustean bed.

This is similar to the concept we learned in first year Civil Procedure class for drafting a complaint. The complaint will detail a general series of facts describing what allegedly happened, but that single set of facts will be used as

A Good Case Theory:

1. **Has internal logic**
2. **Is assembled and presented in a logical manner**
3. **Addresses all legal elements required in your case**
4. **Is easy to believe**
5. **Is based on carefully chosen facts**
6. **Confronts your opponent's key facts**
7. **Must be consistent with your overall strategic objectives**
8. **Does not get bogged down in the details**
9. **Does not prematurely force the jury to conclude that the opposing party is a scoundrel**
10. **Lets the jury know they are righting a wrong**
11. **Applies the theory of Occam's Razor**
12. **Is one that you yourself believe**

ILLUSTRATION 2-8 Characteristics of a Good Case Theory

the basis for multiple causes of action with slightly different legal or factual requirements. These causes of action are usually related to each other, and, as such, are generally complementary. The same applies here—you need a single, unified statement of what happened (this is your overall Case Theory), but that single statement may be sufficient to trigger a series of related Legal Theories.

Having said all of this, let me caution you against thinking you can get around the rule against arguing alternative Case Theories by merely attempting to prove a score of different (and potentially contradictory) causes of action or defenses at trial. Just as you should limit yourself to one Case Theory and thus avoid arguing in the alternative, you should limit your number of Legal Theories to no more (and hopefully less) than a handful; any more will likely confuse the jury. To the extent that you have multiple Case Themes, they should complement, rather than conflict with, each other.

Let me repeat—the ultimate lesson here is to settle on a single Case Theory and then carefully pick a limited number of consistent (or at least not inconsistent) Legal Theories to pursue at trial.

"Why," you might ask, "can't I argue in the alternative? I did so in law school on every final exam." The simplest answer to this is: "Thank God, this is not law school. You do not get a better 'grade' at trial by spotting and arguing every potential issue." For the most part, your audience in a jury trial has never been to law school and is unfamiliar with the legal technique of arguing in the alternative. Not only does this technique of presenting alternative versions with differing degrees of plausibility appear disingenuous to the jurors, it is confusing and makes it difficult for them to keep track of your arguments during deliberations.

According to the psychological theory known as the "economy of hypothesis," people prefer a single explanation to multiple ones. Consequently, most jurors will remember your overall Case Theory better than the individual details or facts. Jurors will often lose confidence in a lawyer who advances alternative theories or inconsistent positions, and they are far more comfortable with a single, central theory that reconciles the greatest number of discrepancies. Multiple possible explanations do nothing but create more perceived irreconcilable problems in the jurors' minds.

The final reason that arguing every conceivable issue at trial is a mistake has to do with time, or the lack of it. Such an approach is a waste of time and, as we will discuss later, time is one of the scarcest resources at trial—do not squander it.

Characteristic Two: A Good Case Theory Is Assembled And Presented in a Logical Manner

The second characteristic of a good Case Theory is that it can be assembled and presented in such a way that each fact leads logically to the next one, and to the next one, and onward. In short, the Case Theory should provide well-lighted stepping stones that, without excessive strain or heavy handedness, will naturally lead the jury to the conclusion that you should win. Formulating such a path can be harder than it initially seems. Nevertheless, one of the best ways to accomplish it is to work hard at refining your story—a process that we will address throughout the balance of this book.

Characteristic Three: A Good Case Theory Addresses All Legal Elements Required in Your Case

All good Case Theories have a third characteristic, namely, they address *all* the legal elements of your case. As we have noted, the Case Theory must provide the necessary compartments that you fill to establish a prima facie case on behalf of your client's claims or defenses. If you need a mental image for this, think of the display boards that coin collectors use to house their collections. These boards have a series of holes, roughly the size of the coin, aligned in parallel rows. Below each hole is a description of what is supposed to go inside the corresponding slot (e.g., a 1956-D Silver Washington or a

1976-S Bicentennial), and most collectors cannot rest until each of the holes is filled. No matter how fluid and convincing your story may be at trial, if it fails to establish even one necessary element, the trial court and/or the court of appeals is not going to let you win. You need to follow the lead of the coin collector and fill *all* of the necessary slots.

Characteristic Four: A Good Case Theory Is Easy to Believe

A good Case Theory needs to be simple and easy for the jury to believe. Whenever possible, it should neither defy common sense nor contradict real-life, everyday experience.

There is a wonderful cartoon by the great James Thurber that was published by the *New Yorker* in 1932. It shows a couple sitting in bed. Behind them on the bed's headboard sits a seal (as in aquatic mammal) that they evidently cannot see. The wife, who looks like she is disgusted with her husband and has finally decided to give up rather than argue any more, is seen saying, "All right, have it your way—you heard a seal bark!"[2]

This cartoon always reminds me that we live in a relatively predictable world. With this predictability comes a willingness to readily accept that which is consistent with our expectations of reality. Conversely, we are reluctant to accept anything that is contrary to what we consider reasonably plausible. We may eventually come around, but it takes extraordinary effort for us to accept anything out of the ordinary.

Sure, by some set of freak circumstances there might someday be a seal hidden in your bedroom, and sure, with enough effort, you may be able to convince your significant other that you heard it bark—but good luck. Such an explanation is so far from the acceptable realm of probability that you will never likely convince anyone, even if the seal is sitting directly over your head. Instead, if possible, go for an explanation more readily consistent with common, everyday, expected reality. If this is not possible, be ready to stay up late arguing that you heard a seal bark and have the evidence to prove it.

Characteristic Five: A Good Case Theory Is Based on Carefully Chosen Facts

A good Case Theory is based on carefully chosen facts, and not all facts are created equal. A good Case Theory must include all the undisputed facts and avoid those facts that are implausible or difficult to prove. A good Case Theory never relies on inadmissible material, no matter how "good" such material is or how much you really, really, really wish you could incorporate it into the Legal Theories. Later in this chapter, we will spend considerable time discussing how you go about weighing and selecting the best facts for your case.

Characteristic Six: A Good Case Theory Confronts Your Opponent's Key Facts

I once worked on a criminal case involving a young man accused of having participated in two gang-related gun battles that occurred at opposite

2. To view this, and other cartoons by James Thurber, visit www.cartoonbank.com.

ends of San Francisco. We had stacks of evidence—I mean, literally, *stacks* of evidence—that our client had not committed the crimes. By contrast, the district attorney had two—and only two—bits of evidence on her side. Unfortunately, these bits were our guy's fingerprint found at one location and his DNA at the second location across town.

Of course, your opposing counsel will have his own favorable facts—sometimes he will have *really* favorable facts. The other side's facts are not going to disappear; the only place they are going is into the record to be used against you—so deal with them!

A good Case Theory deals with the reality that your case has weaknesses. As a result, your Case Theory must find some way to confront these "bad" facts instead of ignoring them. The best thing you can do is to find a way to incorporate these facts into your explanation of what happened.

Ideally (but rarely), you will be able to use what I call "adversarial aikido" or "judicial ju-jitsu" to turn what initially appears to be an adverse fact to your advantage. There are few things more satisfying than taking an adverse fact and, with a mere flip of the wrist, not only rendering it harmless but then, with a slight shift of weight, making it something that works to your benefit.

Unfortunately, you will rarely get this kind of traction from adverse facts. But that does not mean you can afford to ignore them. Instead, confront them head on. Find a way to explain them as part of your overall Case Theory. Do not run the risk of losing your credibility; admit the unfavorable facts that cannot be denied and adjust your case accordingly.

Characteristic Seven: A Good Case Theory Is Consistent With Your Overall Strategic Objectives

Your Case Theory must be consistent with your strategic objectives. Most often, this involves confirming that your Case Theory matches your desired remedy. For example, the story line that you would use for injunctive relief would undoubtedly be different from that which you might use for compensatory damages, which would be different from what you would use for punitive damages.

Characteristic Eight: A Good Case Theory Does Not Get Bogged Down in the Details

The best Case Theories are relatively bare-boned. Engineers who have become lawyers (or lawyers who should have become engineers) sometimes have difficulty coming up with a succinct Case Theory because it is hard for them to let go of the details, especially since they are often vexed by generalities and conclusory statements—both of which are necessary for a good Case Theory.

Remember, your Case Theory is not your entire case; it is only the framework for your case. As with any supporting structure, it will get exponentially denser once you start using it for the purpose for which it was designed, that is, providing support for multiple layers of substantiating material. Starting off with a bare-boned Case Theory prevents your final case from ultimately becoming too dense. By contrast, starting with an overly complicated Case Theory virtually guarantees that what you finally present to the jury will be far too convoluted and thick for most jurors to understand.

Characteristic Nine: A Good Case Theory Does Not Prematurely Force The Jury to Conclude That the Opposing Party Is a Scoundrel

Unless the facts are overwhelmingly in your favor, a good Case Theory does not immediately force the jury to assume that the opposing party did something unethical, malicious, or illegal.[3] Jurors often give people the benefit of the doubt until it is absolutely clear that they can no longer afford to do so. This approach is consistent with the advice one of my wise aunts gave me, "Chris, don't confuse someone who cannot help being stupid with someone who is deliberately trying to be a pain in the butt!" Be sure to consider this as you (1) assemble your Case Theory and (2) decide what Legal Theories you should assert as part of that process.

Some trial lawyers use Case Theories that too quickly accuse their opposition of intentional wrongdoing when all that is really involved (or all that the jury is likely to initially accept as being involved) is mere negligence or (as my aunt would say) "being stupid." Unless your opposing party is clearly evil, be careful when using this approach. Jurors will be reluctant to immediately label someone as "bad" merely because you claim they are. Instead, jurors are more likely to view an early attack as excessive and unduly adversarial. Such an attack at the beginning of your case is more likely to put your credibility into question than that of your opposing party.

Let me be clear here. Of course evil people exist and it is sometimes necessary to identify your opposing party as belonging to that group. I am merely suggesting that the better Case Theories do not hastily apply an unsavory description to the opposition, nor do they require its acceptance *as a precondition* for the jurors to identify with the lawyer's position. Instead, good Case Theories tend to build to this conclusion after the jury has been gradually shown—and has accepted—your negative characterization of the opposing party. Given enough and consistent evidence, jurors will eventually reach the conclusion that your opposing party is a scoundrel (or worse), but it takes time; avoid using a Case Theory that forces the jury to rush the process. If your opposing party is really all that bad, the jurors will see it in their own good time. If they draw this conclusion on their own, they will cling to it with great conviction.

As a corollary to this, let me remind you to avoid sarcasm or otherwise treating your opposing party and counsel with disrespect. The feeling of satisfaction you may get will not last very long once you hear that your jurors hated your smugness and condescension.

3. This rule does not always apply to prosecutors in criminal cases where, despite what the official rules as to presumption of innocence may require, the defendant is often presumed by many jurors to have done something wrong or he wouldn't be on trial.

Characteristic Ten: A Good Case Theory Lets The Jury Know They Are Righting a Wrong

Many of the best Case Theories incorporate what I call a "Don Quixote" element, that is, they encourage the jurors to (1) right a wrong, (2) prevent a wrong from occurring, and/or (3) prevent the perpetrator from profiting from his wrongdoing.

Psychologically, this feeds into the desire of most jurors to be helpful and to fix what they see as broken. I suspect that you have seen signs posted that advise, "If it ain't broke, don't fix it." When I see such a warning, I am reminded just how powerful our need is to "do something." The sign acknowledges our innate desire to tinker, to fix, to correct—even when the situation does not warrant it or the person most directly affected by our actions does not want our help. Your challenge is to foster the jurors' desire to "fix it" as part of your Case Theory.

Characteristic Eleven: A Good Case Theory Applies the Theory of Occam's Razor

The best Case Theories apply Occam's razor, which holds that, "If two theories explain the facts equally well, the simpler theory is preferred." An audience member at a lecture I once gave offered me his own home-grown version of this theory. He said that when he was growing up on a ranch in central California, his father would occasionally remind him, "If you hear hoofbeats, assume it's a horse, not a zebra." In other words, the simpler theory is the one that is most likely to be correct and, therefore, a better bet.

For purposes of jury trials, you can add two corollaries to Occam's razor. The simpler theory is not only the one that is most likely to be correct, but also it is (1) the one that is likely to be easier to prove and (2) the one the jury is more likely to accept as true. These two corollaries by themselves provide enough of a reason, whenever possible, to apply Occam's razor to your Case Theory.

Characteristic Twelve: A Good Case Theory Is One That You Yourself Believe

The best Case Theories are the ones in which you personally believe. My grandfather, who was the most honest car salesman and mechanic I ever knew, used to say, "You can't sell what you yourself don't buy." This is a good recommendation that should be followed by anyone whose business is persuasion.

Without knowing it, my grandfather offered advice consistent with that advocated by Aristotle in his work on rhetoric. The Greek philosopher insisted that one of the three crucial elements to a successful argument was "ethos," the persuasive force that comes from a speaker's personal qualities as an advocate. The melding of positive personal qualities with an argument in which the speaker obviously believes creates a very powerful one-two punch that is not wasted on your opponent nor the spectators who make up the jury.

How to Know If You Have the Right Case Theory

Your Case Theory is the overall formula that you hope the jury will use to rule in your favor. But how do you know if you have a good Case Theory?

In order to judge its effectiveness, I like to apply what I call the "Successful Broadway Musical Test."

Traditionally, New York theatre critics would, in part, judge the success of a Broadway musical by observing if the audience left the theatre on opening night humming refrains from the show's songs. If they were humming the tunes, there was a chance that the musical was good. If no one was humming, the performance was likely to have been a flop.

You can use a similar standard to judge the success of your Case Theory. Specifically, if you are successful, your Case Theory will align with the general position that the jury adopts and will keep humming through deliberations and all the way into post-verdict interviews. Chapters 4 and 5 will discuss suggestions for putting together such a Case Theory and how to test it using such tools as Mental Mining and Feedback Forums to make sure that you have done the best possible job.

Your Case Themes

Case Themes Defined

To succeed at trial, you need to convince the jury that your position is legally correct *and* morally right. For most people, law and morality are not the same thing; each represents something different.

Law is imposed from the outside; it is first defined and then enforced by an impersonal (and never fully identified) "them." Law is linked to rational thought and reason. By contrast, morality springs from the inside; it is defined by the highly personal "me." Morality is linked to emotion, intuition, and instinct.

Law and morality can be viewed as endpoints on a continuum. (Ill. 2-9) Somewhere along the continuum fall social duty and social convention. I visualize social duty as being closer to the Law endpoint and social convention closer to the Morality end of the spectrum.

Scientists have observed a phenomenon they refer to as homeostasis, a form of equilibrium, whereby a system will regulate variables to preserve its internal stability. For example, warm-blooded animals maintain a constant

ILLUSTRATION 2-9 The Law–Morality Continuum

body temperature by raising their metabolisms when the outside temperature goes down and by lowering their metabolism when the outside temperature rises.

The Law-Morality Continuum helps maintain social homeostasis. By acting in a manner consistent with the standards established on the continuum, we help keep ourselves more or less on the straight and narrow. We also create a relatively fixed perspective from which to measure deviation. Consequently, the continuum allows us to determine not only if someone has deviated from this path but also how far he has strayed and how much force society needs to apply to pull the deviant back to maintain social homeostasis.

Jurors are asked to make judgments consistent with the standards of this continuum. At one end are the legal issues, which jurors evaluate using the Legal Theories provided by way of Operating Instructions, a concept that we will discuss later in this chapter. Concurrently, we ask jurors to make moral judgments; that is, we require that they determine whether someone's actions are appropriate or inappropriate, selfish or unselfish, good or bad.

While strict legalists may "pooh-pooh" morality, practical trial lawyers never do so. When our progenitors at the bar decided that a lay jury would decide all factual issues, they effectively guaranteed that human behavior, psychology, and morality would play a role in every jury deliberation. How much of a role varies depending on who is on the jury.

The fact that jurors are neutral observers and do not have a personal investment in the outcome does not mean that they remain unaffected by it. Modern neuroscientists suggest that human beings are hard-wired to judge how third parties affect (and are affected by) others. Specifically, in the late 1990s, scientists discovered "mirror neurons." These are brain cells that fire when a person observes or reflects upon actions being taken by and upon others. When a person sees someone else being hurt, for example, mirror neurons in the viewer's brain are triggered as if the viewer himself is also suffering an injury.

Here (as far as I am concerned) is objective confirmation of juror empathy. Mirror neurons also explain (to my unscientific satisfaction) why jurors take their obligation to find the right answer so seriously—they know (and the neuroscientists would suggest these jurors' brains respond to) the potential degree of satisfaction or additional distress their verdict will cause the parties. As such, jurors have a powerful incentive to get to the "right" decision.

In order to persuade a group of people (such as those likely to be on the jury), you must keep morality and law squarely aligned. On an individual or micro level, certain of your jurors will rely on morality as the Core Value by which they reach their personal decision as to which party should prevail. On a collective or macro level, a decision that aligns the specifics of law and general principles of morality attracts and holds a larger number of supporters than one that does not.

To convince jurors, you need to move them (and your case) beyond a dry collection of facts and the law as provided by your Legal Theory. The jurors need to believe in the morality of your client's position. In short, you need to follow the example of the Berkeley hypsies who decorated my daughter's hair and weave some color into and through the Factual Strand of your Proto-Story. Case Themes add this color.

Case Themes add moral force to your story and appeal more to emotion, intuition, and instinct than reason. For most jurors, emotion and reason supplement and complete each other; they do not substitute for one another. As such, Case Themes drive home why your side is morally entitled to win.

Case Themes are often rooted in people's understanding of fundamental decency; therefore, they must fall squarely within commonly accepted value schemes in order to be effective. Case Themes tend to provide emotional and moral perspective. They supply the lens through which the jurors view your version of the facts and subsequently draw inferences favorable to your client.

Almost all cases have elements of a morality play in them and can be reduced to one or two generally accepted moral lessons. These moral elements are often your Case Themes. The Case Theme is something that everyone can relate to and something that affects everyone. Having said this, I must quickly caution that being affected by a Case Theme is not the same as being convinced by it. The premises underlying a particular Case Theme are rarely absolute. Case Themes are based on values as opposed to undisputed facts. Moreover, other Persuasion Tools can trump valid Case Themes. For example, scientific fact may serve to defeat a commonly held belief. At the same time, commonly held themes can convince some to ignore what might otherwise be widely held scientific fact—something I learned from my great-grandmother who, until the day she died at age 90-plus, refused, because of religious beliefs (one of her life-long themes), to acknowledge that man ever landed on the moon.

Because Case Themes are primarily rooted in morality (as opposed to law) and because they deal with moral entitlements (as opposed to legal entitlements), they will generally have no independent legal significance in your case. They are not technically part of any prima facie requirement that you must meet in order to win on a particular cause of action or affirmative defense. Said differently, a court cannot grant a directed verdict against you for not including a Case Theme as part of your case. But frankly, this should not really affect the overall strategy of your case, because Case Themes matter to jurors, and they matter a lot!

Even though Case Themes are not a legally necessary element, most jurors appreciate their effect and need to understand the underlying themes before they are comfortable making an important substantive decision. For some jurors, Case Themes play an even more important role in their decision making than pure law, as thematic lessons are the lessons learned at mother's knee—a source far more powerful than a distant legislature or regulatory agency.

Most Case Themes can be expressed very succinctly, using only a few words. Amazingly, these few words often have a strong, immediate impact on those who hear them. Let me pause here to make a key point. Being succinct and immediate does not make a message trivial. Rather, these messages can act like a shot of adrenaline and strike on a visceral level. Why? Because Case Themes cut through the barriers of words and thought and hit straight home. A ten-word Case Theme can have a more immediate impact than a logic-based explanation with a hundred times as many words.

Case Themes are sometimes described as "anchoring ideas" because they help to psychologically and emotionally anchor jurors to a few critical points upon which they can safely fall back to justify their position during deliberations. You will often see this happen during an argument, inside or outside of the jury deliberation room. One party to the argument is not sure how to respond to a particularly forceful attack by someone with a contrary view. As a result, the person being assaulted pulls back, cowers for a millisecond, and then, just when he looks like he is about to yell, "Remember the Alamo" or some other deeply ingrained rallying cry, unsheathes the short sword that is the Case Theme and parries the attack.

If you have done your job well, your Case Themes will be immediately accessible to the jurors because they will be based on sentiments already familiar to them. These Case Themes are always within reach and can be quickly seized upon whenever they are needed. Case Themes are particularly effective for two reasons: (1) They are subjective and, as such, hard for the other side to objectively contradict, and (2) because a Case Theme is worth a thousand words and is often emotionally based, it takes considerable effort by the opponent to dislodge it. This does not mean that it is impossible to do so; it just means that it is difficult. At a minimum, the Case Theme provides the attacked juror, described in the preceding paragraph, with enough backup to regroup and try to launch a counterattack.

When and How to Use Case Themes

When it comes to trial, Case Themes are a bit schizophrenic. On the one hand, Case Themes substantially contribute to educating and persuading jurors. They add context that makes it possible to judge the key points that arise throughout the entire trial. On the other hand, Case Themes themselves have no independent legal significance, they are not required as part of a prima facie case or affirmative defense, and they are not strictly admissible as evidence. This creates an interesting predicament: Case Themes are extremely important, but technically irrelevant.

Case Themes are a form of argument, but I consider them to be a *special* form of argument. They are what I call "contextual" or "orienting" arguments, because they help orient jurors and expedite the jury's learning process. As such, I believe that Case Themes are entitled to slightly more favorable treatment from the court and counsel than other, more partisan forms of bickering.[4]

4. What follows in this section are my opinions based on extensive observation of trials. Other than common sense, I do not know of any particular rules that can be cited to support these observations.

The purpose of a Case Theme is to help orient the juror and to provide context and perspective against which the juror affixes meaning to what follows in the courtroom. To this end, by definition, a theme works best when it is allowed to surface at the beginning and is permitted to repeatedly resurface as needed throughout the entire trial. By way of an admittedly imperfect analogy, consider how themes arise and are used in classical music: A theme is first stated (i.e., defined) at the beginning and continually recurs throughout the piece, sometimes in whole, sometimes in part, but always in an identifiable form. Without an expressly stated theme to provide context, the musical variations would have no fixed point against which to be juxtaposed or appreciated by the listener.[5]

Hopefully, you now see the tension between the inherent and beneficial nature of a Case Theme on the one hand, and the restrictions imposed by the rules of evidence and trial procedure on the other. Your challenge is to somehow shape your contextual arguments into the time and format limitations of the various parts of your case, including your opening and case in chief, and not just your closing argument.

Fortunately, trial lawyers do not give up easily and most judges are somewhat forgiving when marginally offensive tactics, such as referring to your Case Themes in opening statement or mentioning them during the case in chief, are motivated by common sense and a genuine desire to assist jurors in understanding what the case is really about. In other words, so long as you do not abuse the privilege, most judges are willing to let you take advantage of the educational benefits inherent in reasonably presented Case Themes, even outside the confines of the closing argument.

Case Themes tend to appear early and throughout a case. Sometimes lawyers raise them implicitly; other times they raise them explicitly. Some potential opportunities to raise your Case Themes are during voir dire, during opening statement, and during witness testimony but, technically speaking, the only time you can raise them explicitly (and generally without objection), is in closing. Whether you can do so explicitly or implicitly at other times depends on your judge, your opposing counsel, and the local customs and rules of your court.

For what it is worth, my general observation is that in jurisdictions that still allow counsel to conduct voir dire, judges and opposing counsel tend not to object if you occasionally work your Case Theme into your questioning of potential jurors. Likewise, most jurisdictions will give you some latitude during opening statement to mention (but not dwell on) your Case Themes, so long as you reinforce these explicit references by previewing the supporting evidence. Do not over do it.

You should make sure that your Case Themes shine in closing. Without being obnoxious, you should not only express the Case Themes early and often during your argument, but also make sure that you help the jury see exactly how the evidence and arguments tie into and fully support your

5. Which raises the metaphysical question: Is a variation still a variation if there is no expressed theme against which the variation can be observed to vary?

themes. Hopefully, your jurors will have identified your Case Themes on their own long before closing, making this more like a "refresher," but, in any event, do not squander this last opportunity to make sure the jurors fully appreciate this important portion of the Factual Strand that helps make up your Proto-Story.

I want to end this section by reminding you that some themes cannot and should not ever be used by the lawyer. Many (if not all) jurisdictions prohibit lawyers from asking jurors to imagine placing themselves in the plaintiff's shoes or to apply the "Golden Rule" for purposes of assessing damages or to appeal to inappropriate prejudices. While some jurors may think of these themes on their own without your having to explicitly mention them, you cannot ever ask them to do so, even in closing. In such instances, established rules as to what is permitted trump any such themes. Honor these restrictions.

The Seven Categories of Case Themes

After working on almost 1,500 cases, my colleagues at The Focal Point and I have noticed that despite what may appear to be an infinite number of variations of facts, Case Themes can generally be classified as falling into one of seven categories. (Ill. 2-10) The first six categories are relatively common; the seventh is less so.

Before defining and describing each category, let me remind you that the fact that there are only a limited number of types of Case Themes does not in any way trivialize how hard it is to successfully organize and try a case.

There Are Seven Categories of Case Themes

1. **Themes that evoke antagonism towards the opposing party**
2. **Themes that evoke empathy towards your side**
3. **Themes that suggest that the status quo should not be disturbed**
4. **Themes that advocate that the status quo must be changed**
5. **Themes that rely on general truisms or adages**
6. **Themes that rely on key phrases specific to your case**
7. **The Nontheme Case Theme**

ILLUSTRATION 2-10 There Are Seven Categories of Case Themes

Instead, this observation is consistent with our earlier recognition of human nature and the limited number of images people have successfully used since time immemorial to tell stories.

Category One: Case Themes That Evoke Antagonism Towards the Opposing Party

The first category of Case Themes includes those that are designed to evoke antagonism towards the opposing party and, by association, to discredit the Proto-Story advanced by the other lawyer.

Of the seven thematic categories, this one is the most common and, while it is impossible to know for sure, I suspect it has the greatest number of variations. I believe the reasons for this are fourfold.

First, going on the offensive has been ingrained in many of us (particularly those of us who became trial lawyers) as a visceral reaction to conflict. To this extent, we have no problem identifying with John Bright, one of England's most radical and brilliant 19th-century orators and social reformers, about whom it was said, "He could not act on the defensive; his mind required attack."

Second, attacking someone's character (which is how this category of Case Themes most often manifests itself) is one of the easiest ways to go on the offensive, as evidenced by the name-calling that is so often spontaneously triggered in children and politicians.

Third, as anyone who has been sued or forced into a lawsuit will tell you, one of the first things you do to make sense of the situation is to try to figure out what moral defects the opposing party has that necessitated the lawsuit. This conclusion often serves as the psychological cornerstone in the edifices we construct to bolster our decisions to prosecute or defend against a legal action.

Finally, there are more ways to convincingly demonstrate that your opponent has deviated from established norms than there are ways to prove that you have adhered to them. While not exactly on point, it is similar to the problem of proving the negative. It is easier to show "Here is what the other guy did wrong" than it is to claim "Here is what I have done 'not-wrong' (i.e., right)."

Examples within this first category of Case Themes that evoke antagonism toward the other party and, by association, the Proto-Story advanced by the other lawyer include:[6]

The other side is a heartless corporation that cares more about profits than about (1) its workers, (2) its customers, and/or (3) the general public.
The other side is behaving like a spoiled child and is vindictively trying to get someone else to be held responsible for its own mistakes.
The other side is being greedy.
The other side is seeking revenge.

6. There is nothing definitive about this or any of the other collections of themes listed in this section.

The other side is seeking unfair advantage.
The other side is lying. [Be careful with this one. Most judges bristle at the use of any form of the word "lie." Additionally, see my earlier caution against prematurely accusing your opposing party of intentionally wrongful acts. If this is one of your Themes, it often has to be offered implicitly throughout your case.]
This is an act of desperation by the other side.
The other side had the opportunity to do the right thing, but deliberately chose not to.
The other side should admit that it caused this problem—but it just can't do so. As a result, it is blaming others.
The other side got "fat and lazy" and is trying to use this litigation to accomplish what it could not legitimately bring about in the free market.
The other side is changing the rules in the middle of the game.
The other side wants the rules to apply to everyone but itself.
The other side has a lawyer who is a bounty hunter and is merely trying to get huge attorney's fees. [This tends to get raised in settlement mediations in class action suits, where the spoils for individual class members are limited.]
The other side is trying to manipulate the system.
The other side has done so many other bad things, it must have done what is alleged here.
The other side gave its word but now wants to break it.
The other side is willing to legally bind others but not be legally bound itself.
The other side wants to have its cake and eat it too.
The other side is pulling an "I'm so innocent" act, which you should not believe.
The other side started off by making a small mistake, but instead of acknowledging it and fixing it, let it continue to grow and is now trying to get the court to help make up for its own negligence.
The other side promised Wall Street (or some other entity) that it was going to make a certain level of profit and decided to fulfill that promise even if it meant lying, cheating, stealing, and hurting others.
What the other side got legitimately just wasn't enough to satisfy it; it wanted more.
The other side should be ashamed of itself.
The other side is relying on a mass of technicalities that you should disregard.
The other side thought it could get away with it and that it would never get caught. But guess what? Surprise!
Things are not as simple nor as straightforward as the other side says.
The other side was sloppy.
The other side was naively opportunistic.
The other side is asking you to ignore your own common sense; don't do so.

The other side is trying to avoid responsibility.
The other side made a promise and broke it.
It is wrong to take something that does not belong to you, and that is what the other side is doing here.
The other side was asleep at the wheel.
The other side wants to be treated differently and better than you and me.
The other side suffers from a lack of control or restraint.
Apparently, only the government has a problem here. No real victims have come forth to complain. What a waste of your tax dollars.
The other side is flip-flopping. What the other side is saying now is not what it said back then.
The other side bet on the wrong horse; it took a gamble, lost, and now want someone else to pay for their losses.
For goodness sake, don't forget it is the Government on the other side. [As in, "The other side (e.g., the government) is being heavy-handed, is more wedded to detail than substance, or is completely wasting our time." Be careful; this is not likely to be a Case Theme that can be raised overtly.]

Category Two: Case Themes That Evoke Empathy Towards Your Side

The second general category includes Case Themes that are designed to evoke empathy, understanding, and sympathy towards you and your client. While this category is commonly used as part of a case's Factual Strand, I suspect that there are not as many variations within this category as there are in the first, for reasons noted above. Additionally, you need to be careful whenever you rely on this category of Case Themes so you do not appear self-righteous or Pollyannaish, or as if your client is trying to escape responsibility for its own actions. In fact, if you use such a theme, be prepared to hear your opposing counsel accuse your client of exactly that.

Examples within this category of Case Themes intended to evoke empathy towards your side include:

We are behaving reasonably (and by implication, the other side is not).
When you work hard, you deserve to earn all of the benefits of your hard work; do not let the other side take these hard-earned benefits from my client.
My client did everything it could, but sometimes accidents just happen; it is not anyone's fault, including my client's.
The Government has singled my client out for selective prosecution.
My client is being persecuted (or prosecuted) for an ulterior motive.
My client is being persecuted (or prosecuted) for who he is, not because he did anything wrong.
My client is a person you trust and need (e.g., a police officer) and performs a service you need. As such, he deserves your respect, support, and benefit of the doubt. Letting the other side hurt him will ultimately hurt you, too.

My client is being made the scapegoat for the wrongs of others.
My client is a good person; there is no way she could have possibly done what she is accused of doing.
The victim is not really the victim—my client is!
My client lived up to his responsibility and continues to do so. [By implication, it is the other side that is not doing what it is required to do.]
My client is a very simple person who only wanted what he was entitled to, and they took everything they could from him.
My client could not help it.
This person needs help, not punishment. [E.g., used when the defendant is pleading insanity or necessity.]
My client did what he thought was right. You would have done the same thing.
My client followed common sense. Isn't that what you would have done?

Category Three: Case Themes That Suggest That The Status Quo Should Not Be Disturbed

The third category of Case Themes focuses on the result of the verdict and specifically suggests that there is no need for the jury to change anything, since the status quo is fair, desirable for society, or deserved by the other side. Examples include the following:

The victim deserved it.
He got exactly what he asked for; leave him just where he is.
The other side got caught in a problem of its own creation and deserves what it got; let them worry about fixing this problem on its own.
Just leave everyone where they are—don't get into the middle of this mess.
It ain't broke; don't fix it.
If you do what they are asking, you are going to cause a huge disruption to something that is already working pretty well.
The other side's proposed change is going to cause more harm than good.
If you do this, it is going to open the flood gates of change, and change is not good.
Technically, what the other side is asking for may be right, but it would be terribly unfair to rule in its favor.
This is already a horrible tragedy; don't make it worse.
Oh, come on, this is ridiculous—there was no harm, there should be no foul.
My client has already suffered enough, leave him where he is.

Category Four: Case Themes That Advocate That the Status Quo Must Be Changed

The fourth category advocates that the jurors affirmatively change existing conditions or alter the status quo. These Case Themes are consistent with the psychological desire jurors have to be helpful and to fix what needs fixing. Such Case Themes include the following:

Would you want this result for yourself? [Be very careful about this Case Theme, which is likely to be seen as being too close to invoking the "Golden Rule" or requesting that the jurors put themselves in the shoes of one of the parties.]
My client harmed the plaintiff but not to the extent he claims; give him only what he is objectively entitled to.
The other side took what was not theirs; make them give it back.
This is not fair; give my client what is fair.
This is going to continue happening unless you stop it.
Make sure this does not happen again.

Category Five: Case Themes That Rely on General Truisms or Adages

The fifth general category of Case Themes include truisms (or, at least, what some substantial portion of the population considers to be truisms), as summarized by a familiar adage or common saying. These Case Themes are often (but not always) used to condone or explain a particular type of action.

Lately, jury consultants have increasingly relied on the concept of heuristics to explain how jurors reason and come to their conclusions, especially in complicated cases. For purposes of this discussion, heuristics may be defined as simple rules of thumb or shortcuts through detailed thinking. Case Themes that rely on truisms or adages would qualify as this form of thinking/reasoning.

My experience is that the definition in the prior paragraph, particularly with its use of the phrase "shortcuts through detailed thinking," leads many people to conclude that heuristic thinking is sloppy thinking. Certainly it can be, as demonstrated by some of our worst prejudices. But this is not always the case. Often there is nothing lazy or shortsighted about heuristics. Many heuristics succinctly distill anchoring principles derived from repeated and detailed observation of human nature. In many ways they are the sound bites (or Case Themes) that summarize the results of centuries of trial and error.

Examples of Case Themes that summarize a commonly held belief or rule of thumb include the following:

No good deed goes unpunished.
All that glitters is not gold.
A deal is a deal.
People who live in glass houses should not throw stones.
Hindsight is 20/20.
Fools rush in where angels fear to tread.
The grass is always greener on the other side.
A courtyard common to all will be swept by none.
Good fences make good neighbors.
It was beginner's luck.

The best things in life are free.
Experience is the best teacher.
Boys will be boys.
Your worst enemy is often a former best friend.
Don't change horses in midstream.
Be careful what you wish for; it may come true.
The apple does not fall far from the tree.
Experience is a dear teacher and some will have no other.
Look before you leap.
You can't teach an old dog new tricks.
Where there is smoke, there is fire.

Category Six: Case Themes That Rely on Key Phrases Specific to Your Case

The sixth general type of Case Theme includes key terms or phrases particular to the specific facts in dispute. These are the headline statements, the memorable phrases or comments that you hear during trial or at a deposition that instantly sum up a key element of a case or are emblematic of the entire problem experienced by one of the parties. Often, you can build your entire story around the Case Themes that derive from these phrases.

Let me give you five examples, each of which needs a bit of context. First, we once worked on a case involving a family dispute. Unfortunately, such cases are generally some of the most vicious fights in our courts. Issues are often blown hugely out of proportion. At the outset of this particular dispute, the mother (who eventually spent $7 million in legal fees against her daughter) turned to face her daughter, who was the primary defendant, and said, "I have suffered for so long, now it is your turn to suffer!" This quotation became a central theme in our defense and provided an explanation of the mother's irrational behavior and motive.

In my second example, a witness to a horrific machinery accident commented that prior to the accident, whenever she looked at the haphazardly maintained equipment, she thought, "This is a disaster waiting to happen!" Despite her concerns, the witness did nothing to correct the problem or prevent the inevitable accident. These facts combined to form a Case Theme that went something like this: "The defendant saw the problem. She will tell you that she knew that this was a disaster waiting to happen, but she decided it was not worth the effort to do anything to prevent this disaster from happening."

Third, we worked on a commercial fraud case against a middle-aged defendant who had set up a sham company, made his eighteen-year-old son the supposed chief executive officer, and then used the sham company to borrow millions of dollars, which were never paid back. The father later claimed that there was nothing wrong with the sham company he created to borrow the money. During the deposition of the teenage son, a lawyer asked this former eighteen-year-old CEO, "What role did you play in the company?" The young man, trying to be helpful, responded, "Well, I was, like, the dude in charge." (Honest, I am not making this up.) Needless to say, the concept of this eighteen-year-old being "like, the dude in charge" became a central theme in this case. This became a thematic response every time the defendant asserted that the transactions had been legitimate and that the company was not a sham. Unable to face the prospect of having to counter this theme at trial, the businessman/father settled.

In another case, the plaintiff claimed he had been injured when a plane he flew crashed—even though he himself had inspected the plane before take-off. Later, he admitted that the inspection he performed had been what he called "quick and dirty." Although the plaintiff's counsel spent considerable time trying to explain away this phrase, it remained a central theme for the defense.

Similarly, we worked on a case in which a trailer had exploded, causing a little girl to burn to death. During the trial, one of the third-party witnesses spontaneously pointed to a photo of the burned-out trailer and said, "Five minutes of additional work [by the defendant] and a $2 replacement part would have prevented all of this." One could not ask for a more poignant Case Theme.

Category Seven: The Nontheme Case Theme

I was originally reluctant to include this seventh category in this section because I am not sure if it is actually a theme or merely a trial tactic. I eventually decided that, whatever it turns out to be, it is sufficiently interesting as to warrant discussion.

I call the seventh category the "Nontheme Case Theme."

Specifically, the Nontheme Case Theme insists that the theme of your case (which you never acknowledge you have) is that themes are neither appropriate nor necessary and, if anything, these devices are nothing more than fluff presented by the other side to distract the jurors from doing what they took a solemn oath to do, namely, to render a verdict based solely on the facts and the law.

If jury nullification is the process whereby the jury ignores the law in favor of the "greater good," the Nontheme Case Theme is the exact opposite. The Nontheme Case Theme preaches (and indeed it often does sound like preaching when you use this Case Theme), that the only thing that matters is the law. In effect, it is the argument that you might expect Victor Hugo's character Javert to have made prior to entering the Parisian sewers in *Les Misérables*.

Let me offer an example.

We worked on a case in which substantial criminal charges were brought against a high-ranking corporate officer for allegedly manipulating the purchase price of his company's stock. In today's post-Enron environment, where jurors do not trust large companies and trust the high-ranking officials in those companies even less, cases such as these are relatively easy for prosecutors to take all the way to a guilty verdict.

Given this, we knew that the prosecutor would have no problem coming up with handfuls of effective Case Themes to use against our client. In response, prior to trial, we repeatedly came up with themes that we hoped would counter the prosecutor's advantage. Frankly, when we tested them in front of a mock jury, absolutely none of our counterthemes worked.

Somewhat in exasperation, we finally decided to urge jurors to reject the prosecution's use of themes as a glib effort to distract the jury from what we believed to be a very weak government case.

Throughout the case, defense counsel kept stressing (both expressly and implicitly) what we called the mantra: "look only to the law and facts, look only to the law and facts, look only to the law and facts. . . ." In closing, defense counsel put up a list of the prima facie elements necessary for a conviction. On another board he then posted each of the prosecution's "themes" that the jury had just heard in closing.

The lawyer pointed to the list of the prosecutor's themes and said:

> Here are the prosecution's themes. He just repeated them this morning in his closing argument. But this case is not about themes. This case is *not* about generalities. Themes are not what you consider in deciding whether or not to send a man to jail. This case is about looking at facts, not general themes, and seeing that the prosecution does not have what it takes for you to convict this man of criminal charges. If he had the facts, why wouldn't he have focused on facts instead of themes?

The lawyer then walked through each of the prosecution's themes and asked the jury to compare the theme to the prima facie requirements necessary for conviction. "Does that general theme establish grounds for conviction?" the lawyer would ask. Of course, each time he did this the answer to his rhetorical question was "No." The lawyer concluded by turning to the list of prima facie elements and showing how the government had failed to prove several of the necessary elements.

Using the Nontheme Case Theme takes some guts, but if no other themes seem to work, it may be a wise move.

Most Cases Rely on Multiple Case Themes Chosen from Several Different Categories

As noted previously, you will ideally have a single Case Theory. That Case Theory may be based on several different causes of action, but all of the causes of action will be based on a single version of what you believe happened, as opposed to multiple versions told in the alternative.

This need for unity does *not* necessarily apply to your Case Themes. In fact, most cases have—and readily benefit from—multiple Case Themes, carefully chosen from several of the first six categories described above.[7] It is not unusual to combine elements from different categories and end up (with more than a little hyperbole) with something like:

7. For obvious reasons, if you decide to use the Nontheme theme, you can't combine this approach with other themes, so the Nontheme theme almost by definition must stand on its own.

> This tragedy did not have to happen! The defendant could have easily prevented it *Category 1.* The plaintiff was a hard-working man who played by the rules and successfully provided for his family *Category 2.* That is, the plaintiff was that way until defendant, who cares more about making money than taking care of the general public *Category 1,* ruined the plaintiff's life. By its own admission, the repair work the defendant did prior to the accident was "quick and dirty" *Category 6.* With just a little bit of forethought and prevention, this tragedy would not have happened—a stitch in time saves nine *Category 5.* The plaintiff deserves better; make sure he gets better than he currently has *Category 3.*

This mixing and matching of Case Themes is appropriate so long as the choices complement, rather than contradict, one another. This makes sense because the collection of themes is, in some ways, a miniature story and the various categories of these themes represent key elements in that story (e.g., "the villain" in Category 1, "the hero" in Category 2, "a crisis that the jurors need to remedy" in Categories 3 and 4, and resolving a problem by using "common wisdom" from Category 5).

Party Motive

Why Party Motive Always Matters

Isaac Newton's First Law of Motion provides that a body at rest tends to stay at rest and a body in motion tends to stay in motion. While this law was originally devised to explain the actions of inanimate objects, its general principles are equally applicable to human beings.

People take action and remain in action only when a force motivates them to do so. Most jurors are aware of this and, as a result, are keenly interested in Party Motive. They want to know "why" the actors did what they did or what prompted them to behave in a particular manner.

Party Motive is sometimes the most overlooked and underappreciated part of the Proto-Story. Often, this is because lawyers make the mistake of assuming that if motive (or the closely related concept of state of mind) is not a prima facie element of the case, then it is not something they have to worry about.

That assumption is wrong. Every juror will wonder about Party Motive, regardless of whether it is a necessary element of a case. For example, while the law does not necessarily care what one of the parties was thinking when he breached his contract—jurors do. While motive and bias are not exactly the same, I often think of them as identical when it comes to evaluating witnesses. The law recognizes that bias (or potential bias) is always relevant when examining witnesses. I consider Party Motive to be equally so.

Why is Party Motive so important to the average juror?

I think it is important for five reasons, which I list here in increasing degree of importance. I already mentioned the first reason: People know that motive exists. Just as George Herbert Leigh Mallory climbed Mount Everest "because it's there," jurors want to explore Party Motive because it's there.

The second reason has to do with a certain voyeuristic tendency that exists in each of us. Jurors want to be able to take a peek behind the curtain to find out what is "really going on." What better opportunity is there to do so? During trial, everyone with a substantial interest and knowledge in the case comes forward, swears under oath to tell the truth, and is subjected to something far more rigorous than a game of "20 Questions." Jurors want to know why people act the way they do, and a trial gives them the perfect opportunity to find out. Be careful about disappointing the jurors by failing to give them this information.

The third reason has to do with how some jurors relate to and empathize with the key characters involved in the dispute. Whether they will admit it to the court or not, certain jurors will privately tell you that evaluating the parties' motives plays a role in their analysis of who should prevail. This is particularly the case with respect to a "good motive." I have been told on multiple occasions by jurors that they were more likely to favor a party whose motive was good because this behavior is consistent with what the jurors wanted to think they themselves would have done if confronted with the same situation. Likewise, other jurors have admitted to being predisposed against a party whose motive they judged to be bad and, thus, contrary to what they believed they would have done if they had faced the same set of circumstances.

The fourth reason to establish motive goes directly to how jurors go about beginning to understand the case. Learning cannot take place in the abstract. No one can start to learn or begin to understand unless and until he can start with something familiar. Regardless of the case, Party Motive is something that every jury understands and to which each juror can relate. It provides the necessary toehold of understanding from which jurors can begin their analysis. Not everyone will understand the complex science or detailed accounting analysis that makes up your case, but everyone understands motive (or believes he understands) and is willing to offer such a view during deliberations.

The final reason is that motive will often help uncover the truth. People behave in a manner consistent with their motives. If a witness's motive and actions do not align, jurors get very suspicious.

Ignoring Party Motive Is Risky

So, what happens if you fail to provide the jury with a plausible explanation of Party Motive as part of your Proto-Story? Just as nature abhors a vacuum and will rush to fill it, jurors abhor narrative gaps and will rush to fill them. The problem with this is that the less help you give them in filling the gaps, the less control you have as to how those gaps will be filled. (Ill. 2-11)

I have repeatedly watched mock juries engage in long, spirited debates about the suspected secret lives of witnesses and parties. I have watched lawyers observe these mock deliberations and sit in shock as jurors debate the existence of potential love triangles, jealousies, secret underhanded deals,

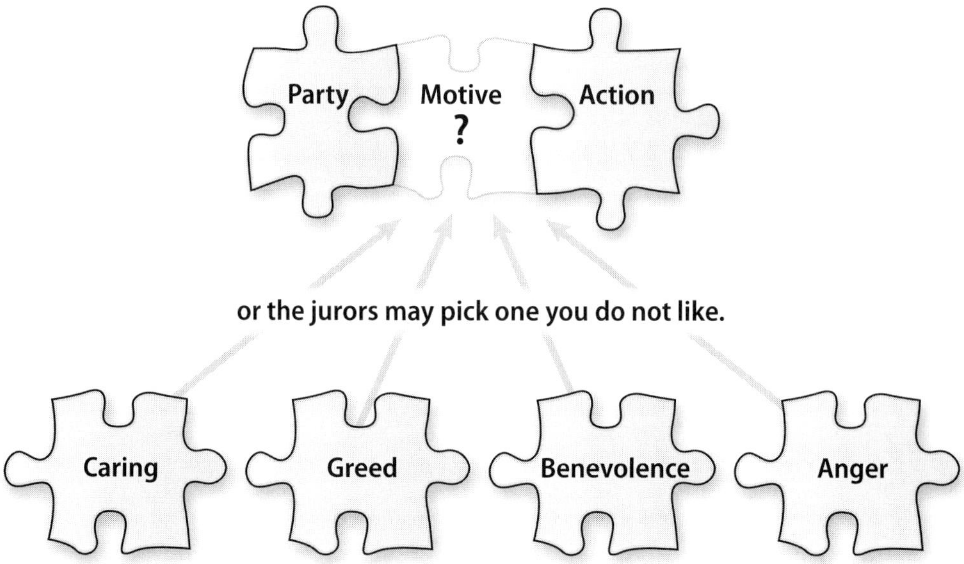

ILLUSTRATION 2-11 Failing to Explain Motive Is Risky

and other fictions—all because the lawyers did not take the time to put forth a plausible explanation of Party Motive.

Do not let this happen; incorporate an explanation of Party Motive in every one of your Proto-Stories. As with your Case Themes, you are not limited to a single explanation of Party Motive in your Proto-Story. As for assigning motives to individuals, it is generally best not to ascribe more than one motive at a time to each character. A person can have a series of motives over time, but attributing multiple motives to the same person at the same time is confusing.

Pulling the Central Cord Together

As I suggested earlier, your Central Cord is quite literally at the center of your case. It is made up of (1) your single Factual Theory and one or more Legal Theories (which combine to form your overall Case Theory), (2) your Case Themes, and (3) your explanations of Party Motive. In this section, I want to concentrate on how to pull these elements together and reconcile any conflicts that may result during this important process.

Let me start with the obvious. Wherever possible, you need all of the above elements in your Factual Strand. Occasionally, lawyers posit a theory without themes or they advance themes without a coherent theory. More commonly, they ignore the importance of Party Motive and leave this gap wide open to be filled (often disastrously) at the jurors' discretion.

The Case Theory and Case Themes provide the formula through which you explain not only why you should prevail but also why the jury, by allowing you to do so, will effectuate a just result. The additional understanding that Party Motive provides helps the jurors understand why key players behaved the way they did. Taken together, the Case Theory, Case Themes, and Party Motive provide the structure around which you can organize your entire case. The Factual Strand serves as a basic touchstone for evaluating almost everything you do at trial.

You must avoid acting in any manner inconsistent with the Factual Strand. Your tone must be consistent with these elements. Your behavior towards the witnesses and opposing counsel are shaped by these portions of the Proto-Story.

But what do you do if there is conflict between or among the elements in the Factual Strand as you are preparing your case? What do you do if your Case Theory, Case Themes, and Party Motive do not entirely mesh? Obviously, the first thing you want to do is to find a reasonable way to reconcile the elements. But let's assume you cannot do so; what do you do then? There is no absolute answer to this question, but as a general rule, when there is conflict, your Case Theory predominates over your Case Themes and your explanations of Party Motive. Said differently, when you cannot reconcile these elements, you generally need to change the Case Themes and modify your explanation of Party Motive to fit the Case Theory, rather than change the Case Theory to fit the Case Themes and explanations of Party Motive.

Why? Because your Case Theory incorporates your Factual Theory, which in turn must include all of the case's undisputed or highly probable facts. You should think of the case's undisputed facts as immutable and the highly probable facts as virtually immutable. If you modify your Case Theory (or at least those portions that are based on undisputed or highly probably facts) to conform to a Case Theme, you run the risk of taking a position that is subject to objective, factual attack. If you lose this attack, which you most likely will, your credibility with the jury will be adversely affected. This is less likely to occur if you modify your Case Themes and explanations of Party Motive to conform to your facts as set forth in your Case Theory.

Case Themes and explanations of Party Motive are, at their core, value judgments. People may disagree with the value, but they do so based on their own judgments, not on objective criteria. Do not get me wrong; these disagreements can be hard fought, but they will tend to be disagreements based on subjective (not objective) criteria. In other words: "I do not value (subjective) what you value (subjective), as much as you value (subjective) what you value (subjective)."

Said differently, if the jurors or your opposing counsel disagree with your Case Theme, there is nothing that they can point to and say, "Liar!" At worst, they can say that your values are not their values. Obviously, this is not exactly what you want if you are attempting to build consensus among the jurors, but at least you will not have lost *complete* credibility, as you would if your theory contradicted an *undisputed* fact, or *partial* credibility if your theory contradicted a series of *highly probable* facts. If your version of the facts, as expressed in the objective Case Theory, is altered to fit the subjective Case Theme, you may very well get caught in a contradiction that can be objectively challenged, with all of the negative consequences of having been caught in what your opponents could characterize as a lie.

The Included Facts

The final element to add to the Factual Strand is the facts themselves, which I want you to imagine strung like beads onto a Central Cord composed of the intertwined Case Theory, Case Themes, and your explanation of Party Motive. The beads are of varying sizes, shapes, and colors, which help illustrate that facts are not all of equal value, weight, or significance. The lawyer carefully chooses from among the facts and strings them on to the Central Cord in a deliberate order.

When I was a kid, I used to watch the television show *Dragnet,* which starred Jack Webb as police Sergeant Joe Friday, the cop who, as he investigated a crime, seemed inevitably to say, "All we want are the facts, ma'am."

With this line, Joe Friday proved why he was a better policeman than he was a prosecutor. Sergeant Friday seemed to assume that facts were somehow judged on a binary scale; that is, something was either a fact or it was not a fact and that was the only determination he needed to make when investigating a crime. While this view may work for police officers, it does not work for trial lawyers. For us, facts are anything but binary; they instead fall along a variety of important continua. As trial lawyers, we need to pick and choose the appropriate combination of these facts to assemble a "truthful" story for our client. We make this determination, at least in part, by assessing (usually subconsciously) where these facts fall along some or all of these continua.

Why is there this difference? Why do police officers judge facts based on a single binary standard, while trial lawyers assess and value facts using a series of continua? I think the difference goes back to the fact that the police are attempting to "find *the* truth" and we, as trial lawyers, are trying to "make our client's version the TRUTH."[8]

How to Evaluate Your Facts

So, how do you evaluate your facts? After helping to prepare over 1,500 cases for trial, my colleagues and I have identified six basic questions that you need to ask when attempting to evaluate the facts of your case. The first three categories are essential and need to be checked against every single fact that you evaluate. Technically, you are not required to ask yourself the final three questions, but they are nevertheless important because the answers provide considerable insight into the relative value of your facts. (Ill. 2-12)

8. Let me quickly add that anyone who has read enough investigative reports knows that while police officers are trying to find the truth, they are also oftentimes trying to create the truth. At least these theoretical differences explain the binary version versus the multiple continua version of judging facts.

Six Questions to Assess the Relative Value of Facts

These three questions are mandatory:

1. **Is the fact admissible?**
2. **Is the fact legally necessary for you or your opponent?**
3. **Is the fact disputed?**

These three questions are highly suggested:

4. **Is there something about the internal characteristics of the fact itself that makes it more or less powerful?**
5. **Is there something about the source of the fact that makes it more or less powerful?**
6. **Is there something about the fact that makes it easier or harder to use at trial?**

ILLUSTRATION 2-12 These Six Questions Help You Assess the Value of Your Facts

Question One: Is the Fact Admissible?

The first question is perhaps the most important: "Is the fact admissible?" While you may have to do some legal research to get an answer, the question is relatively straightforward and its importance is obvious.

No matter how terrific it may be, inadmissible material cannot be used. If the material is inadmissible, then the analysis of that fact stops right then and there, since there is no need to go on asking yourself any of the five remaining questions.

It probably goes without saying, but just because a fact is admissible does not mean that it should automatically be part of your case. All it means is that it is *potentially* available for use. Thus, at this point in the analysis, it is far more important to identify which material is inadmissible than what will pass as admissible, since much of your admissible material will still not be useable at trial for a variety of reasons.

Question Two: Is the Fact Legally Necessary for You or Your Opponent?

This second question measures how necessary a fact is to your case *or* (and this is an important "or") to your opponent's case. A fact is legally necessary if it is required to establish a prima facie element of a claim or a defense *for either side*. Obviously, failure to prove such a fact to the extent that it applies to either your case or your opponent's case will lead to the claim or defense being dismissed.

The answer to this question—"Is the fact legally necessary for either you or your opponent?"—is *not* strictly "yes" or "no;" in fact, I want to analyze five possible responses:

1. The fact is neither legally necessary nor helpful to either side.
2. The fact is not legally necessary, but it is helpful to your opponent.
3. The fact is not legally necessary, but it is helpful to your client.
4. The fact is legally necessary and helpful to your opponent.
5. The fact is legally necessary and helpful for your client.

What you should do with respect to each of these variations may not be completely obvious and, in a couple of instances, may actually be counterintuitive. Let us start with the easiest category, the *material that is neither legally necessary nor helpful to either side*—such material should get thrown away, wholesale.

The *material that is not legally necessary, but potentially helpful to one side or the other,* is a bit problematic if for no other reason than its rather extensive volume. This will obviously be the bulk of what you are gathering for your case. This is the material that you must judiciously sort to have a compelling case, but not a mind-numbingly tedious one.

The *material that is both legally necessary and helpful to your opponent* warrants intense scrutiny. Because this material is legally necessary, you know by definition that it will be included in your opponent's case and, because you know that these facts are helpful to your opponent, you know that when these facts do show up, they are going to sting. It would, therefore, be extremely shortsighted of you not to devise a plan to deal with these facts well in advance of trial and develop possible rebuttal material for that portion of your Proto-Story.

Spend time working on your defense and prepare for what you know is coming. None of this effort will be wasted. If, by some miracle, this material does not show up in your opponent's case against you, consider yourself lucky and move for a directed verdict, citing your opponent's failure to offer evidence on a necessary element of his case. Realistically, you will *not* likely be that lucky; however, you will be several steps ahead in preparing your rebuttal.

Finally, there is the *material that is both legally necessary and helpful for your case.* This includes what I call your "golden beads." These are the facts you know you will automatically include in some form on your Factual Strand. These facts will then serve as the central point from which you add supporting factual material and ultimately argue in your client's favor.

Question Three: Is the Fact Disputed?

The third question assesses the extent to which the fact is disputed. By far, the vast majority of the facts will be. If this were not the case, there would be far fewer lawsuits and far more successful motions for summary judgment.

In reality, undisputed facts are relatively rare, but they do exist and need to be treated with extra care. You must uncover all such facts and make sure that you find a way, at a minimum, not to contradict any of them in your Case Theory. Ideally, you will find ways to incorporate these undisputed facts into your case.

Failure to account for undisputed facts can have disastrous consequences. My favorite example of this is well known, but bears repeating. The case is *Illinois v. Armstrong,* a murder trial set in Cass County, Illinois. The defense lawyer is Abraham Lincoln, and the year is 1858. If any of this sounds familiar, I suspect it is because you have probably seen a reenactment of this famous moment in the film *Young Mr. Lincoln,* starring Henry Fonda.

In this real-life example, Lincoln defended his friend's son, who was accused of murder. The prosecution's main witness claimed that he saw the killing and could identify the murderer even though the crime took place late at night. The transcript of Lincoln's cross-examination of the witness survives and makes for fascinating reading.

Q: Did you actually see the fight?
A: Yes.

Q: And you stood very near to them?
A: No, it was one hundred and fifty feet or more.

Q: In the open field?
A: No, in the timber.

Q: What kind of timber?
A: Beech timber.

Q: Leaves on it are rather thick in August?
A: It looks like it.

Q: What time did all this occur?
A: Eleven o'clock at night.

Q: Did you have a candle there?
A: No, what would I want a candle for?

Q: How could you see from a distance of one hundred and fifty feet or more, without a candle, at eleven o'clock at night?
A: The moon was shining real bright.

Q: Full moon?
A: Yes, a full moon.

The record reflects that Lincoln referred to an almanac and continued his line of questioning.

Q: Does not the almanac say that on August 29 the moon was barely past the first quarter instead of being full?
A: (No answer.)

Q: Does not the almanac also say that the moon had disappeared by eleven o'clock?

A: (No answer.)

Q: Is it not a fact that it was too dark to see anything from fifty feet, let alone one hundred and fifty feet?

A: (No answer.)

Some of the people who were watching the trial later claimed that by this point, a number of the jurors were actively laughing at and mocking the prosecution's main witness. The transcript concludes by noting that the jury unanimously acquitted Duff Armstrong.

Traditionally, when lawyers and historians review this transcript they focus on what Lincoln did right. Alternatively, I want to suggest that we can learn just as much (or more) by looking at *what the prosecutor did wrong.* Specifically, the prosecutor *failed to identify and incorporate all undisputed facts into the story* that he presented to the jury. Were the phase of the moon and the time of its setting undisputed facts? Absolutely! Do not make this same mistake. If you do, it will not take an opponent as skilled as Abraham Lincoln to defeat you and your case. Instead, identify the undisputed facts and figure out how to use them, or at least how to avoid contradicting them.

Uncontested facts come in a variety of forms. For example: (1) the fact is so firmly established by common sense that no one contests the conclusion, (2) the evidence is so overwhelming that to challenge the fact would look foolish and would harm the contesting party's credibility, (3) "objective" science has established the conclusion as being absolute and beyond dispute, (4) the parties themselves have stipulated to or responded to requests for admission in a way that the fact is deemed undisputed, or (5) the court has taken judicial notice of the fact.

In whatever manner the fact is established as being undisputed, you must deal with each such fact. When it is in your favor, embrace it and emphasize its undisputed nature as a way of bolstering your Case Theory. When the undisputed fact it is against you, incorporate it into your case in the most credible way possible.

Likewise, when the evidence is overwhelmingly against you, don't make an ass out of yourself. Graciously cede the point and move on. New Yorker cartoonist Noel Watson captured this point in his 1992 cartoon, which played on the same themes of the James Thurber cartoon discussed earlier in this chapter. (Ill. 2-13)

Question Four: Is There Something About the Internal Characteristics Of the Fact Itself That Makes It More or Less Powerful?

Your objective at trial is to present a case that consists of intriguing evidence punctuated with damning details. Inherent in this description is an observation that I suspect is obvious—not all facts pack an equal punch; that is,

"O. K., have it your way. You heard a seal bark."

ILLUSTRATION 2-13 If You Can't Possibly Win a Point, Let It Go!

some are far more powerful and important than others. You want to find and use as many powerful facts as you can. To do so requires that you make a concerted effort to rank the relative importance of your facts and the degree to which they will hold the jurors' attention. Such an assessment often hinges upon what I call the "internal characteristics" of the facts. More specifically: Is there something inherent in the fact itself that makes it more or less powerful in the eyes of the jurors?

I am not sure that there is a definitive way to make such an assessment. The way I do it is to see where the fact falls along a series of continua, which include

- The Speculation v. Established Fact continuum
- The Trivial v. Significant continuum
- The Unbelievable v. Believable continuum
- The Improbable v. Probable continuum
- The Complex v. Simple continuum
- The Inconsistent v. Consistent continuum

Before moving on, I should note that I have listed these continua (and those in the next two sections) with what is generally perceived as the less desirable state on the left and the more desirable state on the right. In other words, the further to the left the facts fall on any continuum, the less valuable they will likely be as part of your Factual Strand; the further to the right that they fall on the continuum, the more valuable the material will likely be (at least with respect to the specific factor being measured on that particular continuum).

The most desirable of these facts (that is, the ones with internal characteristics that make them more powerful in the eyes of the jurors) are those facts that are (reading down the right hand column of the continua listed above) established, significant, believable, probable, simple, and consistent. Each of these descriptors benefit from an explanation.

The Speculation Versus Established Fact Continuum

One of the issues that you must determine with respect to the internal structure of each fact you hope to use as part of your Factual Strand, is whether it is actually a fact, or if it is a form of less credible (or even inadmissible) speculation or conjecture. Materials that commonly fall along this continuum from left to right include (1) rank speculation, (2) character evidence, (3) certain lay opinions (such as speed and distance), (4) other types of lay opinions (such as intoxication), (5) expert opinions, and (6) facts.

By drawing the continuum this way, I am stressing two points about this material. First, as a general rule, jurors value expert opinion testimony less than they do reliable factual testimony from ordinary percipient witnesses. As previously noted, one of the reasons that the jury system works is that we generally require our witnesses to have actually experienced the events about which they are testifying. We require witnesses to have personally "absorbed" the events through their own senses and then, after having done so, be sufficiently competent to personally relay what it is that they heard, saw, felt, tasted, and/or smelled. In short, we insist that witnesses have personal knowledge in order to testify.

But there are exceptions, the most common of which is the expert witness who, we tell the jury, is qualified to testify based on special expertise or knowledge. Even with this special insight, experts suffer in the jurors' eyes. Jurors expect witnesses to have personal, firsthand knowledge and they discount the testimony of those who lack it. One mock juror summed it up when he described the expert in his case: "He was not there at the accident, so why is he here, except for the money?"

Let me be clear: I am not denigrating the expert nor am I discounting your need for one. What I am suggesting is that every expert starts off "behind in the count." The only way that you are going to get ahead is by carefully planning and selectively choosing your expert who must convince the jury of two key points (regardless of the subject matter of his testimony): (1) that what the expert did makes sense and (2) that what the expert did seems fair. Jurors will never understand the level of detail provided by most experts. But if they believe that what the expert did makes sense and seems fair, you can successfully move his testimony to the right on the continuum.

My final point has to do with the split in lay opinion testimony. Some forms of such testimony are rarely, if ever, considered reliable. The two most obvious examples are opinions as to speed and distance. Common experience tells most jurors that only one person in a hundred can testify accurately about either of these subjects. On the other hand, I have found that lay opinion on other subjects, most notably intoxication, tend to be readily accepted by other lay persons on the jury. I suspect the reason for this is pretty obvious—both the lay witness and the jurors are presumed to have some personal experience in assessing whether someone is intoxicated or not.

The Trivial Versus Significant Continuum

As we have previously noted, time is one of the scarcest resources in the courtroom. You only have so much of it before the jury loses interest, gets bored, stops listening, and then begins to resent you for wasting their time. When I was in law school, an experienced lawyer told me that the best way to avoid this was to never let your case become "a trap for the trivial and a sieve for the significant." I have always remembered this advice and have attempted to apply this standard to each of the cases I have worked on.

This continuum helps to assess whether a fact warrants being included in your Proto-Story. The continuum is relatively straightforward and probably does not need much explanation. Ideally, you will use facts that fall on the right-hand side of the continuum; that is, the facts will be significant.

The Unbelievable Versus Believable Continuum And the Improbable Versus Probable Continuum

The last thing you want is for your jury to be collectively shaking their heads, staring at you and your client and thinking, "You have got to be kidding! Is that it? Is that all you've got?" Remember that the jurors are looking for the truth. Any message you deliver that lacks credibility will be perceived as indicating that you, too, lack credibility. That is a hard obstacle to overcome. The better strategy is to avoid this altogether by carefully assessing the believability of your evidence and the overall story it tells, as well as whether the assumptions you ask your jurors to make seem likely (or probably) true.

As you can tell from the prior sentence, I generally consider believability and probability to assess slightly different aspects of your Proto-Story. "Believability" goes more to the overall theory of the case and the credibility of the evidence. Does the story hang together? Are the witnesses and other evidence to be trusted?

"Probability" assesses gaps and speculation. Inevitably, there will be gaps in your story, parts of what happened that no one knows or someone does not want you to know. For example, what was someone thinking at the time he acted; did he know that what he was doing was wrong; did two or more people secretly conspire to set prices? Even with extensive discovery, there will be gaps. As noted above when we discussed Party Motive, it is potentially dangerous to leave gaps without at least some kind of explanation to fill the space. Probability goes to the likelihood that your gap-filler is the accurate one. The defendant arrived at this fork in the road. Which way did she go? There are no actual footprints, so we use other evidence to infer the most probable answer (an answer that, by the way, must be consistent with your Case Theory and Case Themes).

What the jury finds probable may vary throughout the trial. For example, at the very beginning of a trial, jurors are rarely willing to assume the worst about a party. Most jurors project their own tendency to behave properly onto the parties and witnesses. As such, it may be difficult early on to convince a jury that someone is an out-and-out scoundrel. As the case progresses and the jurors become acclimated to what is going on in the case and the unique behaviors of various people, they may eventually determine that the same person they were reluctant to judge early on is, in fact, an unmitigated rogue.

The Complex Versus Simple Continuum

Whenever possible, choose the simple rather than the complex; that is, choose material to the right of this continuum. As I said before, the best Case Theories apply the theory of Occam's razor, which holds that if two theories explain the facts equally well, the simpler theory is preferred. In other words, the simpler theory is also the one that is most likely to be correct. For purposes of jury trials, you can add a corollary to this position: "The simpler theory is not only the one most likely to be correct, it is the one that the jury is more likely to accept."

The Inconsistent Versus Consistent Continuum

To shamelessly misquote Ralph Waldo Emerson, "Consistency is the hobgoblin of little minds, adored by statesmen, philosophers, divines, and jurors." Whether a story remains consistent is a major factor used by jurors to assess which side's Proto-Story to believe. Just as everyone feels they are capable of determining and stating an opinion as to Party Motive, just about everyone is capable of spotting, judging, and arguing about inconsistencies. Jurors may not be able to determine the applicability and appropriateness of regression formulas, but they can (and do) spot facts that change or are inconsistent. When they see such evidence, they view it with suspicion. Avoid using this material.

In determining consistency, you need to assess the fact from two perspectives. First, is the fact consistent with other facts; that is, is the fact an outlier or is it generally similar to other facts? Second, is the fact itself steadfast, remaining consistent over time, or is it fickle, contradicting itself at different points in the case?

Question Five: Is There Something About the Source Of the Fact That Makes It More or Less Powerful?

Facts do not exist unconnected, by themselves, in some sort of free state. All facts come from, and are metaphorically attached to, a source. For trials, the source of a fact is important for two reasons. First, the fact's relative worth is affected by how credible the source material to which it is attached is perceived to be. For example, does the information come from someone who is a neutral or a partisan source? Is the source considered definitive or does the information come from someone who is essentially a dilettante?

Second, the source is the means through which the fact is ultimately introduced or presented at trial. It is rare for there to be only one source for a particular piece of information. Therefore, the lawyer can typically choose between a number of potential witnesses, each of whom has strengths and weaknesses.

I assess the relative value of the source the same way that I assessed the internal characteristics of the facts in the prior section; that is, I measure it against a series of continua, which include:

- The Not Credible versus Credible continuum
- The Biased versus Unbiased continuum
- The Single versus Multiple continuum
- The Undocumented versus Documented continuum
- The Inconsistent versus Consistent continuum
- The Retroactively Revised versus Contemporary and Unchanged continuum
- The Words versus Actions continuum

The Not Credible Versus Credible Source Continuum and the Biased Versus Unbiased Source Continuum

A single fact can be valued differently by jurors, depending on which witness or piece of evidence you use to introduce that fact at trial. This is often dependent upon two variables: (1) the witness's or evidence's perceived credibility and (2) the witness's or evidence's affiliation or bias.

Credibility is generally a measure of the internal validity of the witness or evidence. It goes to what the ancient Romans characterized as *gravitas,* or internal substance, weight, or dignity. Obviously, you would like all of your evidence to come from a credible source, a person with integrity who is capable of accurately perceiving the events that lead up to the litigation, accurately remembering these events, and then persuasively conveying the facts to the jury.

Bias is relationally based. More specifically, bias is the effect (or apparent effect) of a relationship on the (conscious or unconscious) ability to perceive, process, or testify accurately. The relationship can be to a specific person (e.g., a family member) or it can be to a group-based prejudice (e.g., favoring blue state Democrats over red state Republicans). In general terms, a bias related to a specific person tends to be stronger than a bias for or against a group.

It should surprise no one that we all have biases. What I find amazing is the nature and extent to which biases can affect a person's ability to remain neutral. Being unbiased does not necessarily make a witness or evidence more accurate. Testimony from a neutral source tends to be better received by jurors because it eliminates a perceived variable—witness bias. But you do not necessarily want all your facts in a case to come from unbiased sources, although some lawyers believe that the most influential information comes from neutral sources. In actuality, the most influential information comes from someone who is biased *against* your client. This is particularly the case if the source is your opposing party. For some, it may seem inconceivable that you could ever get that kind of information. In reality, such information is often available. Ironically, some lawyers fail to use this material because they perceive it as easier to get the evidence from neutral witnesses or those affiliated with their own client. If you can establish the same fact during direct examination of your own witness or by way of cross-examining someone who is perceived as supporting the other side, the "admission" on cross is apt to have greater impact.

The Single Versus Multiple Continuum

Jurors naturally take comfort in knowing that verification from multiple sources increases the likelihood that something is true. This principle is applicable to both the number of witnesses who confirm a fact and to the types or sources of the evidence. Oral testimony alone is not as good as having both oral and written confirmation.

The more sources that confirm your fact, the better off you are. Obviously, the greater the disparity between the number of sources who saw it one way and the number who saw it the other, the greater value a jury will place on the credibility of the facts. Said differently, ten witnesses, split six on one side and four on the other, have far less persuasive value than if nine witnesses saw it one way and only one witness saw it the other. This having been said, common sense should tell you that jurors are not merely pollsters; they will not simply accept a fact based on which side has the greater number of witnesses. In fact, some jurisdictions make it a point to instruct jurors that a single, credible witness is enough evidence for them to disregard a multitude of less credible witnesses on the other side.

The Undocumented Versus Documented Continuum

While the adage "An oral contract is not worth the paper on which it is written" may not be technically correct, it does reflect how partial jurors tend to be towards written material. Oral testimony alone requires the jury to balance and counterbalance numerous variables (i.e., Did the witness accurately perceive, remember, testify?). Written testimony has none of these infirmities, but it does suffer from another problem—despite the common objection to the contrary, "documents do not speak for themselves." Written material is most effective when supplemented by consistent oral testimony.

The Inconsistent Versus Consistent Continuum; the Retroactively Revised Versus Contemporary and Unchanged Continuum; And the Words Versus Actions Continuum

Jurors do not like witnesses who change their testimony. While there may be an entirely valid reason for the change, jurors will need some additional persuading in order to disregard this perceived disability.

This is particularly true if the change occurs after it becomes obvious to the parties that they are headed to litigation. Contemporaneous comments made prior to any hint of conflict are usually given (and probably should be given) more weight than comments made after the parties "lawyer up."

There are two important corollaries to this. First, as the adage provides and common sense confirms: Actions speak louder than words. Second, actions taken prior to any perceived dispute are far more persuasive—and are perceived as having come from a more credible source—than actions that take place after the dispute has occurred.

Question Six: Is There Something About the Fact That Makes It Easier or Harder to Use at Trial?

All of the facts in the world mean nothing if you cannot get them admitted into evidence. Some facts will roll themselves into court and others will resist (or be resisted) with hammer and tongs. You need to assess how difficult it will be to use your material at trial.

How easy or difficult it is to use material at trial will vary greatly depending on a number of factors, including the nature of the material itself, its perceived reliability, and the purpose for which it is purportedly being used. It is beyond the scope of this volume to discuss the evidentiary requirements of specific types of evidence. Instead, I would like to make two key points.

First, there are usually a variety of ways to establish a particular fact. While the end result may be more or less the same (i.e., the fact is admitted into evidence), the degree of difficulty associated with the various potential paths may vary widely. Think about this as you lay out your evidence map. In pointing this out, I am not advocating that you get lazy and only offer evidence that is easy to introduce. Instead, I am suggesting that you save your "head banging" for situations where it makes sense.

Second, I want to remind you that there is not always a direct relationship between the amount of energy required to get a fact admitted and the resulting degree of persuasiveness it will have at trial. Using material "for illustrative purposes" often yields a very high ratio of persuasiveness to the amount of energy expended to using it.

Technically, illustrative material is not evidence; it does not officially get admitted and, as such, it rarely becomes part of the official trial record. To say that illustrative material is not evidence is like saying that opening statements and closing arguments are not evidence. While true, it may not matter much when it comes to persuading the jury. Just as no one denies that opening statements and closing arguments have a profound effect on the jury despite not being formal evidence, few would deny that illustrative material can significantly affect the jury.

The court has considerable discretion when it comes to deciding whether to allow the use of illustrative material. Generally speaking, in order to be used at trial, illustrative material must meet only three criteria: (1) the material cannot violate some other evidence rule, (2) the material must be relevant, and (3) the material must be fair, reasonable, and accurate. Still, the judge retains considerable discretion in this area and ultimately decides if the material is appropriate. But think about it—if you can convince a judge that there is a legitimate basis for the material, and if there are not particularly onerous requirements and each requirement is met, you have a fair amount of discretion as to what helps illustrate a key point of testimony or argument.

The Persuasion Tools

If, for the moment, you consider the Factual Strand to be the "truth" (or at least your client's version of the truth), the Persuasion Tools (Ill. 2-14) could be considered the "study guides" for the truth. If the truth is direct and heavily reliant on words to make its meaning clear, the Persuasion Tools are indirect, rely on nuance, and tend to be visually based. Such material can include actual pictures or graphics, but it also includes tools that help convey concepts in the "mind's eye" using analogies, adages, similes, metaphors, and other similar devices.

Persuasion Tools are the communication devices that provide perspective to the jurors. An experienced lawyer uses them at various key decision points throughout the case—points where she can substantially increase her chances of winning if she persuades the jurors to accept her explanation over her opponent's.

I divide Persuasion Tools into two categories. The first include "Operating Tools," which appeal to the Core Values of a particular juror and help that juror appreciate the lawyer's case as being consistent with those values that the juror believes drives (or should drive) the world. For example, certain jurors strongly respond to structure and order. They believe that the greater good is best served when there are definable and predictable criteria with which to judge what might otherwise be a difficult situation. Such jurors want—and favorably respond to—Persuasion Tools that are designed around the jury instructions provided by the court. Such tools might include checklists and items of annotated jury instructions, that is, graphics that directly link the language of the instructions back to the specific evidence that supports that legal element.

The second category includes "Educational Tools," which help jurors better understand the key aspects, or what I call the "Core Details," of the case. Core Details are those bits of information that the typical juror feels he needs to understand before he can comfortably make his decision.

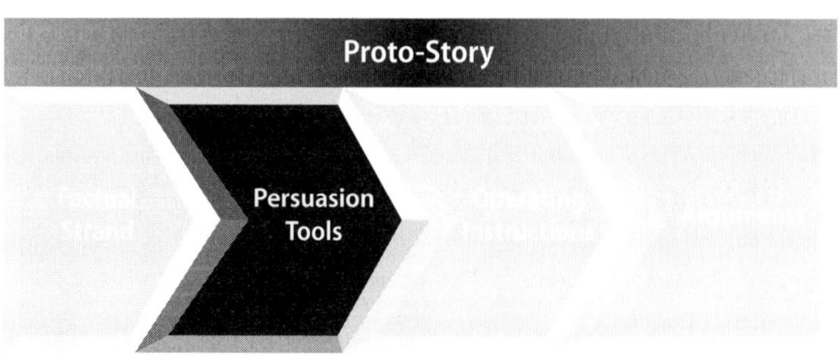

ILLUSTRATION 2-14 The Second Input: The Persuasion Tools

We will be discussing Persuasion Tools and how they affect different types of jurors in considerably greater detail in Chapter 4.

The Operating Instructions

Jury Instructions Are Broader Than Just a Listing of Elements

The "Operating Instructions" (Ill. 2-15) are the jury's understanding of what it is supposed to do and how it is supposed to do it. The jury derives this understanding after listening to—and incompletely digesting—the court's recitation of the law during the jury charge.

I suppose you might be wondering why I refer to this category as Operating Instructions, rather than the more conventional term "jury instructions." I prefer to call them Operating Instructions because far too often we think of jury instructions as being limited to a recitation of the prima facie elements of a cause of action or defense and the definition for burden of proof. Part of this may be due to two factors. First, most of the energy that lawyers put into preparing and arguing jury instructions at the charging conference is focused on those instructions that define a claim or affirmative defense. Second, I firmly believe that most lawyers never really listen to the judge when he reads the instructions to the jury. Depending on when the judge charges the jury (either before or after the closing arguments), many lawyers are either trying to calm themselves down before getting up to argue or they are keeping themselves awake after exhausting themselves during their argument.

I generally see Operating Instructions as providing guidance in three areas (Ill. 2-16):

1. The elements necessary for one side to prevail on a claim or defense,
2. Definitions of key terms the jurors need to understand and use in order to reach a verdict, and
3. Suggested protocols that jurors can use to respond to common, recurring situations that develop during deliberations.

Consequently, I use the term "Operating Instructions" to remind you that such instructions often contain material to which we do not give adequate notice to when preparing our Proto-Story, particularly as that story is expressed in closing.

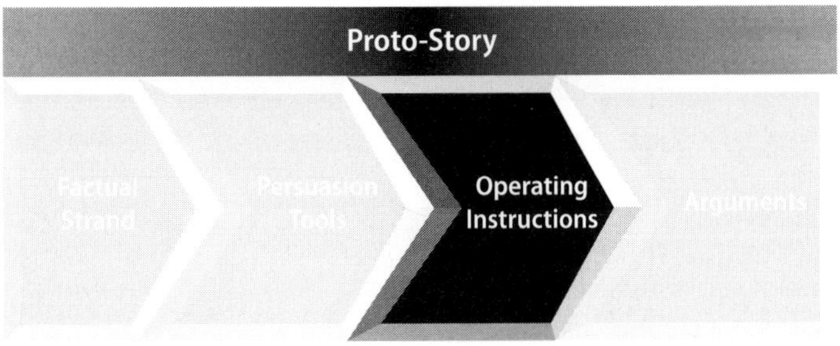

ILLUSTRATION 2-15 The Third Input: The Operating Instructions

There Are Three Types of Operating Instructions

1. Those that list the elements necessary for one side to prevail
2. Those that provide definitions of certain key terms that the jurors need to reach a verdict
3. Those that suggest protocols jurors can use to respond to common situations that occur during deliberations

ILLUSTRATION 2-16 Three Types of Operating Instructions
Lawyers often forget that jury instructions are broader than a list of the elements necessary for a claim or defense. Where appropriate, include all three types of instructions in your closing argument.

Providing a List of Prima Facie Elements That Must Be Proven in Order to Prevail on a Claim or Defense

As suggested above, when lawyers think of jury instructions, they think about instructions that list the prima facie elements of a claim or defense. The way you use these Operating Instructions as part of your Proto-Story is relatively straightforward. These Operating Instructions provide the latticework upon which you and the jury assemble facts and then cross-check them (sometimes literally with a checklist offered for illustrative purposes), to see if all of the elements of a claim and/or defense have been met. Since most trial lawyers already do this, I am not sure there is much more that need be said on this topic.

Defining Key Terms

Defining, and thereby "naming," something is the first step in understanding and eventually controlling it. Operating Instructions typically contain numerous definitions of key terms—terms that are needed and used in a variety of ways during deliberations. Some of these definitions go toward explaining the components or building blocks upon which the prima facie elements of a claim or defense are based. Other definitions explain crucial concepts such as "preponderance of the evidence."

If you look up a word in a dictionary, you will find that the entries usually include both a definition and an example of the word used in context. In some dictionaries, you may even find a small picture to help more fully explain—or illustrate—what the word means. Like a lot of people, I find the combination of a strict definition, an example of use in context, and an illustration to be a highly effective method of definition or explanation.

Formal Operating Instructions usually provide only one-third of what most people need to understand a key term or concept. To use my dictionary analogy, Operating Instructions presented by the court provide only the formal definition portion of the dictionary entry, while the lawyer is left to put the word into a contextual sentence and to provide the accompanying illustration.

It is your job to help the jury understand the definition itself and to understand the definition in the context of the case. You do this by using the facts (plus anything else you are permitted to use—analogies, arguments, etc.) to put the definitions into context and to illustrate them with trial graphics.

Protocols That Jurors Can Use to Respond to Common, Recurring Situations That Develop During the Trial and the Deliberations

One of the most overlooked types of Operating Instructions are those that instruct jurors how to respond to certain events that occur during the trial or their deliberations. For example, one witness gets caught in a lie, another exhibits bias in favor of one of the parties, a third testifies to his previous felony conviction. This type of thing happens fairly regularly in the courtroom. As trial lawyers, we see these things occur while trying our case, we understand their significance, and we listen to the jury instructions that highlight their significance, but we often fail to use the resulting Operating Instructions to our advantage.

Do not make this mistake. Incorporate these Operating Instructions into your Proto-Story and tie the Operating Instruction to the specific event that occurred in your case. For example, if a witness gets caught in a lie, tie that lie to the common instruction that the jury can disregard all of that witness's testimony. Explain this to the jury; show the jury what your opponent's case looks like without the evidence of the perjurer. Finally, remind the jurors that it is not only you who are administering this instruction; it is the law, the law as personified by the judge as she delivers her instructions to the jury.

Some more examples: What should a lone juror do if he finds himself in a minority of one, like Henry Fonda in the movie *12 Angry Men*? What do the instructions say about applying common sense? Can a juror disregard the testimony of an expert witness, even if that expert won the Nobel Prize in physics? Must jurors accept everything the expert says merely because he knows more than they do about a particular topic? Can a juror ignore ten witnesses on one side of the issue in favor of a single witness who testifies to the contrary? What are jurors to think when a witness does not take the stand or insists on a privilege that leaves the jurors wishing they had that missing piece of evidence?

I suspect that you know or can quickly find the answers to these questions. Share these answers with your jurors and—even more importantly—help them understand why the answers matter and should affect the way they deliberate.

Some Folks Are Cooks and Others Are Bakers

Let me explain why you should care about Operating Instructions. This may sound naive, but I did not fully appreciate how much some jurors rely on Operating Instructions until I started observing mock juries on a regular basis.

Don't get me wrong, I knew the instructions were important and I carefully drafted them and argued as forcefully as I could at the charging conference as to why my version was better than my opponent's. But I saw this more as an academic exercise than as a key element to winning a trial.

The truth is that I was wrong. Actually, to be more accurate, I was partially wrong. For some jurors (like those that reason as I do), Operating Instructions are not supremely important. They help orient us, but we tend to rely on other parts of the Proto-Story more extensively when assessing who should prevail. For others, Operating Instructions are crucial and are at the heart of the way they make their decisions.

What accounts for this difference? At their core, Operating Instructions are just that—instructions, and people generally use instructions in one of two ways. Perhaps the best way to explain this is to offer an observation that I have made about people who love to prepare food.

As with everything in life, in the jury room, there are "cooks" and there are "bakers." (Ill. 2-17) It is my experience that really good cooks rarely follow recipes, except by way of general guidelines and to more or less confirm that what they have already done is more or less correct. On the other hand, good bakers keep the recipe closely at hand, and will do nothing without consulting it first.

ILLUSTRATION 2-17 Some People Are Cooks and Others Are Bakers
Some jurors are "cooks" and rarely consult the instructions when coming to their conclusion; others are "bakers" and repeatedly consult and rely on the instructions.

I am the product of a mixed marriage—my mother is a cook and my father, a baker. When they are in the kitchen together, my mother will occasionally complain that my father is "too scientific." This is not a compliment because, as she likes to quickly add with some pride, "We cooks are much less scientific than bakers." Her point is that bakers necessarily rely very heavily on precise directions. On the other hand, my father will mutter to my mother with frustration, "Where is your recipe; how do you know how much [insert ingredient here] to put into your dish?" Baking is much more precise than cooking and it is very disconcerting to bakers that someone might not diligently follow the directions.

Some people consult instructions before they get started on a project and rely on them throughout the building process. These are the "bakers." Others consult the instructions almost as an afterthought or as a way of confirming to themselves that what they have done was done correctly. These are the "cooks."

Jurors are more or less the same way. Depending on their predilections, some jurors use the Operating Instructions from the very beginning of deliberations until a final decision is reached. These folks see the Operating Instructions as absolutely crucial to the decision-making process and they use them accordingly. Others tend to look at the Operating Instructions as verification that their conclusion was the correct one, and so they consult the Operating Instructions only periodically.

You often observe this phenomenon during deliberations that follow a mock trial or focus group. The bakers immediately consult the instructions (either actual copies given to them or the written notes they took while the instructions were read to them). The cooks quietly listen until the bakers are finished reading. Then the debate begins, with bakers focusing on instructions and the cooks usually more intently focused on the facts. These discussions are not (at least initially) at cross-purposes with each other. These two approaches tend to be complementary. However, if the group is unable to reach a consensus, you will see the bakers retreating back to the instructions and the cooks going back to their feelings about the facts.

The Arguments

It is only a slight exaggeration to say that during trial, highly skilled lawyers constantly do one of two things. They are either arguing or they are laying the foundation so they have the necessary tools and supporting material to argue. Pure facts by themselves rarely convince anyone; that is what arguments are supposed to do. Experienced trial lawyers are not afraid to argue *implicitly* throughout the case and *explicitly* during closing. (Ill. 2-18)

As I emphasized earlier in this book, arguing is not the same as fighting. Some lawyers, particularly new ones, believe that to argue, one must be overtly adversarial and must generate considerable sound and fury. This is not the case. One can argue without fighting; one can fight without arguing;

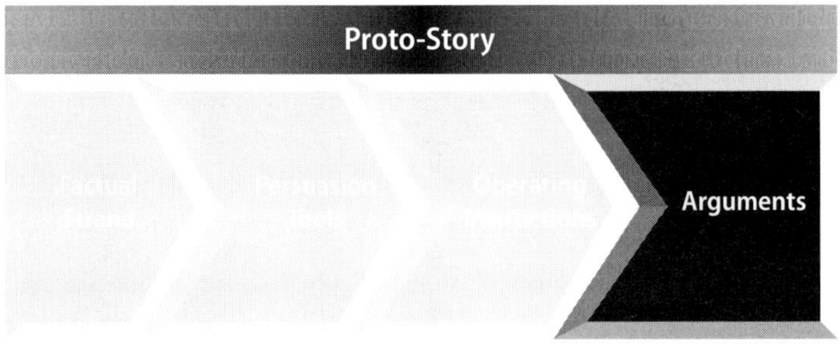

ILLUSTRATION 2-18 The Fourth Input: The Arguments

and one can fight and argue simultaneously. The best lawyers know the difference and how to use the right combination to persuade a jury.

A trial lawyer's job is, within the substantial confines of the law and all applicable ethical restrictions, to win his client's case. There are three common ways of doing so: (1) affirmatively, (2) negatively, and (3) by a combination of these two techniques.

Trial lawyers win their cases "affirmatively" by, as my twelve-year-old friend suggested, making their client's version "the TRUTH." When the general public (and perhaps most lawyers) envision trial counsel winning a case, it likely is by way of the affirmative technique. I would wager that every fictional closing argument you have ever seen or heard—and most of the closing arguments you have ever imagined giving—proved the case affirmatively. With a clear vision and recitation of the facts, a dose of irrefutable logic, and just the right flavoring of passion, you affirmatively made your client's version the TRUTH.

Trial lawyers win their cases "negatively" by trumpeting the fact that the opposing party has failed to make its version the TRUTH. This technique is far less dramatic (but ultimately no less satisfying—a win is a win, after all) than winning your case affirmatively, because winning a case negatively rests squarely on the concept of legal burdens. In the formal sense, it says, "You had a burden and you failed to meet it." In a less formal sense, it is the equivalent of thumbing your nose in the face of your opposing counsel or saying to him, "Nice try, but no cigar. Your case has come up short and, as such, your version cannot be the TRUTH."

In reality, trial lawyers most often win their cases by using a combination of both affirmative and negative techniques. In short, establish that your version is the TRUTH and (for good measure) that your opponent's version is *not* the TRUTH.

There are several reasons why the combination technique is most often used and most frequently successful. First, as a practical matter, that is the way life is—there are both affirmative and negative elements in almost everything that happens. Without overburdening your case with extraneous detail, you will probably do well to include the best of both elements in the story you tell the jurors.

Next, in and of itself, the claim that one side has failed to meet its burden (proving your case by negatively reflecting on your opponent's) is rarely sufficient to ensure a win. The technique may work for some kinds of jurors, for example, those who rely exclusively on the checklists suggested in some cases by the jury instructions. However, most jurors want more than just this; they want to know *why,* and this important element of motive requires the use of affirmative techniques.

Finally, a combination of affirmative and negative elements appeals to the broadest potential constituency on the jury. The affirmative elements will appeal to a subset of jurors, the negative elements to another subset, and a combination of both elements to a third. Hopefully, this broad-based appeal will allow you to create a coalition with a sufficient number of jurors to obtain your desired verdict.

Putting the Pieces Together That Are the Proto-Story

So, what do you do with all of these pieces? The answer is that you pull them together to form your Proto-Story (Ill. 2-19), which, as we discussed earlier, is the sum total of the material you carefully selected to present to the jury to let them know why your side should prevail.

To recap what we have covered so far, the Proto-Story consists of a Factual Strand, which, in turn, is composed of a single Case Theory that is formed by combining your Factual Theory and one or more Legal Theories. Woven through the Central Cord are the Case Themes, which add moral authority to your case, and your explanation of Party Motive, which allows the jury to better understand why the characters acted the way they did.

Strung on to the Central Cord are the Included Facts that you have carefully chosen based on where they fall along the various continua described earlier in this chapter. At a minimum, these Included Facts must incorporate all the facts you need to establish a prima facie showing of your claim or defense. You must also include and incorporate into your explanation all of the undisputed facts, including both those that favor you and those that

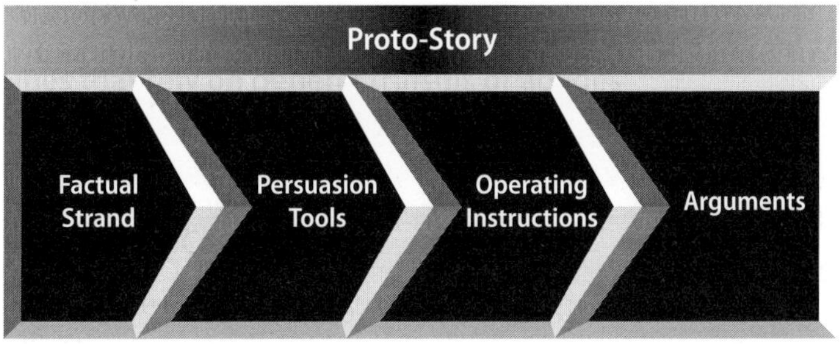

ILLUSTRATION 2-19 The Proto-Story Requires That You Assemble All Four of the Inputs

favor your opposing counsel. In addition, you should include only those facts that add interesting color to your case and/or make it more compelling.

Surrounding the strand and its attached facts are the other portions of the Proto-Story, with those elements necessary to make your case persuasive to the jury. These additional elements include three items:

1. The Persuasion Tools that help explain the facts by making them real and understandable to the jury
2. The Operating Instructions that help define what is legally important and how jurors should process all of the material they receive
3. The Arguments that help synthesize the facts and allow your Proto-Story to make sense

In the next chapter, we will discuss how the jurors take the two Proto-Stories (one from each side) and assess them based on a combination of characteristics, some of which are shared by all of the jurors and others that are unique to each individual. As part of this evaluation process, the jurors break the two Proto-Stories into pieces. Eventually, each juror creates his own Secondary Story based on a variety of elements, some from the Proto-Story and others from sources not presented at trial. Based on these Secondary Stories, the jurors form coalitions and eventually, in the vast majority of cases, reach a verdict.

CHAPTER 3

The Process—How Your Client's Version Becomes "The TRUTH"

"What a long strange trip it's been."

Juror, quoting the Grateful Dead after she and her colleagues finally reached a verdict.

Chapter Overview

Several years ago, I listened to a series of lectures by the historian Joseph Ellis in which he described how John Adams, George Washington, Thomas Jefferson, and Benjamin Franklin each came to the conclusion that American independence was necessary, even if the inevitable price was war with England. Though admittedly I had not given a lot of prior thought to the question, I somehow envisioned our Founding Fathers as a single unit and assumed they had all come to this conclusion in the same way and for more or less the same reasons. Professor Ellis not only corrected my misperceptions but also helped me more fully appreciate (by way of analogy) several important aspects of how jurors reach their verdict.

John Adams, the consummate trial lawyer who only a few years before had successfully defended British troops against murder charges arising from the Boston Massacre, relied on centuries of English common law as support for his conclusion. George Washington, whose interests at the time were primarily those of a Virginia tobacco farmer, came to the same conclusion because he believed that England, through its mercantile system, had imposed such an economic stranglehold on colonial agricultural exports that, save rebellion, he and his neighbors would inevitably be forced into poverty. Thomas Jefferson, although a Virginia farmer like Washington, was drawn to the need for independence based on a highly personalized version of Rousseauian natural law. Benjamin Franklin, the ultimate pragmatist and embodiment of common sense, concluded that revolution was necessary because, after considerable thought and effort, he could find no other alternative. (Ill. 3-1)

As Professor Ellis pointed out, because each of these Founding Fathers began his analysis in a different place and was personally motivated by a

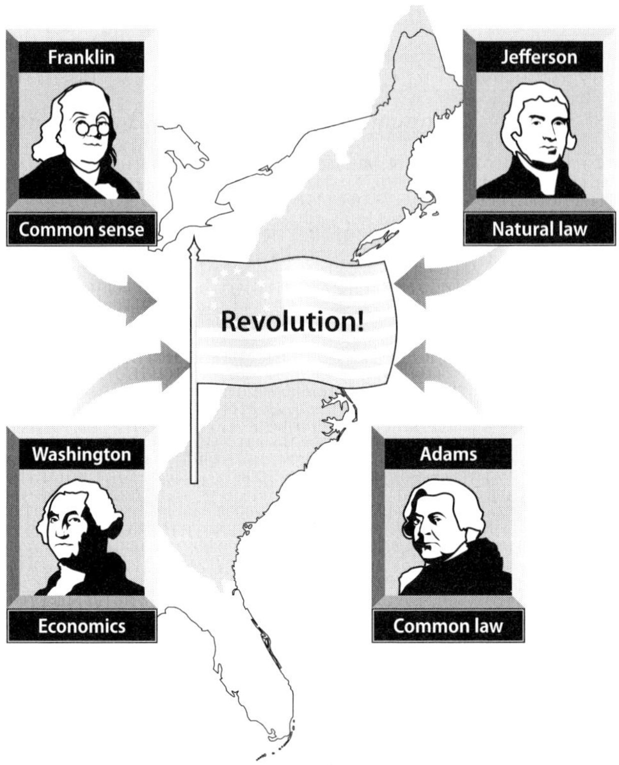

ILLUSTRATION 3-1 The Founding Fathers Each Had Different Motivations for Revolution Each of the Founding Fathers began his analysis in a different place and was personally motivated by a different set of factors. Each forged a different path to their common conclusion.

different set of factors, each forged a different path to their common conclusion. As crucial as each man's individual reasoning was to him during his personal decision-making process, these differences did not prevent any of them from joining the same coalition and working together to expand that coalition by pursuing a common goal—in this instance, political independence.

I am not suggesting that these highly opinionated men ever fully accepted or endorsed any of the others' differing rationales. In fact, I am confident that if any of them had been pressed, they would on the one hand have agreed with Franklin that it was crucial that "We must all hang together, or assuredly we shall all hang separately," while, on the other hand, each would have had no problem asserting that his own personal line of reasoning was far superior to that of the other three.

In short, what united these individuals was a common desire to achieve the same result (i.e., to see that the side they favored won), even if they could not completely agree as to exactly why. Despite personal and philosophical differences, this highly active core group cobbled together a coalition that was successful precisely because its members had powerful similarities *and* profound differences—both of which they turned to their collective advantage.

Specifically, the coalition had a highly focused and motivated core that was committed to driving its original members and all those they eventually recruited toward the same result. At the same time, the fact that each original member came to his own conclusion by way of a different path, the validity of which he firmly believed in and actively advocated, made it relatively easy for him to proselytize, recruit new members from outside with similar backgrounds, and convince these fresh recruits to become equally committed to the coalition members' common goal. (Ill. 3-2)

ILLUSTRATION 3-2 Each Founding Father Recruited Additional Members Who Shared Similar Ideas

As a result, John Adams could appeal to other students of the common law and bring them into the coalition. George Washington could do the same by finding a receptive audience from among other similarly situated farmers who shared his concerns about what they believed was England's unfair trade system. Thomas Jefferson would find allies among other intellectuals who might not be as familiar with Rousseau's writings, but perhaps were very comfortable with Locke's related theory of social contract. Benjamin Franklin . . . let's hold off for a couple of paragraphs before we discuss Franklin because, in many ways, the influence provided by his pragmatic approach was most widely felt by coalition and noncoalition members alike.

I suspect that the opportunity that each Founding Father had to project his personal philosophy outward and do battle with those outside the core group (rather than within) had the additional benefit of diffusing ideological tensions that might form within the coalition itself. Left unchecked, these tensions would potentially have pitted coalition members against one another.[1]

As with any coalition, some of the members would have had multiple reasons for joining. For example, some might have been primarily motivated by Adams's philosophy of common law while secondarily fearing that the English mercantile system would eventually bankrupt the colonies, as Washington feared. Far from dividing them, the fact that some members were motivated to join for several different reasons would strengthen the connections between various subgroups within the coalition. As we will see later, these people with their multiple connections would serve metaphorically as

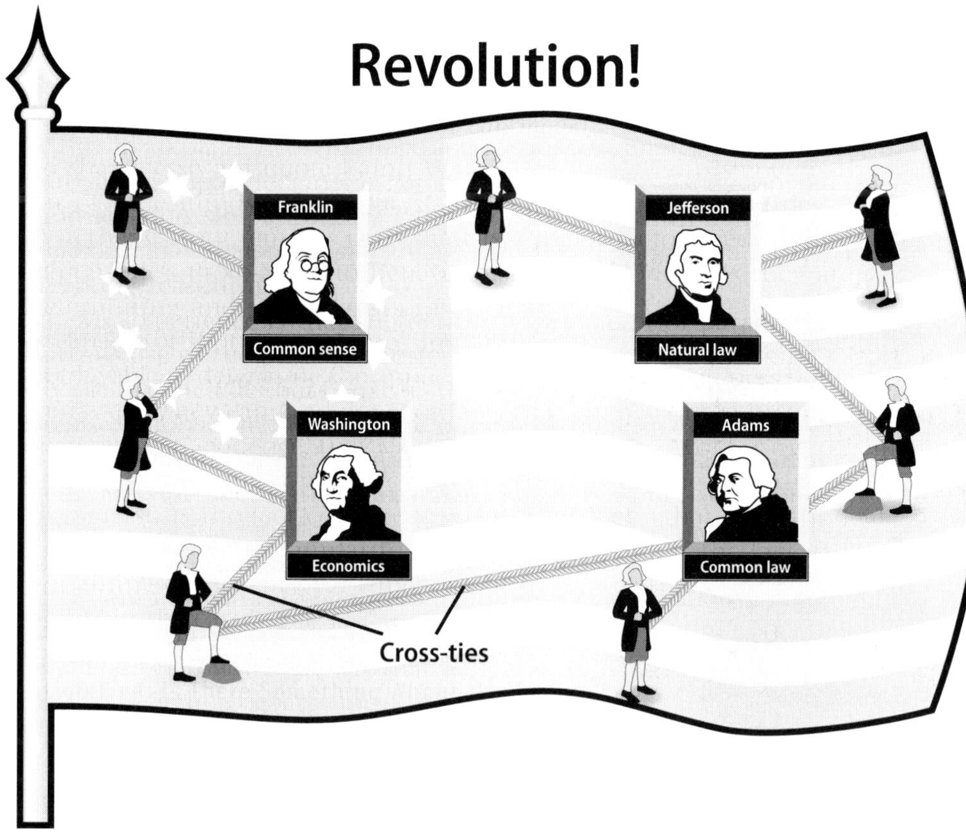

ILLUSTRATION 3-3 Cross-Ties
Some members joined the coalition for a variety of reasons and formed reinforcing cross-ties.

1. When mock jurors deliberate, one often sees this benefit of directing tension outward, thereby preventing a break from occurring within the coalition.

"cross-ties," indirectly attaching Adams to Washington to Jefferson to Franklin. Just as in chemistry, where multiple covalent bonds make it more difficult to break apart a molecule, these cross-ties would have strengthened the coalition by making it more difficult for those who opposed independence to persuade coalition members to split off and defect to the other side.

As the personification of *common sense* and pragmatism, Franklin's contribution to the cohesiveness of the coalition was particularly important. Not only would he have attracted those who directly shared his beliefs, but also his plainspoken approach would have had broad appeal, crossing philosophical lines as well as appealing to and helping bind those whose primary motivations might be closer to Adams, Washington, or Jefferson. Franklin's homespun and commonly shared wisdom (i.e., his "common sense") would appeal to virtually everyone in the coalition and thereby act as mortar, filling in the inevitable gaps that might otherwise develop. This metaphorical combination of mortar and cross-ties would further bind these members together, thereby making it difficult for those who opposed the coalition to strip away its members.

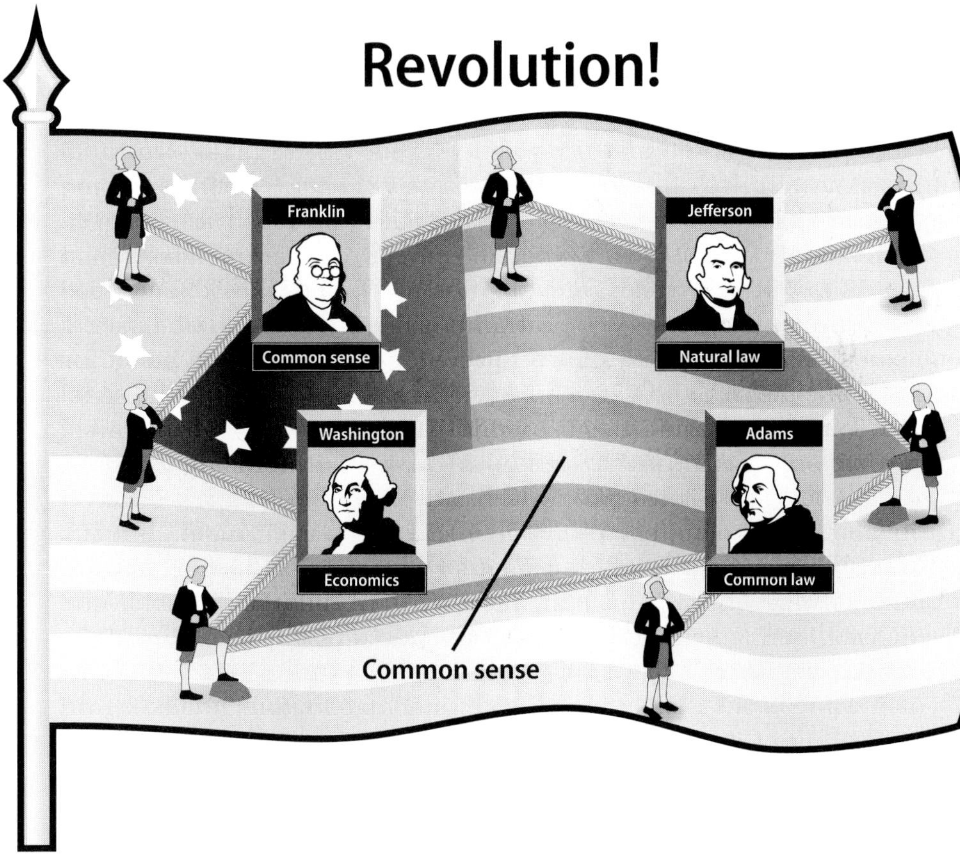

ILLUSTRATION 3-4 Common Sense
The common shared vision or "common sense" appealed to everyone in the coalition and filled gaps that might otherwise have existed between the members.

This coalition, united in a common purpose—even if its members came from different backgrounds and did not entirely agree as to why they agreed—formed, held, expanded, and, as they say, "The rest is history."

Now, fast-forward to the present. Why do I consider this American history lesson so important in understanding your last jury trial or in preparing for the one that is coming up?

Because the *process* that Professor Ellis describes of how the Founding Fathers overcame their individual philosophical differences, bound themselves together in pursuit of a common goal, and developed a critical mass while opposing another group with a contrary opinion is, in many ways, analogous to how modern jurors reach their verdicts.

Like the Founding Fathers:

- Jurors begin their analysis in different places and each is personally motivated by a different set of factors.
- Each juror forges a different path to a common conclusion, based on an individual story unique to that juror.
- The jurors eventually form a broad-based coalition where the members unanimously agree on the end result, although they do not necessarily agree as to why this conclusion is the correct one.
- This prevailing coalition is created, held together, and its membership ultimately expanded through the work of a small number of highly motivated Active Jurors.

This chapter deals with mechanics. It deals with the process through which your client's version becomes "the TRUTH." It discusses how a series of events triggers a dispute that the involved parties cannot resolve and how the resolution comes to rest on twelve randomly selected people who will eventually agree upon the "Ultimate Reality."

"Ultimate Reality"

Underlying every lawsuit is an event that I call the "Big Bang." It is at the core of the dispute; it is the reason the parties are fighting. The Big Bang occurs at such places as on street corners when cars crash, in boardrooms where conspiracies are hatched, and at restaurant tables when friendships fall apart—there are virtually infinite ways for a dispute to begin.

For the most part, a conflict arises because no one, neither the parties nor the witnesses, have any way of objectively knowing exactly what happened at the center of the dispute. In fact, given the imperfections of human nature, I am not sure there is ever a way of "scientifically" making such a determination. Therefore, we are forced to rely on an imperfect substitute method for deciding what, exactly, is "the TRUTH." We rely on jurors to determine "what really happened" leading up to and at the moment of the Big Bang. At the same time that we publicly charge them with this essential duty, we privately recognize that we have committed them to an impossible task and that the most we can possibly hope for is that they agree on an acceptable explanation for "what really happened."

Let me make explicit what we trial lawyers are somewhat afraid to openly admit. In an effort to resolve conflict, the judicial system must, by necessity, make a mish-mash of reality. Using witnesses who have each viewed the same event from differing perspectives, trials attempt "in the present tense" to resolve a dispute that occurred "in the past tense" between two (or more) parties, each of whom has an entirely different view of what really happened. None of this changes the basic fact that we rely on the jury to find the ultimate truth and to determine the Ultimate Reality.

Before proceeding much further, I need to explain what I mean, at least in the context of a jury trial, by "ultimate truth" and "Ultimate Reality."[2] I do not believe that there is an ultimate reality—as in a single, correct, all-knowing view of a series of events (and, if there is, I am not convinced we will ever find it in even the most basic human interactions, let alone in something as complicated and contested as a lawsuit.) In fact, that is *not* how I use the word "ultimate." Instead, I use the word as in "last," or "final."

Establishing the ultimate truth—as in the last or final version—is the best that we as society can hope for, and the most we can realistically afford. It is the best we can hope for precisely because the Big Bang never occurs in a way or in a place where cause and effect can be scientifically isolated and objectively measured. Thus, as a practical matter, we have to accept that it is impossible to know with complete objectivity exactly what happened at the Big Bang. It is the most we can afford because the dispute cannot go on forever; at some point the involved parties and society must accept the jury's decision, deem the dispute resolved, and move on with their lives. In short, the jury's verdict is close enough to what really happened to satisfy society and the adversarial parties.

Given these limitations, what then is this thing that we call the "verdict" and how does it become something that we accept as the "Ultimate Reality" or final restatement of what happened at the time of the Big Bang? In a typical case, there are at least seven sequential versions of reality, with the verdict being the ultimate (last) of these versions. It is important to know what these versions are because understanding this progression will help you to better understand the process jurors go through in reaching a verdict.

As the accompanying graphic shows, these views of reality form what I call a "nonrecurring loop."[3] (Ill. 3-5)

2. To what I am sure is the consternation of certain philosophers, I treat the terms "reality" and "truth" as the same thing, and for the purposes of this discussion, the terms are used interchangeably.

3. It is a loop in that we end up where we started. It is nonrecurring in that once we end up where we started, we stop and do not keep going.

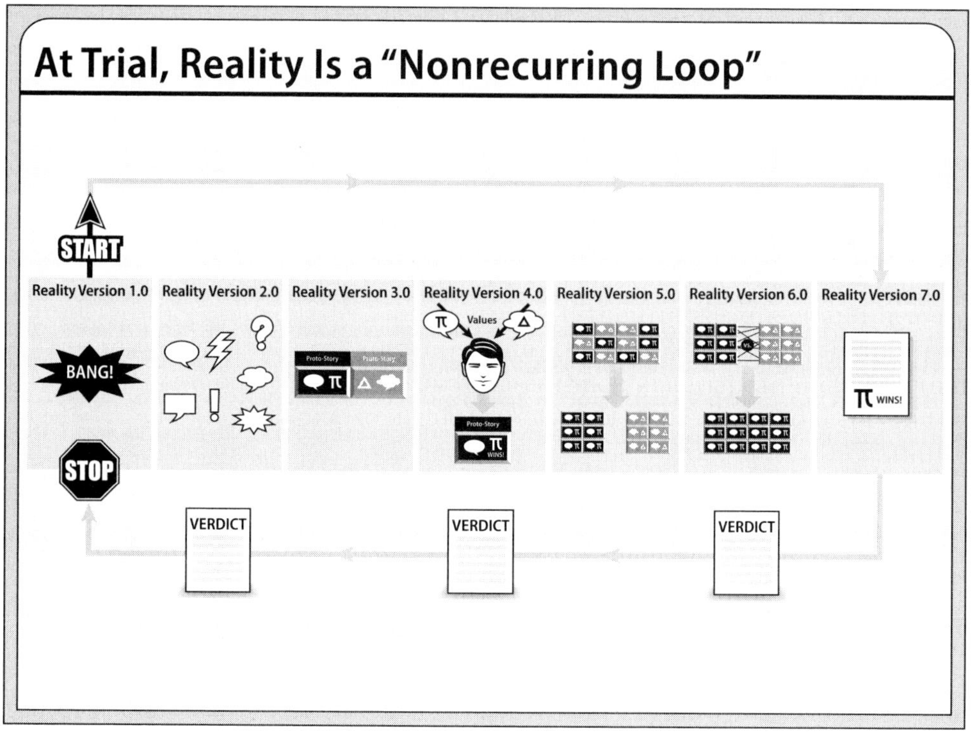

ILLUSTRATION 3-5 At Trial, Reality Is a "Nonrecurring Loop"

The seven sequential versions of reality are:

Reality Version 1.0: The Big Bang
Reality Version 2.0: The Universe of Potential Information
Reality Versions 3.1 and 3.2: The Two Proto-Stories
Reality Versions 4.1 through 4.12: The Jurors' Secondary Stories
Reality Version 5.1 and 5.2: The Coalitions' Stories
Reality Version 6.0: The Prevailing Coalition's Story
Reality Version 7.0: The Verdict

Reality Version 1.0: The Big Bang

Reality Version 1.0 is what "actually" happened just before, during, and after the Big Bang. Unfortunately, the Big Bang never occurs in a scientifically controlled setting where every variable can be observed and objectively quantified. As such, while it may theoretically be possible to put together a single, wholly accurate explanation of the Big Bang, no one—not either of the parties, nor any of the witnesses—can objectively know exactly what that version of reality is. Yet this is exactly what we ask the jury to determine. (Ill. 3-6)

Reality Version 1.0 is where we both begin and eventually end our search for the ultimate truth. Reality Version 1.0 serves as the beginning because, as I have already noted, every lawsuit starts with the Big Bang; it is the reason

Reality Version 1.0: The Big Bang

The Big Bang is an event that triggers a lawsuit. Because we live in a world full of uncertainties, we have no immediate way of knowing exactly what "really happened."

ILLUSTRATION 3-6 Reality Version 1.0 Is "The Big Bang"

the parties are fighting. It is where we end our search because, after going through all seven versions of reality, we come back to where we started since it is not until the jury renders its verdict (Reality Version 7.0) that we can "officially" know which party's account of the Big Bang has been adopted by the jury as the TRUTH.

Reality Version 2.0: The Universe of Potential Information

The Big Bang rarely occurs in isolation; it is usually observed by witnesses. Many of these witnesses will have preserved, in some type of documented form, what they believe to have happened at or during the Big Bang. As with every dispute, none of the witnesses will have a complete understanding of what happened. Likewise, no two witnesses will have perceived and processed the events in exactly the same way. As a former teacher of mine used to say, "That's what makes for a good horse race!"

Reality Version 2.0 is the universe of potential information surrounding the Big Bang.[4] It is the all-encompassing source of the material used by either party at trial. It is the complete collection of what every witness could

4. For simplicity's sake, I am including all forms of evidence, particularly documentary, in this general description.

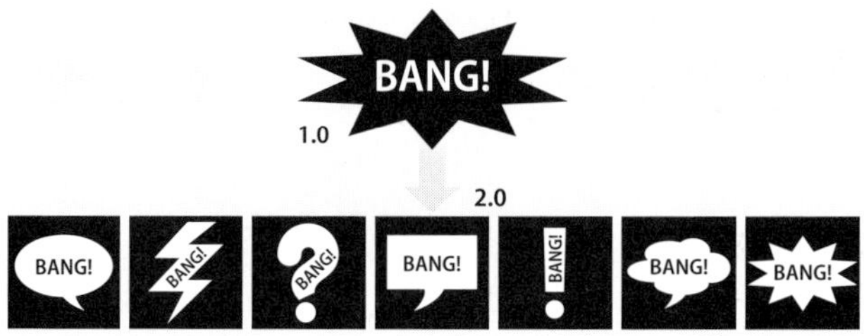

Reality Version 2.0: The Universe of Potential Information

The Big Bang is witnessed by a number of individuals and documented in a variety of ways. This massive pool of information—relevant, irrelevant, material, immaterial, admissible, and inadmissible—constitutes Reality Version 2.0.

ILLUSTRATION 3-7 Reality Version 2.0 Is the Universe of Potential Information

potentially say (admissible or otherwise) and what every bit of information from every possible source could demonstrate (relevant or otherwise). It is the mother lode from which the parties pull the material that is eventually used at trial, the universe of raw material from which the skilled trial lawyer will draw all of the necessary facts and related supporting material for presentation to a jury. As we will see, the bulk of this material is never used and effectively suffers the same fate as the hypothetical tree that falls in the forest when no one is around to hear it. (Ill. 3-7)

Reality Versions 3.1 and 3.2: The Proto-Stories

Reality Versions 3.1 and 3.2 are the parties' competing descriptions or explanations of what they claim "really" happened. These are each side's Proto-Stories, which I described in Chapter 2. Plaintiff presents its version of what happened as Reality Version 3.1 and defendant presents its Reality Version 3.2 in response. Each of these versions (i.e., 3.1 and 3.2) leads to a specific result. One concludes that plaintiff should win and the other favors the defendant. The jury's job is to agree on which of the results should prevail. By collectively choosing one result over the other, the jury favors one party and, in so doing, ultimately endorses one version of reality (or truth) over the other. (Ill. 3-8)

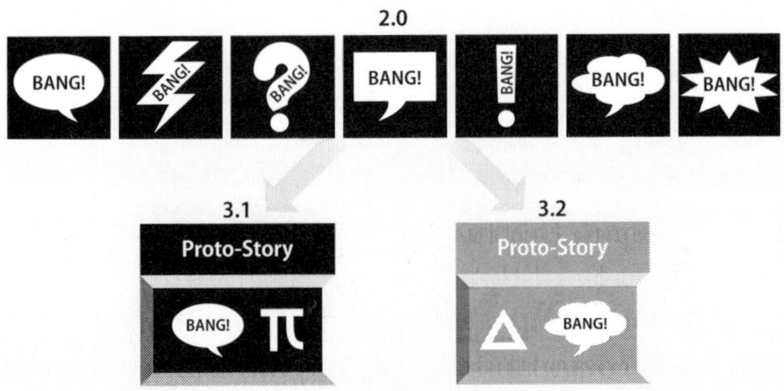

Reality Versions 3.1 and 3.2: The Two Proto-Stories

Each lawyer sorts through the mass of information that is Reality Version 2.0 and creates his client's Proto-Story. Plaintiff's Proto-Story is Reality Version 3.1 and defendant's is Reality Version 3.2. These are the versions of reality presented by the respective parties during the trial.

ILLUSTRATION 3-8 Reality Versions 3.1 and 3.2 Are the Parties' Proto-Stories

It bears repeating that both versions rely on only a fraction of the material potentially available from Reality Version 2.0. For example, while hundreds of people may have been present at the Big Bang, only the "reality" experienced by a handful of these people will ultimately matter at trial. This is because the reality that matters for purposes of Reality Versions 3.1 and 3.2 is that which is favored, carefully selected, and presented by the respective parties. Later in this chapter we will discuss how to go about choosing the right material for your Proto-Story.

Reality Versions 4.1 through 4.12: Each Juror's Secondary Story

Reality Versions 4.1 through 4.12 are the twelve views (one for each juror) of the Big Bang that the jurors develop while listening to evidence and deliberating. It is unlikely that any juror ever fully accepts one party's version of the facts. Generally, a juror accepts a greater number of facts from one party than the other and mixes these accepted facts with other facts unique to that juror's perspective, background, and experience. Each of the jurors will eventually come up with his own "Secondary Story" or personal version of what he believes happened at the Big Bang. (Ill. 3-9)

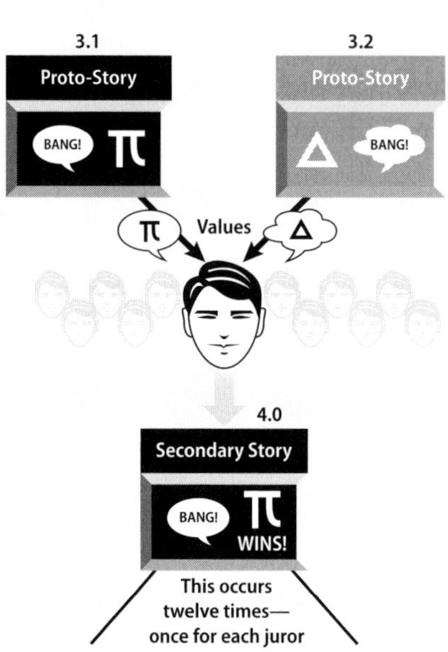

Reality Versions 4.1 through 4.12: The Jurors' Secondary Stories

During and after the trial, each juror combines bits and pieces from the two Proto-Stories with his own individual experience, memories, perceptions, and attitudes to create his own personal "Secondary Story." This personal story is how each individual juror explains his decision to himself and others. Each juror has a different Secondary Story and, as such, there will initially be twelve of them. Collectively, these twelve different Secondary Stories are Reality Versions 4.1 through 4.12.

ILLUSTRATION 3-9 Reality Versions 4.1 through 4.12 Are the Jurors' Personal Secondary Stories

Reality versions 5.1 and 5.2: the two coalitions

During deliberations, the jurors will often split into two different coalitions: one favoring the plaintiff and one favoring the defendant. Each juror joins one of these two coalitions based on the ending of his own Secondary Story, which will conclude either: "Plaintiff wins" (Reality Version 5.1) or "Defendant wins" (Reality Version 5.2). (Ill. 3-10)

Reality version 6.0: the winning coalition

As suggested above, there are initially a multitude of competing versions of jurors' Secondary Stories swirling around during deliberations (Reality Versions 4.1 through 4.12), until they are finally narrowed down to two coalitions (Reality Versions 5.1 and 5.2). After considerable debate, one of the coalitions will likely predominate. In fact, most jurisdictions require that they do so either unanimously or by a supermajority. Reality Version 6.0 is the version reflected in the predominate view of reality collectively settled upon by the prevailing coalition. The process by which this happens is discussed in greater detail later in this chapter. (Ill. 3-11)

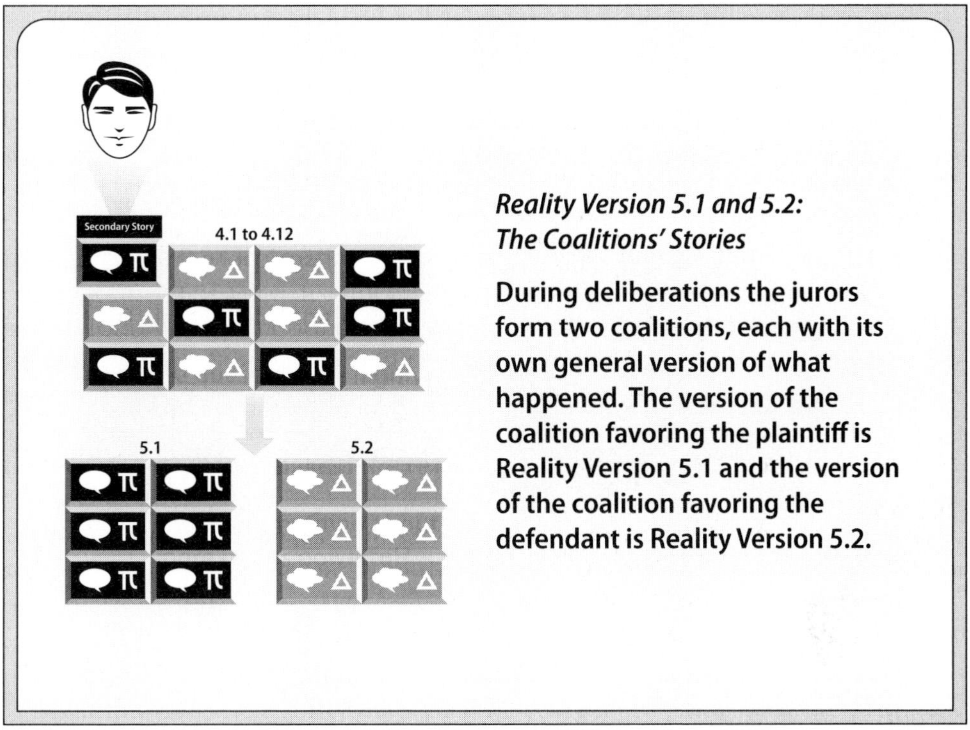

ILLUSTRATION 3-10 Reality Versions 5.1 and 5.2 Are the Coalitions' Stories

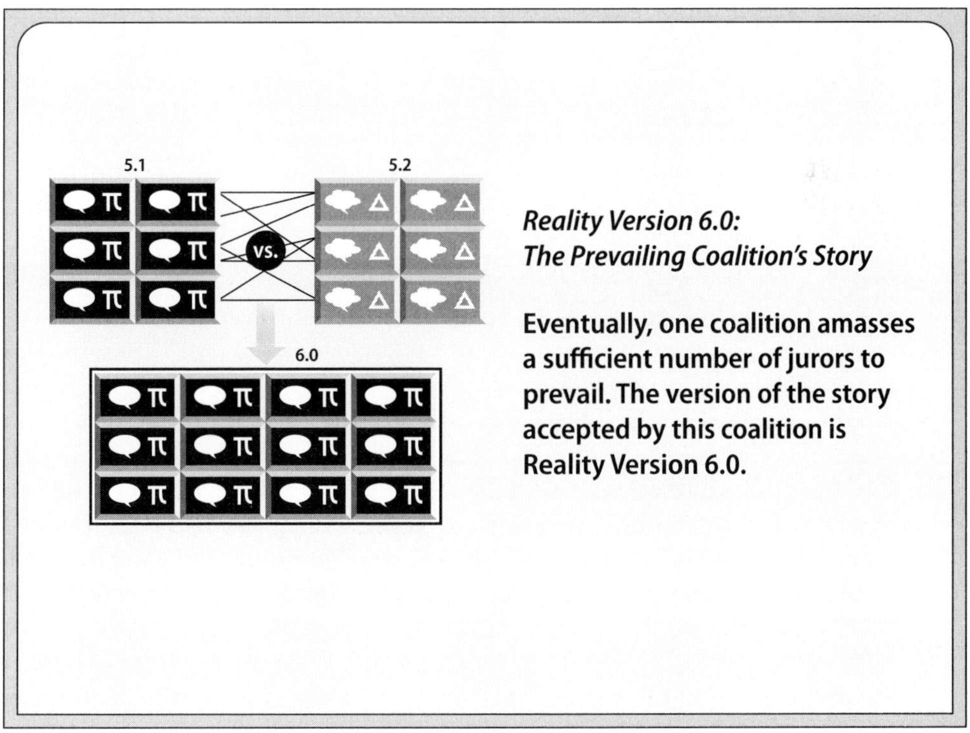

ILLUSTRATION 3-11 Reality Version 6.0 Is the Prevailing Coalition's Story

Though for purposes of this discussion I treat Reality Version 6.0 as a single account of reality, it is a mistake to say that jurors ever completely agree on all aspects of what happened as part of the Big Bang or why one side is entitled to prevail. Even if there is a unanimous verdict, it is usually more accurate to say that, at most, the jurors agree as to which party should win, but for slightly different reasons. The same holds true for special verdicts or jury interrogatories that require more specific information than a general verdict. I strongly believe that while they may agree on the answers, the factual underpinnings for those answers will rarely be identical for all twelve jurors. The fact that the jurors never completely agree on a definitive or single version means that what we actually end up with is, at best, a cloud of accepted reality that surrounds one of the party's versions of the facts.

Reality Version 7.0: The Verdict

Reality Version 7.0 is the written memorialization of the consensus reached by the jurors, as collectively expressed in the verdict. For all practical purposes, the side listed in the verdict as the winner is deemed to have accurately defined what "actually" happened at the Big Bang. Hence, we come full circle back to Reality Version 1.0, in that Reality Version 7.0 becomes our socially agreed-upon description of "what really happened." With this determination, society (and hopefully the parties) considers the matter resolved.

Once the verdict is rendered, one party is generally considered to have "won" the lawsuit. That lawyer is considered to have made her client's version "the TRUTH" and, for all practical purposes, the client who prevails is deemed to have been the one who accurately described what happened at and as a result of the Big Bang. (Ill. 3-12)

From the "Big Bang" to Final Verdict: The Mechanics Of How Jurors Determine Ultimate Reality in Four Steps

Enough time has passed that I can admit that, for many years, I had the same fear at the conclusion of every trial: "There is no way this jury will ever reach a verdict." It was not so much a fear that they would rule against my client (that is a different kind of fear) as it was being completely convinced that the jurors would never reach *any* verdict, the court would declare a mistrial, and we would be forced to start all over again.

Of course, the vast majority of times, the jurors came to a verdict and I found myself wondering why I had ever doubted their ability to do so. I would then move on to the next case, but when that trial ended, up would spring that same fear again, "This time, I know for sure, there is no way this jury will ever reach a verdict. . . ."

This fear did not reflect a lack of respect for the jurors because, as I hope you know by now, I have considerable admiration for the jury system. My skepticism was more like the feeling that I sometimes get when I see a piece

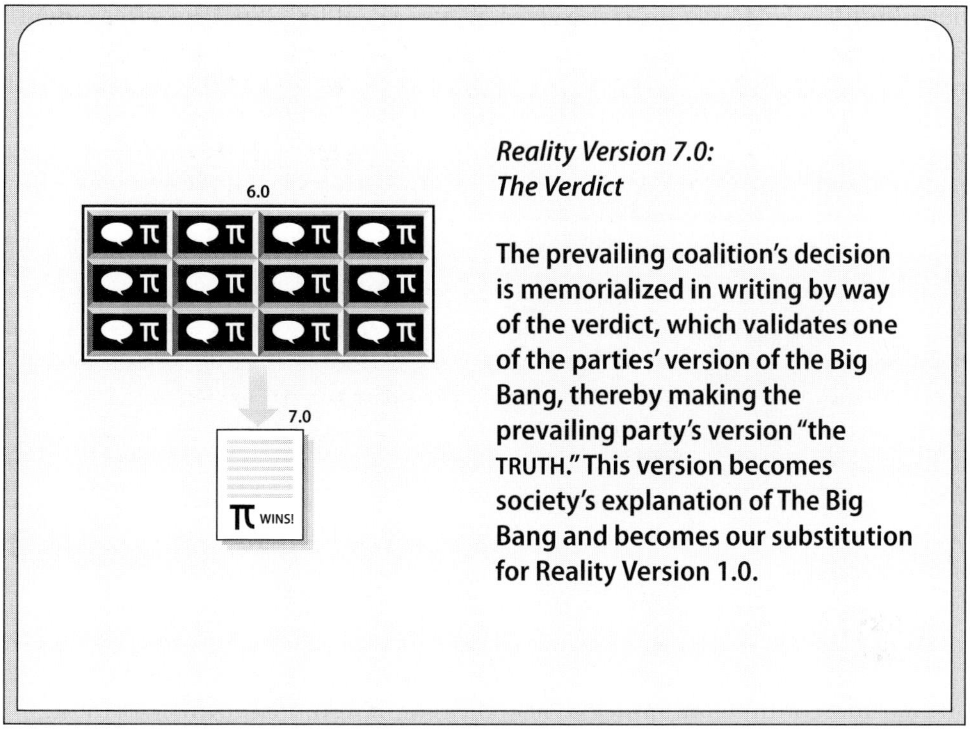

ILLUSTRATION 3-12 Reality Version 7.0 Is the Verdict: The Ultimate Version of Reality

of complex equipment for the first time and I find myself thinking, "How in heaven's name can this thing possibly work?" Despite my trepidation, the vast majority of times, things do exactly what they are designed to do—and, of course, the jury system is the same way.

While I still worry about not winning (everyone has that fear), I no longer worry as much about the jury not being able to reach a verdict and the court forcing the parties to retry the case. I think this change occurred because, after watching several hundred mock juries deliberate, as well as talking to and seeing data from hundreds of actual juries, I now realize that jurors generally behave in ways that substantially increase the chances that they will reach a verdict, despite the apparent diversity that exists among the various members.

Obviously, no two juries are exactly alike and each will reach a verdict in a slightly different way. But, having made this obligatory disclaimer, I can readily point to patterns in the mechanics of how one side eventually prevails. In the broadest sense, the process proceeds in four steps: (Ill. 3-13)

Step One: Each side assembles its Proto-Story and presents it at trial.
Step Two: For each juror, two Proto-Stories go in and one Secondary Story comes out.
Step Three: The jurors initially form various coalitions.
Step Four: One coalition grows and eventually prevails.

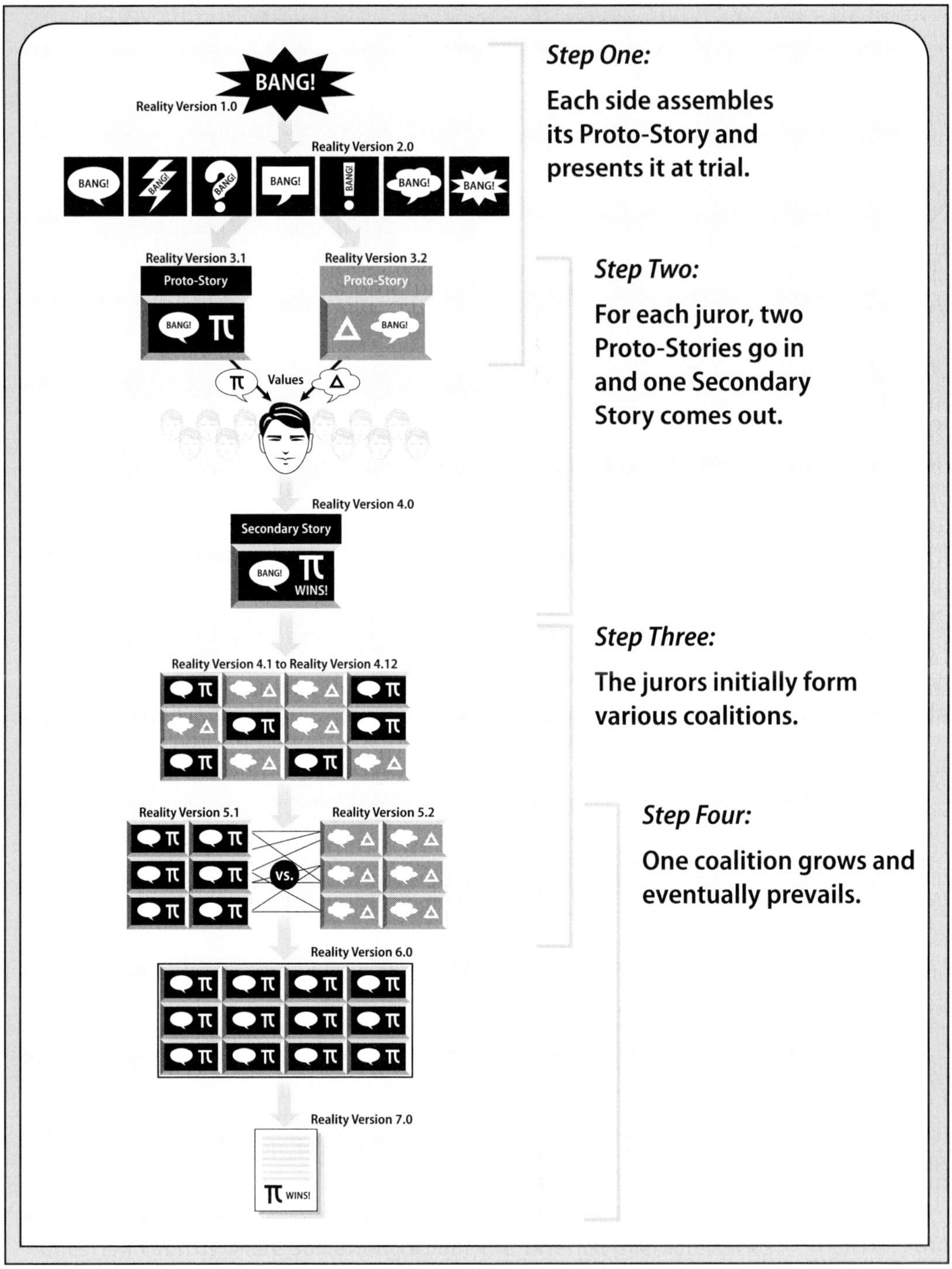

ILLUSTRATION 3-13 The Four Steps in Reaching a Final Verdict

Step One: Each Side Assembles and Presents Its Proto-Story

I have previously introduced the concept of the Proto-Story, which I described as the party's best version of why it should prevail. It is how each side would respond if you challenged: "Go ahead. Give me your best shot! Tell me why you should win." In Chapter 2, we discussed the various subparts or elements of the Proto-Story and some of the factors that apply in determining which pieces you should include in it. But what are the mechanics for assembling this material and creating a Proto-Story?

I wish that there were a formula I could impart to you that would make the process of sorting, weighing, and assembling simpler. For example, I wish I could just say, "You need five red parts, one blue, and none of the green. And this is the order you need to put them in." But that is not how it works. The best I can do is to provide you with some simple guidelines.

Some of these guidelines are already familiar to you. For example, you know that you must make sure that you are able to substantiate, with admissible evidence, each of the prima facie elements of your legal theory or affirmative defense. You know that you need to account for *all* undisputed facts, not just the ones you like, and that by failing to do so, you would leave your own Proto-Story vulnerable to easy attack. You know that you should avoid advancing alternative Case Theories. You know that when there are alternate possibilities, the simplest one is preferred because it is most likely to be the correct one and the one that the jury is more likely to accept as true. (Ill. 3-14)

Using the Twitch Test

By definition, choosing your facts requires applying a standard and weighing the relative value of these bits and pieces. I have already suggested a series of continua with which to accomplish this task. For purposes of this discussion, I want to switch to a more macro level, an elevated view, to concentrate on how you make an *initial* cut through all of the facts. To do so, I often apply what I call the "twitch test." While you may not have heard of such a test, it is one of the simplest, most effective ways of helping you determine what to potentially include in your Proto-Story. It is also a test that most lawyers readily apply without consciously thinking about it.

As you prepare for trial, certain facts will cause you to pause and, for lack of a better description, make you twitch. These twitches are then almost always followed by an immediate sense of either glee or dread. I refer to those facts that lead to a sense of glee as "twitch positive." These are the facts that you need to at least consider including in your Proto-Story as part of your affirmative case.

I refer to those facts that cause you to twitch with dread as "twitch negative." These are the facts that you need to find a way to counter as part of your rebuttal—or even preemptively include in your case in chief—because as much as they are causing you to feel dread, these facts are likely leaving your opposing counsel feeling very optimistic about the case.

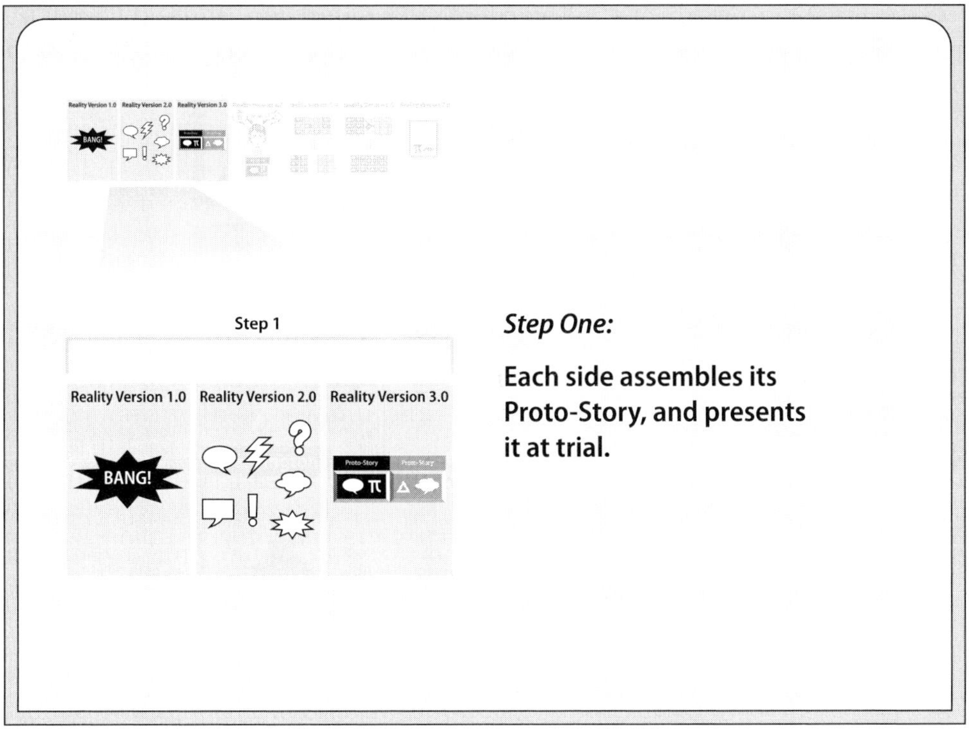

ILLUSTRATION 3-14 The First Step: From Big Bang to Proto-Story

I suspect that you will have little or no trouble finding the facts that are twitch positive; they always seem to jump out at you and, as such, are a joy and a thrill to find. Finding such facts is rarely a problem; the problem is figuring out which of them are the most important. You do so by consciously applying some or all of the six basic questions described in Chapter 2.

As a general rule, you should be finding an equal number of twitch positive and twitch negative facts. If, as you review the underlying facts of your case, you have difficulty finding the negative material, you need to be more cynical about your case and make an extra effort to search such places as your opposing counsel's pleadings, summary judgment motions, motions in limine, settlement conference statements, and other places where she is likely to tip her hand as to how she is likely to proceed at trial.

Never Forget: It's a Story, So Make Sure You Put Together a Good One

At its core, a Proto-Story is a story!

If that prior sentence seems to be stating the obvious and/or this definition seems redundant, please bear with me. Many lawyers, particularly those with limited trial experience, seem either to forget this fact or are not entirely sure what constitutes a good story.

There is a reason that people refer to storytelling as an "art." And there is a reason why the most successful trial lawyers are often master storytellers, making their cases come to life for their jurors. The reason is that *stories mat-*

ter and, as such, a good story is key to any trial! As we have previously noted, stories are the deepest and most obvious way that humans organize, communicate, receive, and digest facts. Since prehistoric cave dwellers painted narratives on cave walls, all human cultures have told stories as a way of entertaining each other, transmitting ethical and religious beliefs, and explaining natural processes.

Children today beg for stories (in the form of books and videos), even at very young ages. And, despite the much-decried decline in reading in modern years, grown-ups still consume copious numbers of stories in the form of books and periodicals, dinner party and watercooler chatter, films and plays, television and radio programs. Reading may be in decline, but storytelling definitely is not and probably never will be.

As Christopher Booker notes in *The Seven Basic Plots: Why We Tell Stories*:

> At any given moment, all over the world, hundreds of millions of people will be engaged in what is one of the most familiar of all forms of human activity. In one way or another they will have their attention focused on one of those strange sequences of mental images we call a story.

Let's start with what a story is not. Far too often, inexperienced trial lawyers confuse a chronological listing of facts with a story.[5] *There is a substantial difference between the two.* At its best, the chronological listing of facts is a train schedule, listing stations along a fixed route. Stories are much more than this.

A good story in a trial has all the elements of a good story in other media, including a coherent beginning, middle, and end; character development; foreshadowing; conflict; metaphors; analogies; scene setting; dialogue; shared assumptions (i.e., values); and the telling of stories-within-stories to explain factors like motive and prior knowledge. Well-constructed stories command attention and rely on elements familiar to all listeners, including basic themes and an explanation of human motives. Stories provide the perfect platform for some of our most important teaching tools, such as metaphors, similes, trial graphics, and analogies—all of which enhance the story and simplify what otherwise might be complicated information. Additionally, remember that these stories will be the vehicle through which you will offer the various Persuasion Tools that we will be discussing in greater detail in Chapter 4.

Unlike a dull recitation of facts, something happens in a story—something that jurors find interesting and to which they can relate. Stories provide context with details of time and place. There are characters in these stories that attract or repel jurors. A good story also provides toeholds of understanding for your jurors. The human mind learns by relating new, unfamiliar information to concepts it already understands. If your story builds on elements with which your jurors are already familiar, your jurors become confident

5. As Henry Adams accurately noted with some derision, chronologies, or as he called them, "time-sequences," are "the last refuge of the hapless historians."

that they can understand your basic version of the events, even if those events include intellectual property disputes, securities law, or other complex legal issues.

Remember, too, that your story has to be versatile enough to be told succinctly, engagingly, and clearly three times in the course of trial: in your opening statement, during the case in chief (albeit with interruptions from questions, delays, and objections), and in the closing argument.[6] As noted earlier, these retellings help you in two ways. They provide an opportunity for constructive repetition, which, as we have seen, is an important teaching technique. And they provide an opportunity to tell the same basic story in slightly different ways and using slightly different Persuasion Tools, which means you have a greater chance of appealing to the many different backgrounds, learning styles, and Core Values your jurors bring to the jury box.

Why is this important? Any lawyer who thinks that his way of analyzing and understanding a given set of facts is the only—or even the most common—way to do it is likely to alienate large portions of the jury. It is counterproductive to take that approach in a legal system in which you prevail only by convincing a supermajority of your jurors that you are right. Besides, lawyers bring to their analyses highly specialized training that most jurors have not had. It stands to reason that the jurors will need to learn and process information in a different format than an attorney does.

By way of summary, great case stories share at least nine basic characteristics (Ill. 3-15):

- They are told in a carefully chosen sequence.
- They incorporate and neutralize the facts likely to be stressed by your opponent in his story.
- They are never told in a factual void.
- They involve characters whose "character" you develop during the trial.
- They explain the motives of key participants.
- They are supported by the details.
- They are in accord with common sense.
- They touch a common emotional element shared by the listeners (the jury).
- They have a strong beginning and a strong ending.

If these characteristics seem familiar, they should! Many of these same characteristics have already been discussed in the context of what constitutes a good Case Theme or good Case Theory (neither of which are by themselves stories, but both of which are key elements to any successful story).

6. See discussion in Chapter 2 regarding the value of telling your story three times during trial.

Great Case Stories Share Nine Basic Characteristics

- **They are told in a carefully chosen sequence.**
- **They incorporate and neutralize the facts likely to be stressed by your opponent in his story.**
- **They are never told in a factual void.**
- **They involve characters whose "character" you develop during the trial.**
- **They explain the motives of the key participants.**
- **They are supported by the details.**
- **They are in accord with common sense.**
- **They touch a common emotional element shared by the listeners (the jury).**
- **They have a strong beginning and a strong ending.**

ILLUSTRATION 3-15 Great Case Stories Share Nine Basic Characteristics

Granted, learning to find and tell a good story during trial is more work than just reciting a bunch of facts or narrating a blow-by-blow timeline. But I can promise you this: It will make your case more interesting (both for you *and* your jurors). It will make your presentation more engaging and, as such, will increase your chances of prevailing in the end.

Before going on any further, I must offer one of the most accurate assessments of how we go about putting together the story that we tell to the jurors. This analysis comes from Professor Edward Chalfant's description of how skilled biographers work. I suggest that these observations are equally applicable to successful trial lawyers.

> Biographers will be better understood when it is more widely recognized how completely they depend upon three things: evidence, intellectual honesty, and imagination. What the biographer does is tirelessly imagine story after story until a story comes to mind which is in every respect sustained and in no respect undermined by all the available evidence, precisely understood. Then the biographer tells that story. But the matter does not rest there. For the story, when told, is likely to seem—and in one sense is—a mere statement of facts. Thus the hapless biographer, after an effort in imagination which has to be made to be appreciated, and after developing many stories in the

course of finding one, is given the appearance of an unimaginative person, only adept at amassing evidence and exercising intellectual scruples.[7]

Carefully Choose the Order in Which You Tell Your Story

A good story has a distinct beginning and ending but, as suggested above, the story does not have to be told in strict chronological order. Instead, the trial lawyer should tell the story in an order that makes the most sense and will most effectively capture the attention of the jurors. While there is no absolute right or wrong way to tell the story, some ways tend to be more effective than others. Before you automatically default to telling the story in sequential order, ask yourself if there is a better way to do it. I suspect that the vast majority of the time there is.

Let me illustrate this last point with a few examples.

Jurors like mysteries; they like conflict; and they really like mysteries with conflict. As a client of mine once confessed, "Jurors like finding the dead body right at the beginning and then figuring out how it got there. So I give it to them right up front. Fortunately, it is usually not a real body." Said differently, jurors pay attention when they realize that something is not right. Human nature causes us to wonder why things have gone amiss and what can be done to correct them.

You may notice a contrast between my advice of starting with a major issue ("the dead body") and the way most lawyers tell their stories. Specifically, rarely do you find much mystery or conflict at the beginning of a story when you tell it in strict chronological order. This, by itself, is a major reason to consider *not* defaulting to telling your story in pure chronological order. Remember: You are telling a story, not reading through someone's appointment calendar.

One of my absolute favorite stories of all time is Homer's *The Odyssey,* which deals with the decade-long struggle of Odysseus to make his way home to his family in Ithaca after the Trojan War. It frightens me to think about how a typical lawyer would tell this tale. I suspect it would be told straight on from Odysseus loading up his ship with plunder from Troy through his killing the suitors at his home in Ithaca. Told this way, it would be a good story, but not a great one.

Because Homer is a much better storyteller than the typical commercial litigator, he knows better than to tell his story in strict, chronological order. Instead, Homer developed a technique that he called *in medias res,* or as he would define the term, "in the midst of things" or "in the middle of all the action."

So, for example, in *The Odyssey,* Homer starts his story ten years after the Trojan War; eventually he works the story's narrative back to the war, and he bounces the story back and forth between "then" and "now" before ulti-

7. Chalfant, Edward, *Both Sides of the Ocean: A Biography of Henry Adams, His First Life, 1838–1862,* Archon Books, 1982, 391–92.

mately bringing it to an end a month or so in real time from where he started the narrative. More specifically, Homer starts *in medias res* with an impending crisis at Odysseus's home where the unwanted suitors are threatening to kill his son, to force his wife to enter into a marriage that she does not want, and to wipe out everything that rightfully belongs to him.

And where is Odysseus? Nowhere in sight! In fact, Homer does not even introduce us to him until nearly 2,500 lines into the epic poem, and when we meet him, there is something wrong. What we see is not *polytropos* Odysseus, the crafty man who engineered the destruction of Troy through the use of a wooden horse. Homer does not introduce us to the man envied and emulated by his peers. Instead, our first vision of Odysseus is that of a beaten man, alone and crying on the beach of a small island, unable to get home, despite the fact that "all the rest who left behind them headlong death in battle or at sea had long ago returned, while he [Odysseus] alone still hungered for home and wife."[8]

With this contradiction (i.e., what Odysseus should be and what he is, at least temporarily), comes the first of a number of mysteries. Something is not right. Homer shamelessly captures our attention. He keeps us spellbound for the next several hundred pages, unraveling what happened and, all the while, we are rooting for Odysseus' eventual success.

You, too, can capture your audience's attention, particularly if you carefully choose the order in which you structure and convey your story to the jury. Whenever possible, consider doing so *in medias res*. Telling a story this way is usually not easy; it certainly takes considerable preparation, but it is far more engaging and it potentially commands greater sway over jurors than the same set of facts told by way of a chronological storyline.

As proof of this, let me give you two real-life examples of telling a story outside of strict chronological order and how doing so made the story all that more persuasive to the jury.

As I noted earlier, jurors like a mystery; they like finding the "dead body" and then figuring out how the body got there. Unfortunately, my first real-world example did involve an actual dead body. This was a case in California, where a couple owned two huge dogs. The dogs, which originally belonged to this couple's adult adopted son (who, by the way, was a member of a white supremacist group and a prisoner in a maximum security federal prison), had been bred and trained to protect illegal drug laboratories.

Needless to say, these were not particularly nice dogs. For months, the dogs had displayed vicious behavior and, as a result, the couple had been repeatedly warned that the dogs would likely kill someone someday. Sadly, that is exactly what happened. One of the dogs, which one of the defendants took on a walk without a muzzle, attacked and killed the owner's next-door neighbor. The couple, who were eventually charged with second-degree murder, insisted by way of their defense that they did not know and, in fact, had no prior warning that the dogs might possibly be dangerous.

8. Homer, *The Odyssey*, translated by Robert Fitzgerald, Farrar, Straus, and Giroux, at 14.

The conventional way to tell this story in opening on behalf of the prosecution would have been to tell it in chronological order, starting with the couple getting the dogs and ending with the young woman's death. Frankly, that approach lacked any sense of mystery, since the jury knew how the story in this highly publicized case would end.

We decided that a better way to tell the story would be to reveal the facts by starting with the ultimate form of crisis—the killing of the young woman—and then proceeding "in reverse chronological order," that is, starting with the death and working backward, examining in reverse order all of the instances before the fatal attack where the dogs had been violent. So, for example, we described a violent act by the dogs that occurred a couple of days before the killing. Then we talked about another violent incident a few days before that, and then how another violent act had occurred a couple of weeks before that, and so on. This process went on through over thirty instances where the defendants were clearly aware of how violent their dogs were and, yet, chose to do nothing about it.

Why tell the story this way? Because, as I said, if we had told the story in strict chronological order, starting with the first day that the defendants acquired the dogs and proceeding onward to the death, the story would not involve any mystery, particularly as to how the story would end, since all the jurors already knew what happened to the poor young woman. But, remember—the defendants claimed that they had known nothing before the attack. This was untrue; they obviously did know. The only mystery was, how far back did they know? How much of the claim that "they did not know" was a lie? For how long had the defendants chosen not to protect others from their violent dogs?

By telling the story in reverse chronological order, we kept pushing back the earliest possible date that the defendants knew their dogs were violent. Each time we pushed the date back by revealing another earlier incident, we not only kept the jury interested but also got them to wonder, "My goodness, how much farther back does this go? How much worse can this get? How much more evidence is there that the defendants knew about this danger and chose to do nothing?"

In the end, no one believed the defendants' claim that they did not know that their dogs were violent. At the conclusion of the trial, the jury convicted both defendants, including one for second-degree murder.

The second example of *not* telling the story in strict chronological order relies on what I call the "picket fence" technique. I use this phrase because anyone who has looked through a picket fence knows there are certain things that you cannot see. While you can see between the pickets where there is open space, the pickets themselves block your vision and prevent you from seeing what is directly behind each of them. In other words, you see some—but not all—of the picture and, hopefully, the parts you can see intrigue you enough to make you want to examine the story even more carefully to find what is hidden or what you may be missing.

I will illustrate the "picket fence" technique by telling you about a different case I worked on that involved a man who had been driven out of business by a powerful competitor's unfair practices. In this specific case, we started by briefly showing that everything that the plaintiff had done, he had done correctly. In fact, every possible problem was anticipated and taken care of before the plaintiff poured his life savings and his soul into this business project. We then quickly jumped forward two years to the end of the story. Based on all the hard preparation, blood, sweat, tears, and money expended by the plaintiff, one would expect for him to have been a success. Instead, his whole effort ended in complete failure. Something had happened in the middle that destroyed all of the plaintiff's best laid plans. Something had destroyed the happy future to which he should have been entitled as a result of all his hard work.

To use my picket fence analogy, the jury could see both the beginning and the incongruent end of the story. What they could not initially see was the middle. This was the point covered by the "picket." This was where the mystery was; this was where the jurors needed to go if they were going to figure out what went wrong for the plaintiff or what caused all of his careful planning to be for naught. Not surprisingly, this was exactly where I wanted the jury to go. Even less surprisingly, the intentionally bad actions by the defendant that had derailed all of the plaintiff's hard work (the bad actions that were the basis of the lawsuit) were behind this picket.

When to Start Assembling Your Proto-Story

Unfortunately, most lawyers wait until after discovery is completed to determine what their case is really about. The standard way of conducting a case is to cast the broadest possible net in discovery and to gather every potentially relevant document and depose every person associated with the dispute. This process continues until discovery closes and then, once it does, there is a mad dash by counsel to develop a coherent plan for trying the case.

There are at least three problems with this approach. First, it often results in excessive and wasteful discovery. Since the lawyer is not really sure what he is looking for, he errs on the side of doing too much discovery in a "shotgun" fashion. If you doubt this fact, count how many volumes of deposition transcripts are neither reopened nor used after discovery is completed. Look at all the forgotten answers to unnecessary interrogatories that sit around in numbers too great to count.

The second problem with waiting until the end to figure out what the case is about is that it is the ultimate form of developing your case from the outside in. The problems associated with this approach have already been discussed in Chapter 1.

Finally, waiting until the end to figure out what the case is about does not give you time to correct your course if you are on the wrong track. By the time you find the problem, you have little or no time to fix it and, perhaps even worse, since discovery has closed, you have no formal way to get the information that you now realize you need.

How to Know if You Are on the Right Track

Relatively early in a dispute, lawyers need to find ways to come up with an initial assessment of what their case is about and test it on people like those who will possibly be on the jury.

I am always surprised by the extent to which some lawyers object to my suggestion that this evaluation must be done early on, well before discovery closes. Some lawyers' protests border on the obsessive–compulsive: "How can I be expected to tell you what my case is about until after I have done every single bit of discovery? How will I know what is going on until I have overturned every rock and shined a light into every cave? What if I miss something?"

Let me start my response to these fears of missing something by letting you know that you most assuredly *will* miss something, regardless of whether you take the time to determine what the case is about early on or as you are walking into court for trial. No one catches everything. Hence, the crucial question is not whether you will miss something, but instead, it is whether (and how quickly) you can recover after you discover you've missed something or, even worse, if you discover you are on the wrong path entirely.

You do not create a Proto-Story and then just forget about it. Instead, you must constantly check what you have developed and, where appropriate, modify your approach. For the most part, these modifications do not involve huge swings or 180-degree changes in course. If you have done a good job assessing what is at the core of the case, these changes tend to be small-to moderate-sized course corrections.

But sometimes you are just plain wrong—you started off on the wrong path and stayed on it for too long. For example, I worked on a case where our client, a highly paid corporate lawyer, was convinced that he had a foolproof defense to a civil fraud claim brought against him and his company. In order for this defendant to be found liable, the plaintiff had to convince the jury that our client (who was really a very good attorney) knowingly violated the law, thereby intentionally furthering the alleged fraud. The defendant adamantly stated that he did not know he had violated the law, and there was substantial evidence to this effect. Our client was certain that no rational jury would unanimously conclude that he could have possibly known everything that was required for him to be found liable, and he convinced his entire trial team of that certainty.

As a result, for almost a year we pursued and developed this lack of knowledge/intent defense to the virtual exclusion of all others. Less than a month before the trial, we decided to test the effectiveness of this approach in a traditional mock trial. Twenty-four mock jurors heard the client's argument and *none* of them accepted it! "Baloney!" the mock jurors concluded. "The guy is a lawyer; of course he had advance knowledge that this was illegal. Lawyers always know these things!" Discovery had already closed, the trial was only a few weeks away, the case had already been continued several times—we were, as they like to say, up the creek without a paddle and sinking fast.

This case stands out because (fortunately) it is an extreme example. What can you do to reduce the chances of this happening in your next case? To some extent, the answer to this question comes from Blanche DuBois—you need, wherever possible, to "depend on the kindness of strangers." More specifically, you need to conduct either a formal or informal Feedback Forum.

A Feedback Forum is your opportunity to talk to a group of people who are not lawyers to gauge what they think about your Proto-Story before you formally present it to the jury. You need to do this with enough time to make changes (including conducting additional discovery, if necessary) in a reasonable manner before trial.

There is no single way to conduct a Feedback Forum. Instead, these sessions, which usually last three to four hours, tend to share certain characteristics, depending on such variables as type of case, number of disputed issues, complexity, budget, and so on. Keeping this in mind, let me describe what typically goes into one.

Usually, there are four types of participants in these sessions. (Ill. 3-16) The first includes between six and twelve Evaluators. Hopefully, these Evaluators

Participation in Feedback Forum

Role	Description	# of People Involved
Evaluator	• No prior case knowledge • Serve as surrogate jurors	6 to 12
Presenter	• Lawyer capable of presenting abbreviated version of case	1 to 2
Moderator	• Neutral participant responsible for encouraging discussion	1 to 2
Observer	• Constantly monitors the proceedings	1 to 4

ILLUSTRATION 3-16 In a Feedback Forum, There Are Four Types of Participants

are not lawyers and, to some extent, are at least a couple degrees removed from lawyers. You want, as a colleague of mine once half-jokingly suggested, "people who still have their common sense." However, I want to point out that the beauty of Feedback Forums is that they can be as informal as you want them to be and, as such, I have seen several highly effective sessions in which the Evaluators were friends, family, or coworkers of the lawyers presenting the case. The main thing that you want to ensure is that your Evaluators are ready, willing, and able to offer candid assessments about what they really think, without worrying about how you might respond.

The second category of participants includes at least one Presenter.[9] This person's job is to offer (initially by reading and later more spontaneously) material to the Evaluators. The Presenter needs to be familiar with the case. The Presenter can be a lawyer, so long as she realizes that, except in those places where it is expressly agreed she should do so, her role is not to be an advocate for any position. I mention this because some trial lawyers simply cannot control themselves—they advocate and confront, they advocate and confront, and (did I mention?) they advocate and confront. There will be times during the Feedback Forum when advocacy and confrontation are appropriate; there are many more instances where such behavior is counterproductive to your overall objective of getting a third party to evaluate your case.

The third category of participants includes at least one Moderator, whose job is to be scrupulously neutral and nonjudgmental, and to encourage meaningful discussion among the Evaluators. This person has to be willing, when necessary, to gently push the Evaluators to explain and expand on their comments. I mentioned that you want at least one of these people. If you have twelve Evaluators, you probably want to break this group in half and will, therefore, need one Moderator for each group.

The final category of participants consists of at least one Observer, but no more than two per group of six Evaluators (otherwise the process can get unwieldy). As the descriptor implies, the Observers are attending the focus group to observe—not casually, but with considerable intensity.[10] They are there not only to listen to what the Evaluators say and how they react, but also (and perhaps more importantly) to watch what the Evaluators do *not* say and when they do *not* react.[11]

The overall format of the Feedback Forum consists of a series of sessions, alternating between periods wherein the Presenter offers information to the Evaluators and periods wherein the Evaluators discuss (facilitated by the Moderator, if necessary) their responses to what they have just seen/heard. I imag-

9. While not ideal, the duties of the second, third, and fourth categories (Presenter, Moderator, and Observer) can be performed by a single person, if necessary.

10. To the extent that it is feasible, these sessions are often recorded—but this does not substitute for an astute live Observer.

11. My daughter, who is an accomplished stage actor, insists you can learn the most about a particular evening's audience by observing when they do not laugh during the performance. As someone who delivers scores of lectures each year, I know she is right.

ine the information provided by the Presenter to the Evaluators as forming a V shape, with the information starting off as relatively general and becoming increasingly focused and partisan as the sessions progress. When I say partisan, I do not mean confrontational; I mean biased in favor of your client. Said slightly differently, the information starts off broadly objective and eventually narrows to your client's best arguments as supported by the Proto-Story.

There are typically three separate discussion sessions in each Feedback Forum. Each discussion becomes increasingly focused on the details of your case. (Ill. 3-17)

As we will see, this narrowing process usually takes place in three steps. After each presentation of material, the Evaluators have an opportunity to offer comments, usually through a discussion facilitated by the Moderator. For example, the First Narrative Session (which I imagine at the widest part of the V) usually starts with a neutral statement of each side's position. This statement is made by the Presenter and should take no more than fifteen minutes. The tone of this presentation is intentionally nonadversarial; it is primarily an effort to say, "Here is what A says. Here is what B says in response."

Following this initial presentation, the Moderator typically asks the Evaluators to do three things: (1) offer their general impressions of what they heard, (2) identify areas where they feel they need additional information, and (3) offer the best argument they can for both sides after there has been a

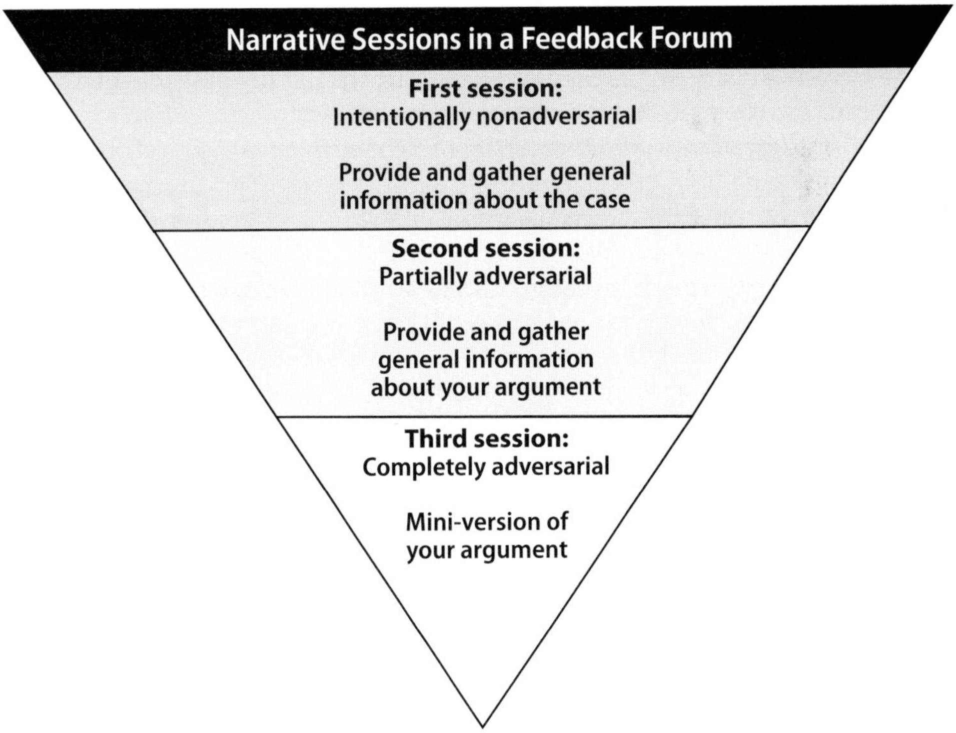

ILLUSTRATION 3-17 Feedback Forums Become Increasingly Focused

sufficient general discussion on these first two topics. Throughout this process, the Observers record what they see and hear, both with respect to the Evaluators and with respect to how the Observers themselves are responding to what is taking place.

An important part of this first discussion is to listen for areas of confusion as well as to ask what additional information the Evaluators feel is missing. Obviously, these are areas that warrant additional explanation and/or discovery.

The focus of the Second Narrative Session is on your client's potential arguments: not only those that you have prepared for evaluation at the Feedback Forum, but also those that were inevitably suggested by the Evaluators at the end of the First Narrative Session. I see this level of inquiry to be at the middle of my metaphorical V-shaped hierarchy of information to be presented at the Feedback Forum.

Specifically, the Presenter makes the arguments, preferably in a nonconfrontational way, and the Moderator asks the Evaluators to assess these various arguments: What do they find persuasive? What is less so? Why? How could you make the various arguments more persuasive?

After this is done, the Moderator asks the group of Evaluators to come up with an agreed-upon best argument for your client. Notice that, in this particular discussion, the Moderator is asking the group to work collectively. The Observers are interested in both individual responses as well as those responses that large portions of the group can and do endorse. In effect, the Observers are looking for comments that might be part of a future juror's personal Secondary Story as well as those ideas that may have sufficient appeal to serve as a basis for a coalition of like-minded jurors.

The focus of the Final Narrative Session is at the point of the V and, as such, is the most adversarial of the presentations. Here, the Presenter takes on the role of the advocate and makes a short closing argument on behalf of your client. The presentation includes your main affirmative points as well as those key rebuttal arguments that you anticipate making in response to your opponent.

This final presentation should reflect the tone that is likely to be used in the actual closing argument at trial. If you anticipate that you are going to be sarcastic in closing (and I am not suggesting you should be), then you should adopt such a tone in this portion of the Feedback Forum. If your closing is likely to rely on an appeal to justice, include that in this final presentation. If you are going to argue that the other side lied, use that specific word (even if your actual court will not let you do so) to see how the Evaluators respond. The point is that you want to get a quick read of how the Evaluators respond to substance *and* tone. At the conclusion of this miniature closing argument, the jurors are asked to critique what you have said and to see what part of the argument they are likely to accept.

Before moving on to another topic, I want to answer what are usually the four most common questions about Feedback Forums.

First question: Does the Feedback Forum have to be as structured as outlined above? No, it does not have to be. The beauty of this evaluation tool is that you can modify the format according to what makes sense for your particular case.

The fact that you do some form of this Feedback Forum is far more important than following a specific format. In fact, I am informally conducting these studies all the time. When I am driving with my family, I mention an argument or a set of facts and get their comments (perhaps that explains why they do not like to travel with me). I do the same with friends over dinner. Obviously, you need to be careful not to breach any confidences during this process, but the point is, get feedback and get it early enough that, if necessary, you can do something with it.

Second question: Do I need to hire someone to do this for me? No, as noted in the preceding paragraph, you can do much of this on your own with help from family members or friends of family members serving as Evaluators. If you want something more structured but do not want or need help from a third party, it is amazing how far a free dinner or a gift certificate in exchange for a few hours of time will go to convince potential Evaluators to help you assess your case. Getting feedback in any format will benefit your client.

Third question: Will this process give me all of the demographic data necessary to pick a favorable jury? Not entirely, no. Jury selection is not the primary purpose of this exercise.[12] The sample size is too small and, while you want to try to get Evaluators who reflect attitudes similar to those you anticipate finding at the actual trial venue, I do not profess that you will know all that you necessarily need to successfully select a jury. That said, there are things you can do to increase your chances of getting a relatively accurate sample of people, including using a professional recruiting company. Nevertheless, Feedback Forums are not intended to substitute for a professionally conducted attitude survey or a mock trial with carefully selected participants from whom demographic data can be drawn.

Fourth question: How are Feedback Forums different from traditional mock juries conducted just before trial? I have considerable respect for well-run mock trials and routinely encourage clients to conduct them when possible and appropriate. But I think that lawyers try to force too much, too late into a mock trial to effectively shape their Proto-Stories. It is too late if you wait until a month before trial to see what your "audience" thinks. By waiting this long, you will be in trouble if you discover that your way of thinking is not their way of thinking.

If you have the luxury of time and resources, I recommend doing both a Feedback Forum (again, even an informal one) well in advance of trial *and*

12. It is worth remembering at this point that you don't actually "select" your jury. Instead, you "deselect" them by excusing a limited number of potential jurors you do not want to serve.

a mock trial shortly before the actual trial begins. This allows you to get the best from both tools and use each for that which it was designed.

To the extent possible, I would use a Feedback Forum to:

- Test early on whether your Proto-Story has the impact you think it does.
- Eliminate alternative theories and settle on the one that works best.
- Catch your own prejudices or myopic views of what ordinary people expect from your trial team and, based on what you find, make adjustments early on. (We all have these shortcomings and tend to hold onto them until we actually see them being rejected by others.)
- Find the holes in your case and use the time remaining in discovery to fill them.

Once you are confident that you have the Proto-Story that you will use at trial, I recommend that you schedule a more traditional mock trial. At that mock trial:

- Test the effectiveness of your first-chair lawyer (or the person most likely to present the opening and closing) by having him present your Proto-Story to the mock jury. Use this opportunity to confirm that this person is comfortable delivering the message and can do so effectively. If not, make changes.
- Observe which types of potential jurors respond most favorably to the proposed first chair and his story. Use this information to get an idea of who your ideal jurors will likely be.
- Modify your final presentation. Generally, because you have done one or more Feedback Forums and are coming to the mock trial with an already refined Proto-Story, these changes will be minor.
- Spend this time prior to trial developing additional teaching and Persuasion Tools that enhance your Proto-Story. Don't waste time and resources trying to salvage a Case Theory that is not believable to potential jurors.

STEP TWO: FOR EACH JUROR, TWO PROTO-STORIES GO IN AND ONE SECONDARY STORY COMES OUT

The obvious targets for your Proto-Story are sitting in the jury box, staring at you. Specifically, they are the 12 jurors who have been selected to decide your case. As far as targets go, these are particularly difficult ones for the following reasons: each one is different; you are not entirely sure what you need to persuade any one of them; you are not entirely sure what will happen when you do; and none of the targets remains perfectly still throughout the trial. Nevertheless, these are your targets and you need to make the most of the situation.

So, you load up your Proto-Story, take it into court, spend days or weeks presenting it to the jury, and when all that is done, you walk nervously and helplessly around the courtroom, hoping for someone to bring you some news.

At this point, many lawyers consider the adversarial process to be over, with waiting all that remains to be done. In reality, the adversarial process is not over; just the participants and location have changed.

I think that court-issued jury summonses should include a warning label similar to those you see on the outside of large boxes at your local warehouse store—"SOME ASSEMBLY REQUIRED." You see, most jurors are not comfortable—nor are they allowed—to just sit around passively and wait until the end of closing arguments to decide which side should win based solely on Proto-Stories. The second step, through which each juror must pass in reaching a verdict, requires far more activity and work by the jurors.

This second step is the one in which each juror processes the two Proto-Stories (one from each party) and assembles her own personal "Secondary Story," with which that particular juror initially decides who should win. For reasons that I will explain in greater detail, I refer to this second step as one where "two Proto-Stories go in and one Secondary Story comes out" for each juror. (Ill. 3-18)

As you know, each side creates a Proto-Story (each side's best version of what happened, inclusive of the Four Inputs described in Chapter 2) and presents it to the jurors. This is what I mean by "for each juror, two Proto-Stories go in." Both Proto-Stories are repeatedly processed by each juror in real time throughout the trial. Each juror, in a manner that I liken to recombinant DNA, pulls apart the two Proto-Stories and breaks down the individual parts. Each juror, based on her own individual experiences, attitudes, and characteristics, then adds additional elements to this mixture.

Eventually, each juror individually makes sense of all these bits of data by creating her own version or story of what she believes happened. These versions are nuanced and shaped (often unconsciously, but not always) by each juror's own personal characteristics, experiences, and motivations, until the juror herself formulates her own private or "secondary" story. This is what I mean when I say "one Secondary Story comes out."

Since there are typically twelve members on a jury, this process occurs at least once for each of the twelve jurors. I say "at least once" because the process of formulating the Secondary Story is often repeated multiple times by each juror throughout the trial and deliberations.

As I have already suggested, the Secondary Story created by each juror is not the same as either of the Proto-Stories offered by the lawyers and witnesses during the trial. Sometimes the individual jurors will make key elements of the lawyer's Proto-Story part of their Secondary Stories; other times, these same jurors may use their own Secondary Stories to explain (or explain away) key elements of the Proto-Stories. In any event, each juror will include "supplemental elements" in her Secondary Story that are as important as they are highly personal to that individual juror. The exact origins of these supplemental elements are not always consciously identifiable, even to the

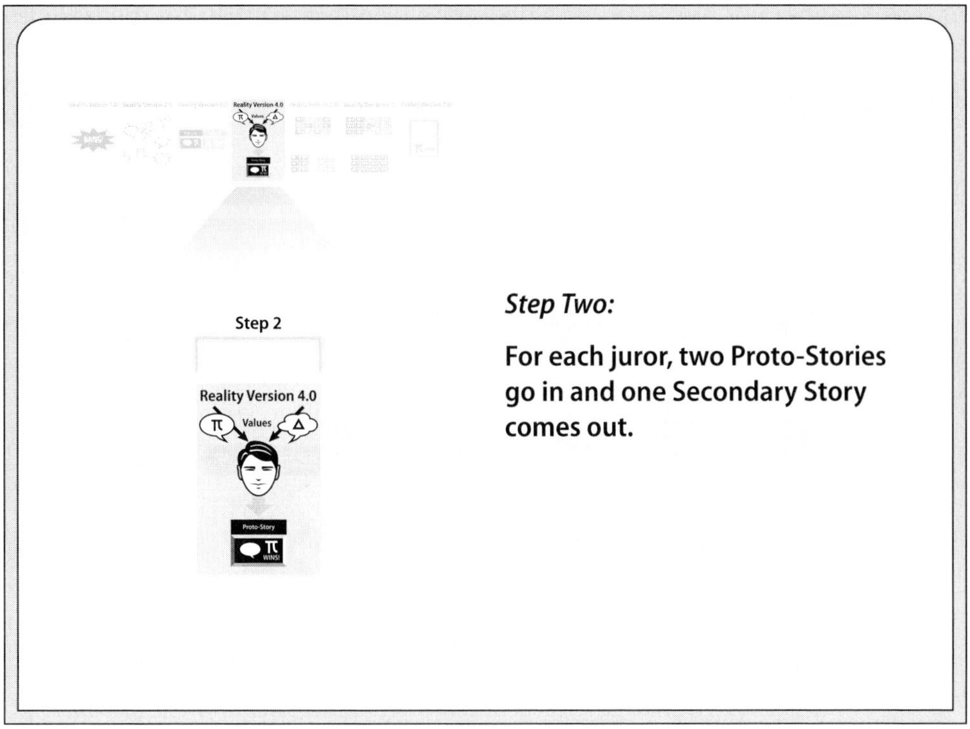

ILLUSTRATION 3-18 The Second Step: From Proto-Stories to Secondary Stories

juror who supplies them. Some of the jurors will have Secondary Stories that are very similar; others will overlap, but only in the most rudimentary details; still others will have no commonalities at all.

At the end of step two, each Secondary Story must end in one of *three* ways: (1) "Plaintiff should win," (2) "Defendant should win," or (3) "I don't know who should win." The balance of this process reduces these three possible conclusions to one.

Step Three: Coalition Forming

The third step involves the process of "Coalition Forming." Specifically, the jurors form two coalitions, one favoring the plaintiff and the other, the defendant. Each juror eventually joins one of these coalitions based on whichever side he thinks should prevail, as reflected by the conclusion of that juror's particular Secondary Story. (Ill. 3-19) While members in each coalition may agree as to which side should win—as with the example of the Founding Fathers at the beginning of this chapter—they may never entirely agree on the reasons why, nor do they follow the same path to get to that conclusion.

One of the first things to happen when the jurors assemble in the jury room is that they take an initial poll to identify how their Secondary Stories initially end. Once a juror decides who he thinks should win, a fundamental

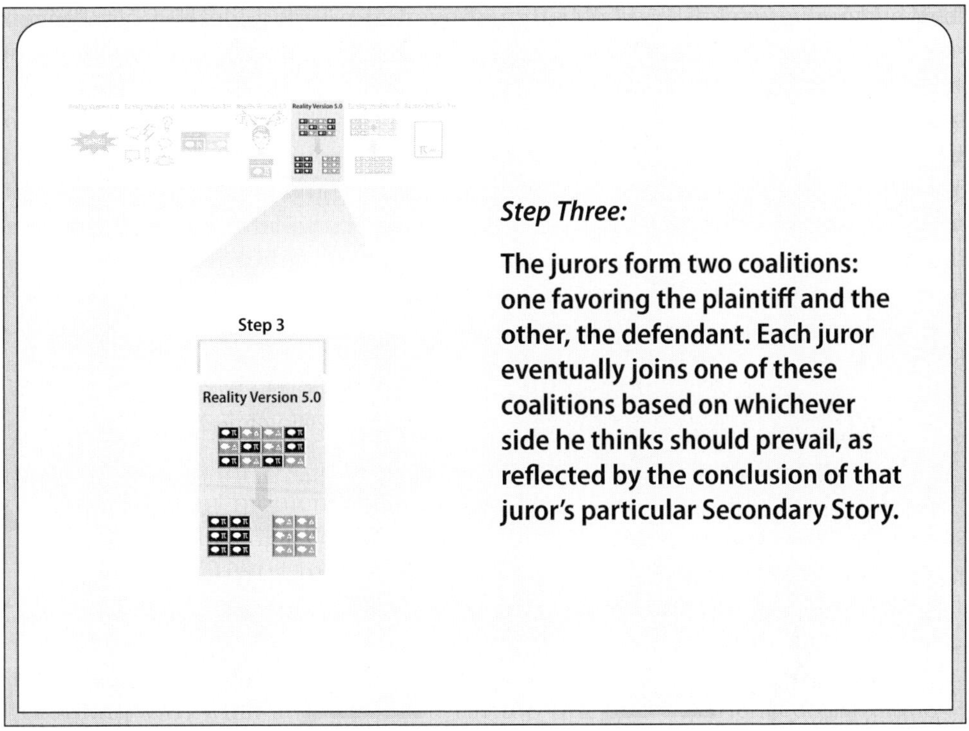

ILLUSTRATION 3-19 The Third Step: Jurors Form Their Initial Coalitions

shift occurs in the way that juror views himself and the case. At this point, the juror is no longer just a juror, he is a "plaintiff's juror" or he is a "defendant's juror." As we will see, such a designation can change if the juror is convinced to change sides during the process of the deliberations. But so long as that juror is identified with one side over the other, the designation of whom the juror supports is more important than exactly why or how he came to that decision.

The process of individual jurors aligning themselves with other jurors whose Secondary Stories end the same way marks the beginning of the third step through which jurors pass on their way to a verdict. This is the step I call "Coalition Forming."

As the name implies, Coalition Forming is the point at which jurors form two coalitions, one favoring each of the parties. You can visualize this process by imagining the two coalitions at the opposite ends of a continuum. Which coalition the juror joins is determined by how his particular Secondary Story ends. Those jurors who have concluded that "plaintiff should win" cluster at one end; those jurors who have concluded that "defendant should win" go to the other end; and those undecided jurors—that is, the ones whose Secondary Story ended with "I have no idea who should win!"—mill around like good agnostics in the middle, between the two extremes.

As with the Founding Fathers, while members in each coalition agree on the result, they may never entirely agree on the reasons why, nor is it likely that they will ever fully appreciate how other coalition members reached their decision. There is nothing wrong with this. In fact, I am convinced that the entire system would break down if complete uniformity were required. Remember that in order for one of these coalitions to eventually win, it needs to get all—or a supermajority of—jurors to agree on who should win. Expecting the jurors to agree as to Why and How this conclusion should be reached is too much to ask if the system is ever going to work.

Step Four: Coalition Building

With respect to jury trials, simple majorities just do not cut it. In order for one side to win, it needs to get a supermajority (for example, nine out of twelve) or a unanimous agreement in favor of one side. As a result, most jury deliberations cannot end after Step Three because, typically, there is neither unanimity nor a supermajority and, as such, most cases have to go through a fourth and final stage that I refer to as "Coalition Building."

As part of Step Three, I described how the jurors can be classified along a continuum stretching from those whose Secondary Stories favor the plaintiff, to those whose Secondary Stories favor the defendant, with those who are undecided somewhere in between.

In order to understand Step Four, we need to examine a second continuum, a continuum that measures how actively each juror is willing to advocate on behalf of the side he favors and believes should ultimately win the lawsuit. At one end of this second continuum is what I refer to as "I Just Am" Jurors; at the other are those I refer to as Active Jurors.

I Just Am Jurors get their name because when they are challenged to justify why they are voting for one side over the other, they always seem to say the same thing: "I don't know why I am voting for plaintiff/defendant—I just am!" As you might suspect, these jurors do not generate much influence over the deliberations. Don't get me wrong, their votes count as much as anyone's on the jury, but few other jurors will be persuaded by those who cannot or will not actively articulate a reason for their beliefs. Likewise, while there are always exceptions to the rule, I Just Am Jurors are usually more easily persuaded to change their vote and join the other side, particularly if by doing so the I Just Am Juror can join the winning side, bring the deliberations to an end, and help everyone go home sooner.

Unlike I Just Am Jurors, Active Jurors exert considerable sway over the deliberations. At some point in the proceedings, Active Jurors come to a strong conclusion as to which side should win and they can clearly articulate the reasons why this should be the case. Active Jurors are willing to fight for the side they want to prevail. In effect, these jurors are no longer "searchers for the truth" and, instead, have become "advocates for the truth" or, more accurately, advocates for the side that they believe is telling the truth. (Ill. 3-20)

Usually (but not always), the side with the most Active Jurors is the one that will likely prevail. These Active Jurors become the parties' surrogate

Differences Between "I Just Am" Jurors and Active Jurors

"I Just Am" Jurors

- **Cannot articulate their reasoning**
- **Have very little influence over other jurors**
- **Lack conviction and can easily change their minds when confronted with opposing arguments**

Active Jurors

- **Can easily articulate their reasoning**
- **Strongly advocate their position**
- **Take their jobs as jurors seriously**
- **Take on the plaintiff's or defendant's side as their own**

ILLUSTRATION 3-20 The Differences Between "I Just Am" and Active Jurors

advocates during deliberations. It is in this role that the Active Jurors often play a crucial part in Step Four.

Remember, in Step Three the jurors are divided into at least two coalitions, neither of which has enough members to announce a verdict. Something has to change; specifically, one of the coalitions needs to increase its membership until it has the necessary numbers for there to be a final decision.

The people who bring about this change are the Active Jurors and they do so by "Growing the Coalition." (Ill. 3-21) This growth requires that the Active Jurors do two things. First, they need to go outside the coalition to recruit members. There are two such sources for these additional members: they can come from the undecided jurors or they can come from the other, opposing coalition.

The second thing that the Active Jurors must do is to prevent any of their colleagues that are within their particular coalition from deserting and going over to the other side. Getting new jurors to join is crucial, but it is meaningless if jurors who were formerly part of the coalition are simultaneously recruited by an Active Juror on the other side. Remember, at this point, it really is a numbers game.

So, how do the Active Jurors do it? How do they both recruit for and defend their coalition? The short answer is that there is no single method. Instead, I have identified at least four such methods, which are best illustrated by going back to our discussion of the Founding Fathers at the beginning of this chapter,

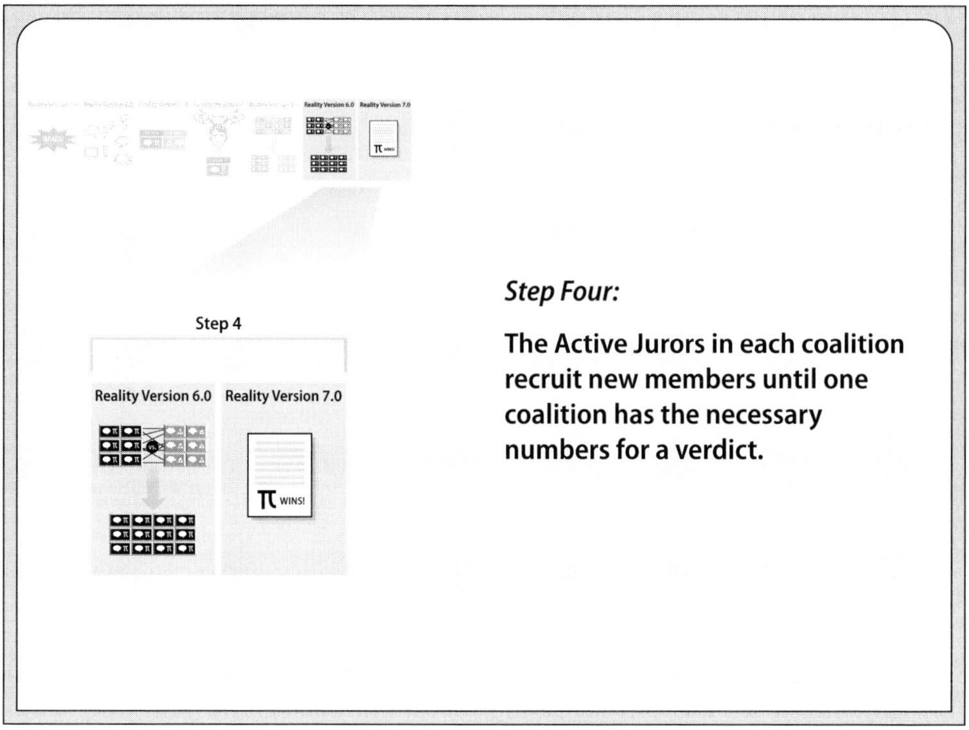

ILLUSTRATION 3-21 The Fourth Step: One of the Coalitions Grows and Eventually Prevails

and to the mock mock-jurors who helped me in the tragic case of the insane woman who drowned her three sons (as described in Chapter 1). Specifically, Active Jurors advocate by projecting what personally motivated them:

- By relying on their cross-ties with other jurors,
- By appealing to overall common sense,
- By using specific tools provided to them by one of the lawyers.

Active Jurors Advocate by Projecting What Personally Motivated Them

An Active Juror joins one side of the dispute (as opposed to the other) because that side has identified, reached, and satisfied at least one Core Value of that Active Juror. By way of analogy, the revolutionary forces appealed to John Adams's instinctual respect for the common law, which the British had disregarded and dishonored, and they convinced him. Likewise, for one of my mock mock-jurors, the scientific testimony by an expert as to the connection between Parkinson's disease and schizophrenia satisfied his basic trust and reliance on the certainty of science, and convinced him that the poor defendant was sick and needed treatment, not punishment.

One of the most common ways that Active Jurors build and maintain their coalitions is to appeal to other jurors using the one or two key facts or arguments that personally motivated and inspired them. This approach makes sense and can be very effective for essentially the same reason—it is something that appeals to and motivates these Active Jurors (often, passionately).

As I have already noted, no two jurors are the same, so this personal approach rarely leads to an "identical soul-mate," that is, someone else on the jury who completely agrees with or is in sync with a particular argument. However, sometimes those arguments personal to the Active Juror are enough (to at least begin) to get one or more of the uncommitted jurors to shift toward the side being advocated by the Active Juror.

Rarely do such recruits agree completely with the Active Juror who is recruiting them; the new recruit rarely says, "I agree with you one hundred percent." A much more subtle form of agreement usually takes place, with the Active Juror hitting a nerve or touching upon something that is sufficiently compelling for the recruit to be motivated to join, even if the reasoning that is triggered is not identical to that advocated by the Active Juror.

The fact that Active Jurors within a particular coalition arrive at their shared conclusion by different paths increases the chances that they will be able to persuade others to join or remain with the coalition. So, if the factor that persuaded Active Juror One does not work on others outside the coalition, perhaps the reason that motivated Active Juror Two will do the trick. Active Juror Two will be happy to have contributed to the coalition by bringing in a like-minded individual, and Active Juror One, while not necessarily agreeing with the new recruit's reasoning any more than he does with Active Juror Two's, will nonetheless welcome the new coalition member.

Active Jurors Advocate by Relying on Cross-Ties

Some coalition members will form cross-ties between and among certain Active Jurors. With respect to our example of the Founding Fathers, we talked about how certain people who advocated revolution did so based on multiple reasons. For example, a colonist might have insisted on revolution based on the economic fears that motivated George Washington as well as the violations of natural law that motivated Thomas Jefferson. A similar situation exists during jury deliberations.

Cross-ties often work to maintain a coalition and prevent members from leaving. A person with cross-ties finds it more difficult to leave because she has to be convinced to sever multiple sets of ties. Furthermore, should that person feel tempted to desert, she will likely face intense lobbying efforts from multiple Active Jurors, who may not agree on the reason why they joined the coalition, but are equally motivated to keep the potentially wayward colleague in their common group.

Cross-ties can be particularly important in those occasional cases where the best you can honestly hope for is to hang the jury—for example, a criminal matter where a hung jury might convince the prosecutor not to retry the case, or in a civil matter where a hung jury may inspire the parties to reach a previously unreachable settlement. Such instances require that a small group of jurors (usually at least two, but potentially only one) refuses to join the overwhelming majority in voting for one party over the other. This takes endurance, guts, and conviction—all of which are easier to possess when the dissenting jurors are bound together through a series of cross-ties.

Active Jurors Advocate by Relying on Common Sense

Question: What do my mother and Benjamin Franklin share in common? Answer: A heavy reliance on "common sense."

As you may remember from earlier in this book, Benjamin Franklin used common sense to come to the conclusion that revolution could not be avoided, in much the same way that my mother adamantly supported her belief that a murder defendant was insane. Both relied on similar, common-sense assessments.

Common sense is the great equalizer of the deliberation room. It both attracts members to a coalition and keeps them there. As a result, it can be thought of, as I previously described at the beginning of this chapter, as the mortar that holds everything in place. Active Jurors rely on it all the time, both to make up their own minds as well as to encourage others to join or remain in the coalition.

Common sense is so powerful precisely because it is so . . . *common*. Said differently, common sense is powerful because it is commonly shared not only by those on the jury, but by society as a whole. Appealing to common sense in a meaningful way will not guarantee that you will win, but it will go a long way toward enhancing a position or argument.

Active Jurors Advocate by Relying on Tools Provided to Them by Counsel

Counsel have a substantial opportunity to influence how Active Jurors come to their own decisions and how effectively these Active Jurors will persuade others during deliberations. This opportunity comes from providing Active Jurors with Persuasion Tools. Not surprisingly, the side with the most effective Active Jurors is the one that is most likely to prevail. Active Jurors are most effective when the side they favor has taken the time to "arm" them with a spectrum of Persuasion Tools. The types of tools—and how counsel designs and uses them—are the subjects of the next section of this book.

Coalitions Are Necessary in the Jury Room

In summary, because our system requires that more than a mere majority of the jurors favor a party in order for there to be a verdict, the coalitions initially formed at the beginning of deliberations often lack the necessary numbers for either side to win outright. A select number of particularly engaged jurors eventually emerge from within each coalition. These Active Jurors aggressively lobby to recruit additional members to join their coalition and fight to keep the original members from deserting to join the opposing coalition. As the number of members in one coalition grows, there is a corresponding decrease in the number of undecided and opposing jurors. Eventually, one of these two coalitions will amass enough members for a verdict. That side is ultimately declared the winner and its version of what happened at (and as a result of) the Big Bang is deemed "the TRUTH." Occasionally, neither side gets the numbers needed for a verdict and the court declares a mistrial, thereby making my earlier fear of having to retry a case an unfortunate reality.

SECTION TWO

Selecting the Right Tools

CHAPTER 4

Tools for the Jurors

Chapter Overview

It has been said that of the cases a lawyer takes to trial, one third can never be won, one third can never be lost, and it is the battle over the final third that makes or breaks a trial lawyer's reputation. Up to this point, we have concentrated on the *process* by which a lawyer puts together his Proto-Story and the *process* by which jurors reach their conclusion as to who should prevail. As important as understanding the process is, as a practical matter, it is equally important for trial lawyers to find the right *tools* to use throughout the process to influence how jurors make their decisions and, thereby, increase their clients' chances of prevailing on the cases that make or break lawyers' reputations.

The battle to persuade jurors does not end once both counsel finish their closing arguments. As we have discussed earlier, the battle continues; the only things that change are the venue and the participants. Specifically, the fight shifts from the courtroom to the deliberation room, where the Active Jurors (as opposed to counsel) struggle to convince the other jury members why the side they favor should win.

Two things should not surprise you: (1) the party with the most effective Active Jurors is usually the one that prevails and (2) the most effective Active Jurors are often those who are most comfortable using the Persuasion Tools provided to them throughout the trial by counsel. Active Jurors initially use these attorney-provided Persuasion Tools to decide for themselves who they think should win. These Active Jurors then use these same Persuasion Tools as ammunition to convince others to join their coalition over the other. (Ill. 4-1)

One of the ways I determine whether a mock trial has been effective is by observing what the Active Jurors do when the closing arguments end and deliberations begin. I know that counsel has done a good job persuading mock jurors when I see the Active Jurors picking up where the lawyer left off in closing argument. Whenever this happens, it means two very important things have occurred. First, these particular jurors have made the crucial transition from being neutral seekers of the truth to being adamant advocates for one

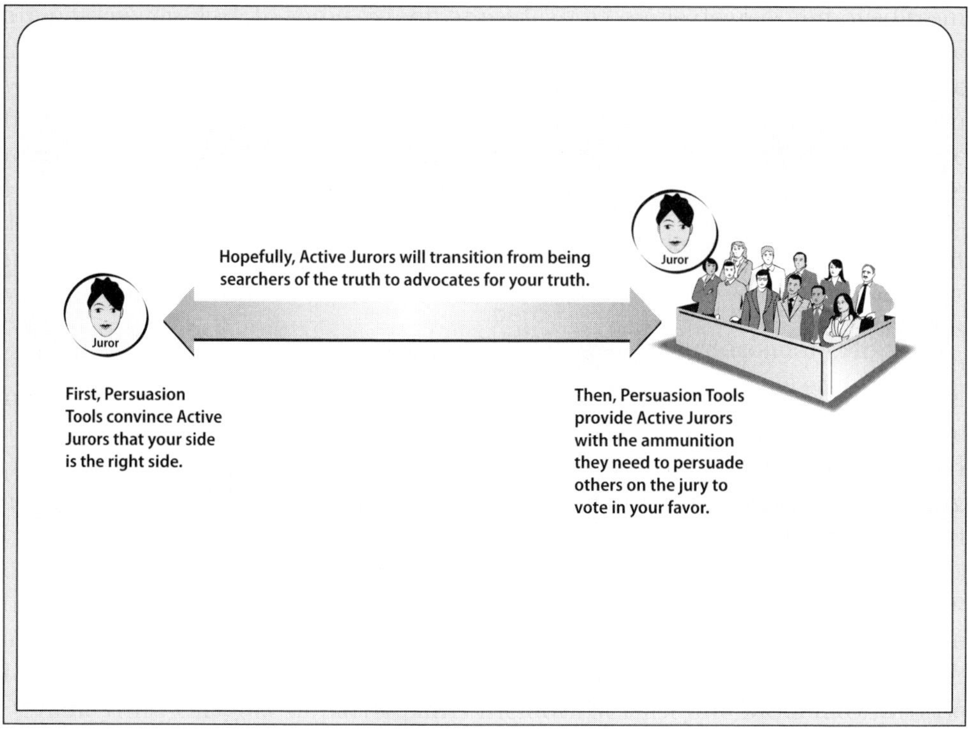

ILLUSTRATION 4-1 Persuasion Tools Serve Two Functions

of the two parties and, as a result, have begun the essential coalition-forming process described in Chapter 3. Second, these jurors have made this crucial step by using Persuasion Tools provided by the trial lawyer.

This chapter is all about those Persuasion Tools—the ones that a lawyer provides to her jurors so that they will vote in her favor and act as advocates for her client during deliberations.

This chapter consists of three sections. The first section defines what I mean by "Persuasion Tools." As we will see, there are two types: (1) Operating Tools, which provide basic guidance to jurors based on their Core Values, and (2) Educational Tools, which help jurors better understand the key aspects, or Core Details, of the case. In this section, we also discuss areas where jurors typically need (and benefit from) Educational Tools and review the kinds most commonly used to assist jurors in these recurring situations.[1]

The second section of this chapter examines why it is important for trial lawyers to use a variety of tools when attempting to influence different members of the jury. While the members of the winning coalition will agree as to *who* should prevail, they will rarely agree in full as to *why*. Likewise, while they all may mark the same box on the verdict form, these jurors usu-

1. For a more extensive treatment of trial graphics and full-color examples (including many that have been used in actual trials), see Ritter, G. Christopher, *Creating Winning Trial Strategies and Graphics,* American Bar Association, 2004.

ally reach their decision via differing routes. Hence, you can maximize your chances of winning by finding ways to convey a *single message* in a variety of ways, using an *array* of Persuasion Tools.

The third and final section examines the four characteristics common to all effective Persuasion Tools. Specifically, these tools rely on common, everyday language; they connect to already-familiar concepts; they are memorable; and they create a "buzz."

An Introduction to Persuasion Tools

Persuasion Tools are the communication devices or learning apparatus through which you bring context and perspective to jurors with respect to the "Key Decision Points" of your case. The Key Decision Points are those select places where you substantially increase your chances of winning if you can persuade the jurors to accept your explanation or position instead of your opponent's. (Ill. 4-2) These crucial moments often occur when one side convincingly employs Persuasion Tools that are more compelling than the opposing party's.

Persuasion Tools are not merely messages but, instead, are a hybrid of *vehicle* and *message*. They are the media through which you communicate or reinforce certain fundamental points to your jurors and ultimately help these jurors value and make sense of your core message and the key details necessary to understanding that message.

Persuasion Tools align with the ways jurors perceive the world and, consistent with those perceptions, how they make important decisions. Persuasion Tools not only explain concepts, but they serve as platforms from which a juror can satisfy himself that your version of the case is consistent with the guiding principle that he (i.e., that specific juror) personally relies on to make key decisions.

Persuasion Tools can take on a variety of forms. They can be offered to the jurors explicitly or implicitly. They can be presented directly or indirectly. They can be tangible, as in a trial graphic, or they can be intangible and conveyed verbally, as in an analogy or story.

There is a correlation between tangible Persuasion Tools and what we more commonly think of as "illustrative material." Likewise, there is a relationship between intangible Persuasion Tools and what is often (but not always) referred to as "argument." Material that is offered for illustrative purposes is not evidence, just as argument is not evidence. Instead, intangible Persuasion Tools can be thought of more like study guides for the evidence.

The fact that this material is something akin to a study guide as opposed to "the real thing" should not discourage you in the least, nor should it lead you to conclude that it is somehow inferior to or less powerful than actual evidence. On the whole, Persuasion Tools in the form of illustrative material and argument can have as much (or more) impact on jurors as the actual evidence, because all Persuasion Tools explain and clarify the evidence. There

ILLUSTRATION 4-2 Provide Your Jurors With the Appropriate Tools
Jurors repeatedly come to key Decision Points. The side that provides the jurors with the appropriate Persuasion Tools at these crucial points generally has a better chance of prevailing.

can be greater power in secondary or explanatory information than there is in the dry, primary source material that is often purely technical.

To avoid confusion, I should point out that not every illustration—nor every argument—is a Persuasion Tool. Similarly, you do not want to expend resources on every illustrative and argument to make them Persuasion Tools. Too much of anything (including Persuasion Tools) is not a good thing.

As we will see, not every Persuasion Tool will affect every juror the same way or to the same degree. Some will strike deeply, while others will not form a crucial part of that juror's thought process and will barely be noticed. The fact that no single Persuasion Tool will satisfy all of your jurors should neither surprise nor disappoint you. Remember, jurors who vote for the same party

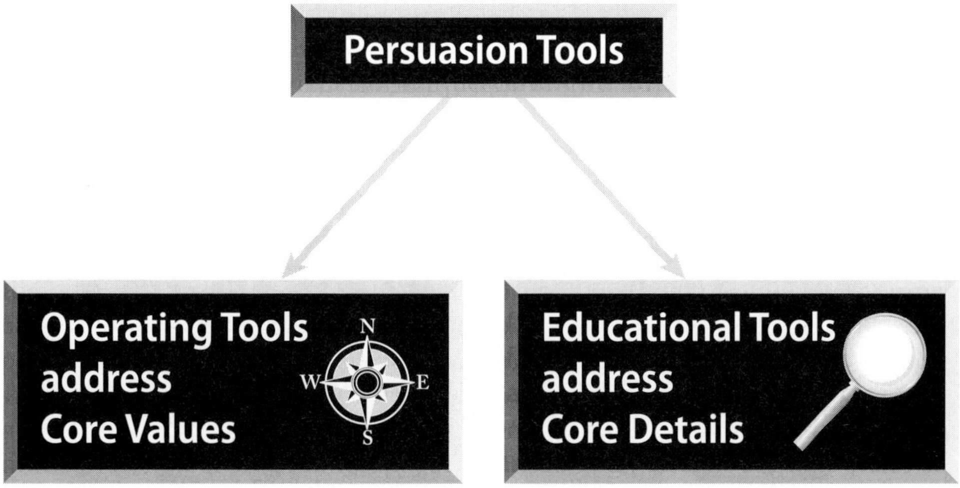

ILLUSTRATION 4-3 There Are Two Types of Persuasion Tools

(hopefully, your client) may not entirely agree as to why, nor do they always get to the conclusion the same way. As we shall see, this is further reason why you need to offer your jury an *array* of Persuasion Tools.

There are two different types of Persuasion Tools: Operating Tools and Educational Tools. Operating Tools address the "Core Values" and Educational Tools address the "Core Details" of your case. The distinction between these two different types of tools is, particularly at its intersection, somewhat artificial. But (and this is an important *but*), it recognizes that the most effective jurors are the ones you have captured with "Educational Tools" *and* "Operating Tools." These are the jurors who have committed themselves to your case because you have persuaded them at both an intellectual level (through the use of Educational Tools) and at a deeper, Core Value level (through the use of Operating Tools). (Ill. 4-3)

Operating Tools Address Core Values

Operating Tools help jurors make sense of—and ultimately value—the essence of your Case Theory. They appeal to the Core Values of a particular juror and help her appreciate your case as being consistent with those values that she believes drive (or should drive) the world. (Ill. 4-4)

By way of a real-life example, let us go back to the tragic case of the schizophrenic mother who believed God had ordered her to drown her three children. As I indicated in Chapter 1, I prepared for this case by periodically describing the events to a variety of people, whom I affectionately referred to as my mock mock-jurors. I exposed each of them to the same Case Theory, Case Themes, facts, and arguments, which, in an abbreviated form, went something like this:

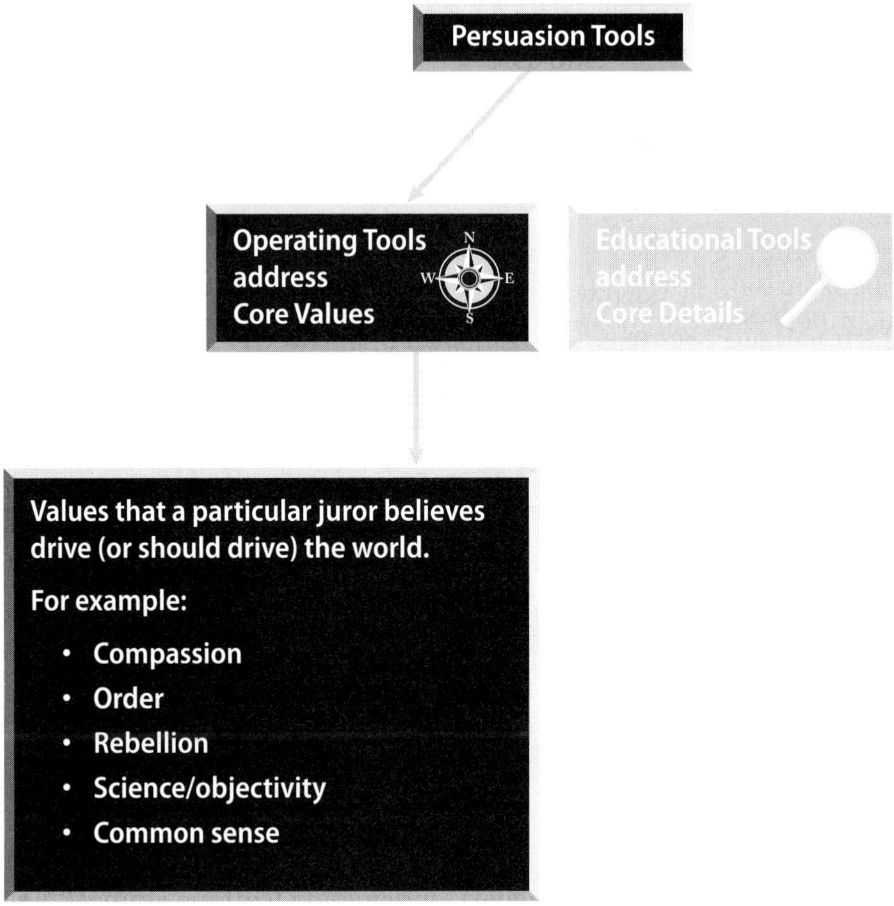

ILLUSTRATION 4-4 Operating Tools Address Core Values

Four things are absolutely clear in this case; in fact, the prosecution does not deny them. First, the defendant loved her children as much as any parent could. Second, despite this love, she killed all three of them. Third, she did so because a voice in her head, a voice that she truly believed to be that of God, ordered her to do so. Fourth, she was immediately tested for drugs and none were found in her system—neither illegal substances nor the prescription medication previously prescribed for her schizophrenia.

The prosecution wants you to convict her of first-degree murder and send her to prison for the rest of her life. The prosecutors want you to do so even though she is clearly insane. The prosecutors want you to ignore the fact that she has been forcibly sent to psychiatric wards at least seven times for being a threat to herself and to others. They want you to ignore that, despite being hospitalized seven times in at least two different states, nobody cared enough or bothered to keep her there for extended treatment or to protect her children. In

> short, up until now, no one cared enough about her or her children to see to it that she got the help she needed.
>
> The prosecutors want you to convict the defendant of first-degree murder, even though we can show that she meets all of the legal requirements for being found insane. They want you to send her to prison for the rest of her life, despite the fact that we have scientific evidence that her mental illness is real and caused by a devastating, verifiable chemical imbalance in her brain.
>
> She is insane—of course she is insane, common sense tells you that. After all, what kind of mother who loved her children as much as she did would do this without being insane?
>
> The prosecution wants you to ignore all of this. Don't do it! Do the right thing: Confirm what is obvious to everyone, including the prosecution (but they won't admit it to you)—this poor woman is insane. Don't be the eighth group to ignore her. Send her to a place that can finally help her and prevent her from hurting herself and others.[2]

After hearing this message, all of the mock mock-jurors concluded that this poor woman was clearly insane. As I suggested earlier, I had expected them to do so, but what really interested me was why and how this group of potential jurors made their decisions.

While my mock mock-jurors agreed on the conclusion, each of them reached that decision differently. Specifically, some elements of the story resonated more deeply with some of the mock mock-jurors than the others. As we examined earlier:

- Some of my mock mock-jurors were moved almost entirely by sympathy or compassion.
- Others went through a mental checklist ("here are the elements, she has met this one, and this one," etc.) to conclude that all of the necessary elements for insanity were met.
- Some of the mock mock-jurors wanted objective scientific proof of the defendant's mental illness before making a decision.
- One mock mock-juror was indignant that the "authorities" had not fully helped the woman when she was previously hospitalized for mental illness and, since they had not done so, wanted to make sure she got the help that she obviously needed.
- Some, like my mother, relied on an innate resource that they described as "common sense."

2. This is an example of what I call an opening argument (a combination of opening statement and closing argument). It makes explicit many arguments that you want to steer your Active Jurors toward, but that you would probably be prevented from making openly in court. That said, everything in this summary (except, perhaps, the fact that the prosecution knows she is insane) is supportable by the evidence and, if given the chance, could be proven at trial. [I actually told the mock mock-jurors a far less adversarial version of the case, but I am including this for pedagogical purposes.]

ILLUSTRATION 4-5 The Jurors Reached the Same Verdict via Different Routes
By choosing one route over another, each juror revealed his or her Core Values.

By choosing one of these routes over another, each mock mock-juror revealed something very important and deeply personal about himself. Each revealed his Core Values, the value that he personally believed should direct the way the world should work. (Ill. 4-5)

Specifically, the first set of jurors valued compassion above all else. They were especially moved by situations where they felt compassion was needed, and they were ready to act in ways consistent with this value.

The second set of mock mock-jurors valued order. They sensed that the "greater good" would be best served if there were clear rules that could be easily followed. In such instances, results would be predictable and efficiently reached by comparing a particular situation to a predetermined set of rules.

The third group valued scientific objectivity and, once established, had no difficulty ruling in accordance therewith.

The fourth group was provoked by what it perceived as an injustice that needed to be remedied. Those in the final group were most comfortable with the wisdom of common sense.

Members of each of these groups needed—and responded differently to—different Operating Tools. Each reached the same ultimate decision: "Defendant is insane." But to get there, each juror had to be pointed down the path that included that Core Value most important to him as an individual. For example, the juror impressed by the objectivity of science had to have his curiosity initially piqued—and then his basic values satisfied—by knowing that there was a verifiable biochemical explanation for what caused the tragic series of events.

Likewise, the juror who primarily cared about orderly standards needed to know that there were preexisting, officially sanctioned criteria for making a determination of insanity and that he could refer to these standards instead of concerning himself with the subjective imprecision of emotion. Once this juror was directed toward a checklist-type Operating Tool, he was able to follow a well-ordered, logical path to conclude that the defendant was insane.

Operating Tools appeal to the Core Values of jurors and reassure them that they can reach a verdict in a way that is wholly consistent with their personal Core Values. I do not want to exaggerate the effectiveness of Operating Tools. They are necessary, but they are not, in and of themselves, sufficient for a successful verdict. Operating Tools can point your jurors in the right direction, but they cannot take them all the way to a verdict. You will still need a wide range of other material (supporting evidence, consistent law, and powerful arguments, for example), to prevail at trial.

Now that you understand the necessity of Operating Tools, we can look at how they are used. Let's continue with the case of the insane mother for some examples.

In this particular case (as we try to in every case), we employed a three-pronged strategy. First, we determined what the Core Values were likely to be. Second, we acknowledged each potentially influential Core Value by including it (along with the four others we had identified) as a consistent element in our Proto-Story. Finally, and most importantly for purposes of this immediate discussion, we provided the jurors with at least one Operating Tool that reinforced each of these Core Values. (Ill. 4-6)

For example, for those jurors whose Core Value was the objectivity of science, we provided them with scientific proof by way of a short tutorial to explain how Parkinson's disease and schizophrenia were related conditions caused by an imbalance of two chemicals (dopamine and acetylcholine) in the brain. Too much of one chemical and not enough of the other results in Parkinson's disease; the opposite imbalance is found in schizophrenia patients. Here are the tools we devised to make this point. (Ills. 4-7 through 4-9)

For the jurors whose Core Value was compassion, we emphasized the tragedy that was this woman's life. We provided an Operating Tool consisting of a timeline of events that traced her troubled life, including a difficult and

Follow a Three-Pronged Strategy to Develop Persuasion Tools

- Determine what the Core Values of your jurors are likely to be.
- Acknowledge each potentially influential Core Value by including it as a consistent element in your Proto-Story.
- Provide at least one Operating Tool that reinforces these Core Values.

ILLUSTRATION 4-6 Follow a Three-Pronged Strategy to Develop Persuasion Tools

The Science of Schizophrenia

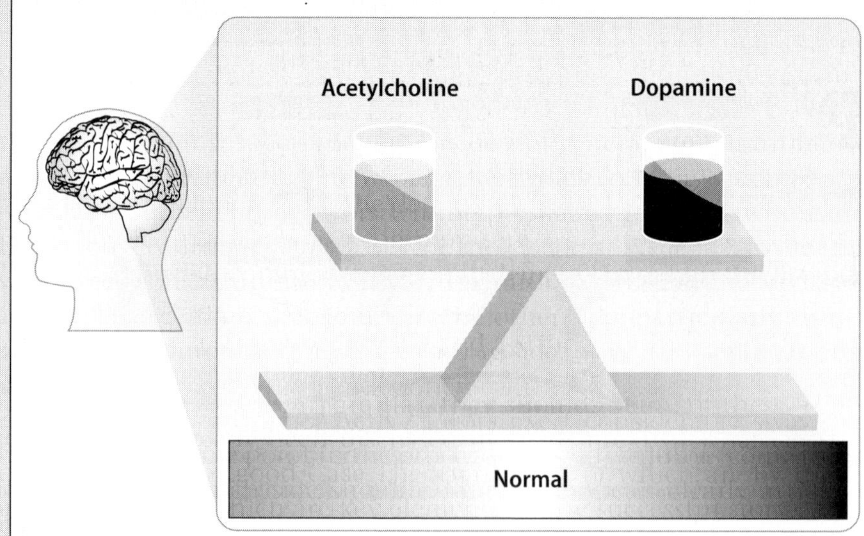

ILLUSTRATIONS 4-7 THROUGH 4-9 Examples of a Persuasion Tool
This Persuasion Tool helped to explain the chemical basis for schizophrenia. While a scientist might argue with the details, these illustrative graphics helped jurors whose Core Value was science/objectivity to conclude that the defendant was legally insane.

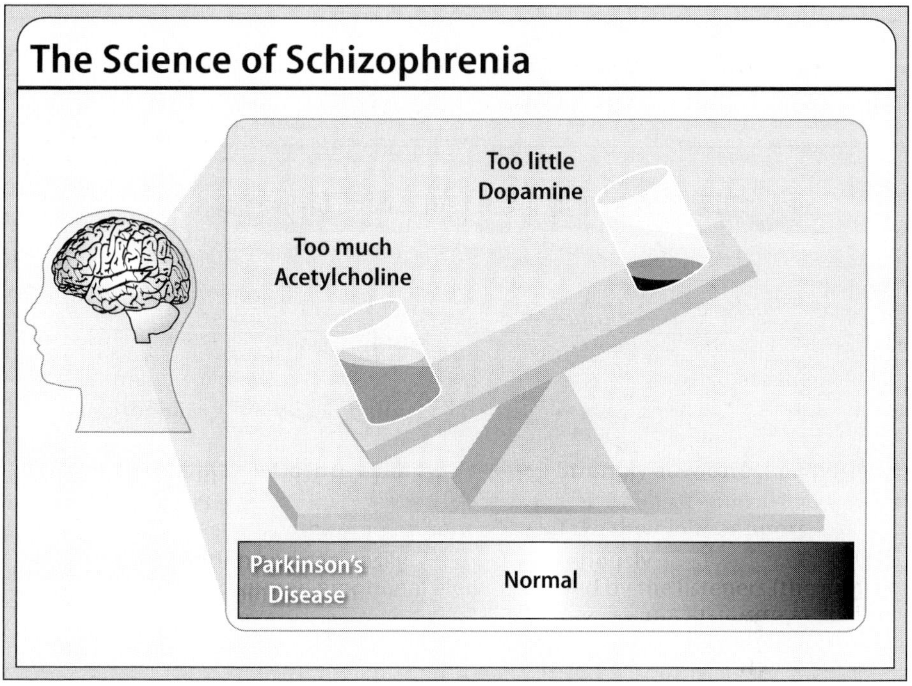

ILLUSTRATION 4-8

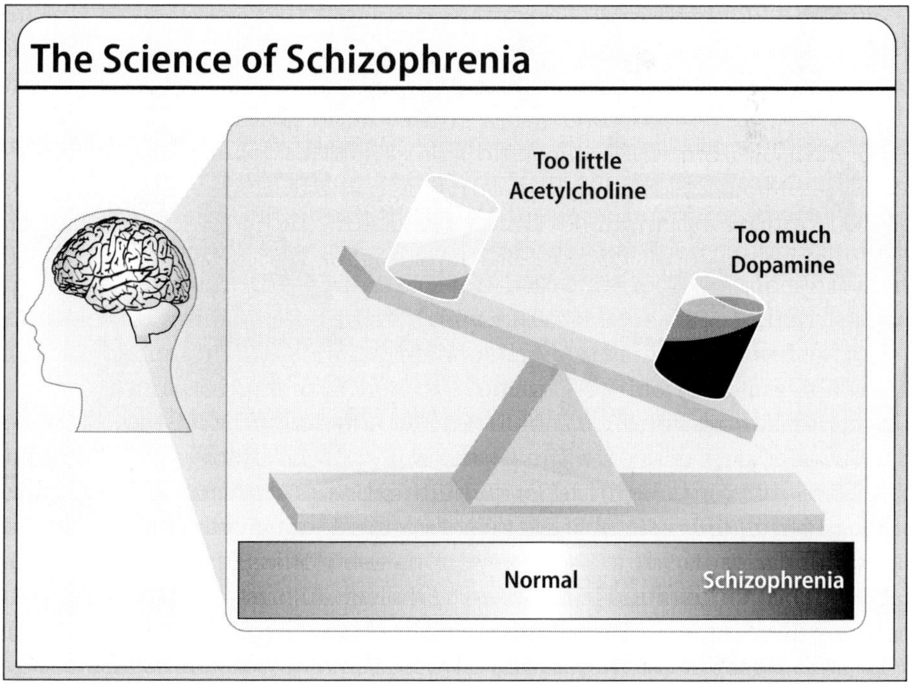

ILLUSTRATION 4-9

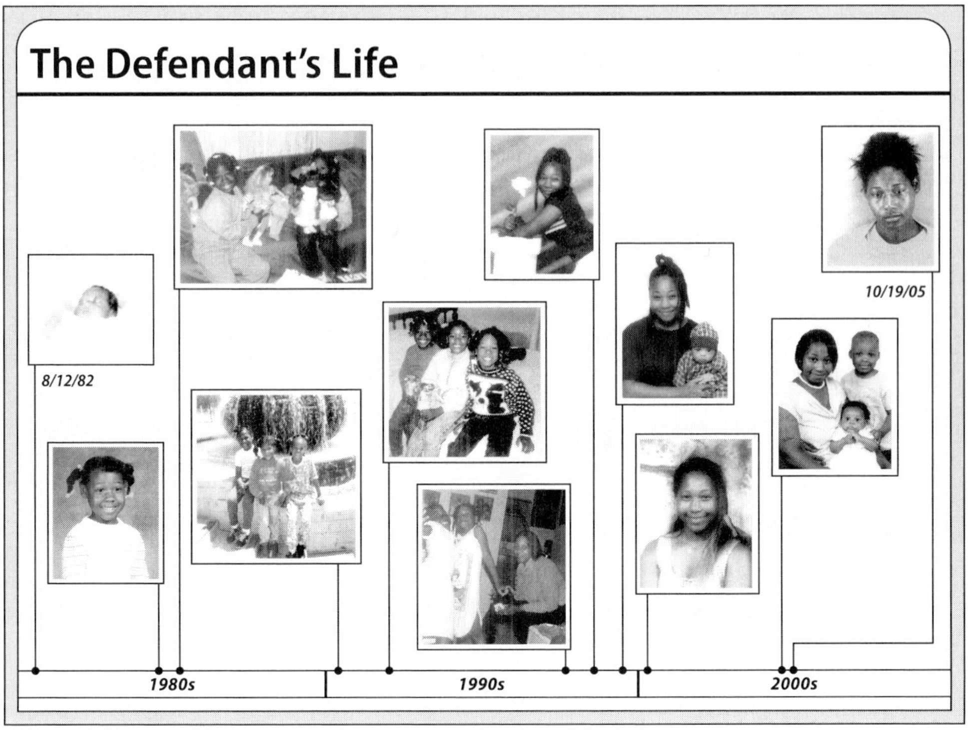

ILLUSTRATION 4-10 Example of a Persuasion Tool
This Persuasion Tool appealed to jurors whose Core Value was compassion. It showed the incredible difficulties the defendant had faced in addition to her severe schizophrenia.

impoverished childhood, becoming pregnant at sixteen years old, dropping out of high school, having three children in quick succession, repeatedly failing to hold down a job, and living in a shelter with her three sons. The timeline was fleshed out, bit by bit, during the opening statement, allowing the lawyers to fully describe each tragic event as it was added to the woman's history. (Ill. 4-10)

For those jurors who felt that injustice permeated the world, we created another timeline that documented the seven instances that officials had committed the defendant to a mental health hospital, without having done anything to protect her or her children from harm. (Ill. 4-11)

As you can see, these Operating Tools appeal to different types of jurors and the messages they convey complement one another.[3] Collectively, the tools help emphasize slightly different points in the Proto-Story's Case Theory. Individually, we designed these tools to affect each particular type of juror we anticipated would be on the actual jury, and to point that individual juror in our desired direction.

3. In addition to the examples shown here, we prepared other Persuasion Tools to appeal to the other Core Values we expected to encounter in the jury.

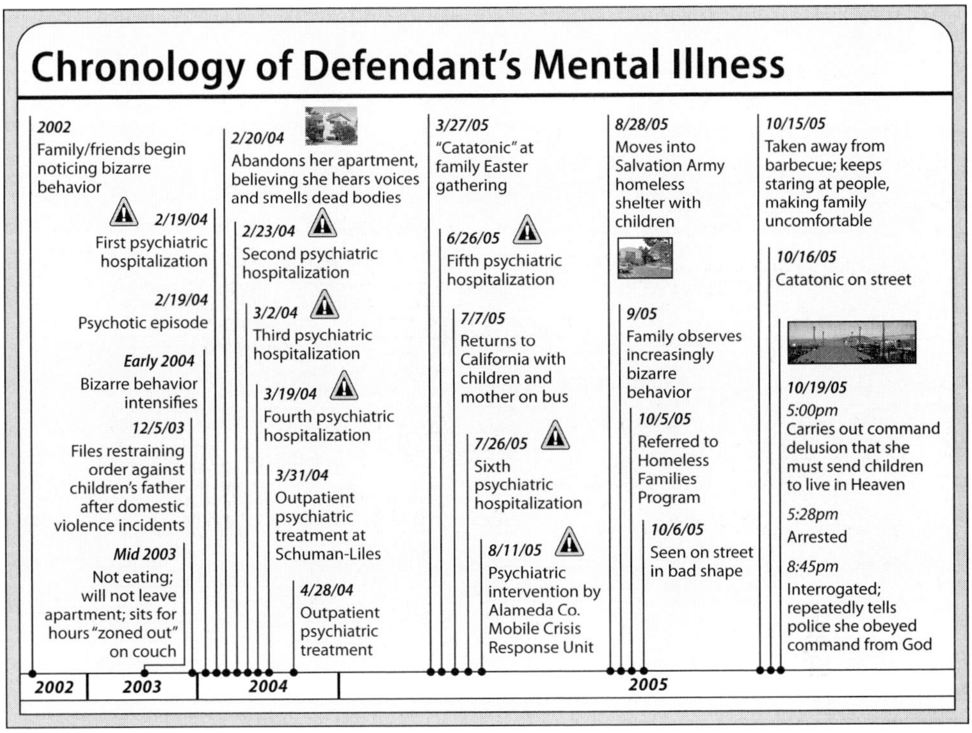

ILLUSTRATION 4-11 Example of a Persuasion Tool
This Persuasion Tool documented the instances where people could have intervened but either failed to do so or did so only temporarily.

The above examples are tangible versions of Persuasion Tools. But remember, not all such tools have to be conveyed in a tangible format. In fact, we reinforced each of the Core Values by including intangible Persuasion Tools as well, by using analogies, stories, arguments, and other verbal tools.

EDUCATIONAL TOOLS ADDRESS CORE DETAILS

Educational Tools are no less important than Operating Tools, but they typically address subjects that are more pedestrian than the Core Values addressed by Operating Tools. Educational Tools address what I refer to as the "Core Details" of your case.

Not all details are of equal value. In the course of trying a case, you inevitably uncover certain details that jurors want to understand in order to feel comfortable making a decision. These are the details that resolve a fundamental factual question or correct an omission in your presentation of the facts. When you fail to provide this information, jurors are left feeling unsettled and comment during their deliberations, "I wish they had told us more about [fill in the blank]." You need to anticipate what these Core Details are and address as many of them as possible. (Ill. 4-12)

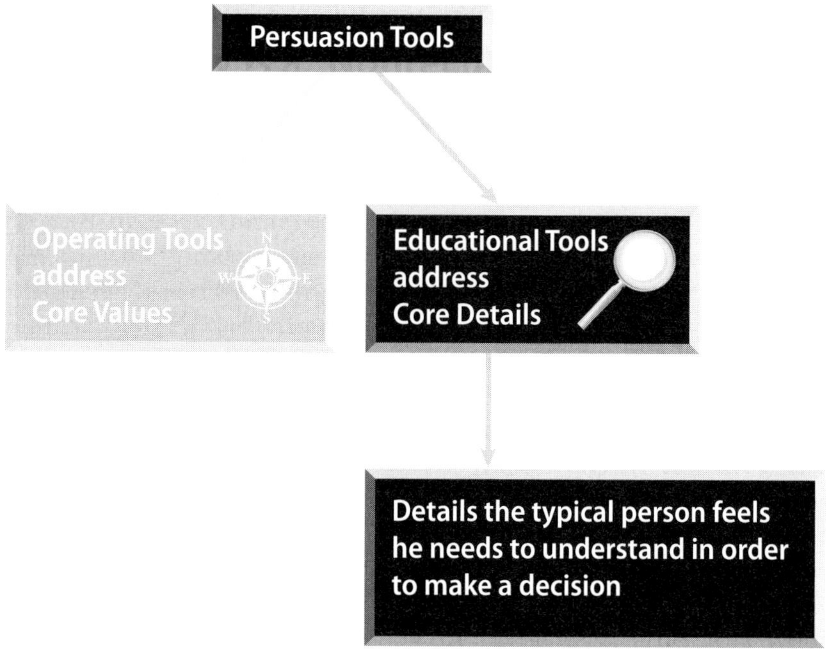

ILLUSTRATION 4-12 Educational Tools Address Core Details

Don't get me wrong; your jurors will make a decision, with or without this information. In fact, the court will force them to do so if the situation arises. But by anticipating and providing this information to the jurors, you make the process easier for them and increase your chances of a verdict in your client's favor.

Situations When Jurors Typically Need and Benefit from Educational Tools

Unfortunately, there is no definitive way of knowing in advance exactly what the Core Details are going to be in a particular case. Fortunately, there are certain recurring situations where you can assume most jurors want and will benefit from your providing them with this additional detail.

While I do not believe it is possible to predict all of the times when jurors will likely need and benefit from Educational Tools, experience tells me that the vast majority of such instances fall into eight categories. But, before I list these categories, let me suggest how you might use this information.

Your case will benefit substantially if, during its preparation, you keep this list of eight instances in mind. As you prepare a witness, structure testimony, or organize an argument, ask yourself, "Do any of the eight situations on the list exist here?" If the answer is yes, take the time to see if you need to include an Educational Tool. Remember, you do not actually need a tool every time such a situation exists in your case—in fact, to provide such "assistance" would likely overwhelm your jury. But in every instance where you identify one of these situations, you do need to at least think about the issue and consider if your case would benefit from such tools.

These are the eight instances where jurors typically need and benefit from Educational Tools:

- Situations where such tools are needed to bridge the gap between what is familiar and what is unfamiliar
- Situations where they need help getting organized or getting their "hands around" a concept or fact
- Situations where they need help comparing and contrasting information or testimony
- Situations where they need understandable definitions or explanations of key terms
- Situations where they need help summarizing your argument
- Situations where they need to understand how things relate chronologically or sequentially
- Situations where motive or precipitating events are important in understanding the case
- Situations where you have "cool stuff" that will pique and hold their interest in a key aspect of your case

Jurors Often Need and Appreciate Educational Tools in Situations Where Such Tools Bridge the Gap Between What Is Familiar and What Is Unfamiliar

By now, you should not be surprised that I mention this first instance in which jurors benefit from Educational Tools. Learning cannot take place in a knowledge vacuum. Jurors, like all students, require at least a toehold of prior understanding in order to begin to learn about the unique, factual elements of your case.

Even under the best circumstances, learning something new invokes a certain amount of stress. In such instances, learning takes place in two steps. The first involves the natural human tendency to try to relate that which is unfamiliar and new to something (whether it a fact, concept, or emotion) that is already familiar and comfortable. The second step—developing understanding incrementally or by way of baby steps—occurs only after this connection is established.

You can help your jurors' learning process by providing Educational Tools that supply the toeholds necessary to assist them in building a bridge between the unfamiliar and the familiar. Be warned: if you do not provide this link for your jurors, they are likely to make sense of the new material by supplying their own connections, appropriate or not. Based on what I have observed, I doubt you want to run the risk of letting them find these initial connections unaided.

Some of the most effective ways of communicating new information to a jury include offering metaphors and analogies, not being afraid to step back and simplify your presentation, providing short tutorials that introduce key concepts in a nonthreatening way, and offering familiar, real-life examples that are related to the subject matter.

Jurors Often Need and Appreciate Educational Tools in Situations Where They Need Help Getting Organized or Getting Their "Hands Around" a Concept or Fact

Albert Einstein is reputed to have claimed that the hardest part of coming up with the theory of relativity was figuring out how to think about or envision the problem. I believe him, not because I think that any other part of the theory of relativity is easy, but because I think we have all been in situations where the answer becomes clear once we figure out how to frame the question (or we find an organized way to think about solving the problem).

Jurors often need and appreciate Educational Tools that help them get their hands around how to solve a problem. Simply by organizing your presentation and arguments in such a way, you will implicitly provide this assistance to your jurors. But, when the situation requires it, there are a number of more concrete Persuasion Tools you can provide, including checklists, flowcharts, outlines, and annotated Operating Instructions that link the prima facie legal requirements to the supporting evidence.

Jurors Often Need and Appreciate Educational Tools in Situations Where They Need Help Comparing and Contrasting Information or Testimony

Because of the way that the parties present their material (particularly during each party's case in chief), evidence at trial is often presented in a rather disjointed manner. Since evidence is not presented topically, but rather by party and witness, key related facts can be separated by days of unrelated testimony. Jurors appreciate Educational Tools that make it easy for them to compare and contrast the evidence that has accumulated over the course of the trial, and they often use such a summary as a scorecard for assessing which side's arguments are supported by the evidence and whose witnesses corroborate or contradict each other.

You can illustrate this information in a variety of ways. One of the most common techniques is to compare your opponent's flimsy evidence on one side of a ledger to the overwhelming support to the contrary on your side. Alternatively, you could present a listing of bullet points that identify your opponent's "claims" versus what is actually supported by the evidence.

Jurors Often Need and Appreciate Educational Tools in Situations Where They Need Understandable Definitions or Explanations of Key Terms

Educational Tools that define key terms or explain key concepts in a way that is fair (yet favorable to your position) assists both you and your jurors. These definitions can take a number of different forms. You can provide written definitions; you can orally explain the concepts to the jury; you can use illustrations or verbal pictures conjured up through analogies. One of the simplest ways to help define a concept is to illustrate it in context, by using an analogy or real-life example. The point here is that you have numerous options and you should not hesitate to use them if they will help your jurors understand or feel more comfortable with your case.

Jurors Often Need and Appreciate Educational Tools in Situations Where They Need Help Summarizing Your Argument

One way to determine if you have effectively argued your case is to see if the jurors latch onto the primary arguments you made in closing, and continue to advance your position during deliberations. Checklists, outlines, bullet points, flowcharts, and other similar Persuasion Tools help reinforce your arguments in the jurors' minds, help them remember your position, and give them the confidence to advocate on your behalf once they are in the jury room. Something as simple as a series of bullet points can be a very effective Persuasion Tool.

Jurors Often Need and Appreciate Educational Tools in Situations Where They Need to Understand How Events Relate Chronologically or Sequentially

Chronological order is the most common way of understanding how events occurred and what action precipitated a subsequent action. While I do not always advocate that you tell your story in chronological order, I do understand that it is important to be prepared—and able to offer—Educational Tools that relay events in sequential order. The most obvious way to do this is with a timeline or flowchart.

Jurors Often Need and Appreciate Educational Tools in Situations Where Motive or Precipitating Events Are Important in Understanding the Case

Jurors need to understand motive, and they need to do so even in those cases where establishing motive or state of mind is not required to establish a prima facie cause of action or affirmative defense. At a minimum, you must work this element into your Proto-Story. Consider highlighting the content of key documents that explain motive. Or, if appropriate, create a special timeline that emphasizes the cause and effect relationship between the party's actions, illustrated with all the plaintiff's actions in chronological order on top of a time bar and all of the defendant's responses below the bar. This type of graphic allows the jurors to see "plaintiff did this, which caused defendant to respond by doing that, which further caused plaintiff to do something else. . . ." These tools, which I call "action-reaction timelines," often serve as very effective Persuasion Tools.

Jurors Often Need and Appreciate Educational Tools in Situations Where You Have "Cool Stuff" That Will Pique and Hold Their Interest in a Key Aspect of Your Case

Occasionally, a case will have a series of facts or a collection of topics that can only be classified as "really cool stuff." For example, I once worked on a matter central to which was our ability to trace the origin of so-called "anonymous" e-mails. Our expert witness at trial was able to explain how to perform sophisticated forensic analysis on computers to trace e-mails surreptitiously sent by people who were trying to hide their identities. This expert had formerly led the federal government's team responsible for protecting the President by tracking down and assessing the threat level of menacing e-mails. Consequently, she had a great deal of information germane to developing and uncovering the techniques employed to protect the President—the same techniques that had been used to find the author of the e-mails in dispute in our case. The witness's professional history and the techniques she developed are examples of what I call "really cool stuff." Of course, we decided to share some of this material with the jurors; after all, what self-respecting, intellectually curious person would not want to know more about these subjects?

Why You Need to Offer a Variety of Persuasion Tools to Your Active Jurors

Two facts consistently impress me about the jury system: (1) jurors generally get to the right answer, and (2) the vast majority of times, they get there by a unanimous verdict (or at least one requiring a supermajority).

One of the fundamental reasons that these results are possible is that our system is designed so that you can provide (and, in fact, you need to provide) a variety of Persuasion Tools to your Active Jurors. By offering jurors an array of Persuasion Tools (as opposed to just the one that most impresses you as the trial lawyer), you allow different people to come to the same conclusion as to whom should prevail, but you allow them to do so from a variety of different directions, through the process that we detailed in Chapter 3.

This system provides both benefits and challenges to the trial lawyer. The benefits are relatively easy to observe and cannot be overstated. Most particularly, the way we structure a trial gives the lawyer multiple opportunities to be a better teacher, which, as I have previously argued, is a role most great trial lawyers play for their jurors. Specifically, we tell the story to the jurors three different times, thereby increasing the chances that they will understand our position. As we do this, we integrate a variety of different tools into the process, each potentially appealing to and educating different jurors with potentially different interests and learning styles.

This system also presents a substantial challenge to the trial lawyer; it requires that the lawyer constantly avoid what I call "Excessive Personalization." Let me illustrate this concept with a personal story.

Many years ago, my family took a trip from our home in northern California to my parents' home in southern Indiana. To our children, who were very young at the time and had only lived in urban northern California, this trip must have seemed as if we had traveled to another planet. All the houses in Indiana had huge yards; the trees and shrubs were unfamiliar; there were these magical things called fireflies (which we did not have in California);

the landscape was considerably flatter; thundershowers with giant cumulus clouds and lightning were common. These differences delighted and fascinated our children. As a result, they constantly commented on how different everything was compared to things in California. At one point, almost overwhelmed by these differences, one of my sons announced that he had noticed another thing that was different, but not necessarily better; "California's moon and Indiana's moon look a lot alike! But I think California's is at least twice as big as the one in Indiana!"

This is an example of Excessive Personalization, the human tendency to perceive one's own ideas, objects, or experiences as being superior to everyone else's. For a small child, this can be endearing, as in, "My moon in California is better than the moon in Indiana." For a trial lawyer, this kind of thinking can be disastrous.

A successful trial lawyer should never assume that her way of reasoning is superior to any other. She cannot lose sight of the fact that not all of her jurors will think the same way she does, nor will they be motivated by exactly the same evidence and arguments that she personally finds persuasive.

You need to remember this and constantly ask yourself, "What else is out there that my particular set of jurors is likely to find interesting, helpful, and persuasive, even if I don't?"

Having said this, I want to remind you that this perspective needs to be balanced against a couple of principles, which we have already discussed. Your case will not automatically get better simply by adding more material to it; your case will get better when you take the time to use more carefully focused material in it. In addition, you do not need to provide a separate Persuasion Tool for each member of your jury. Although I have repeatedly praised the jury system, I consider some jurors to be outliers, the "exceptions to the norm" that skew data until it cannot be explained in terms of standard deviation. It is *not* your job to pander to these folks at the expense of the other jurors; your job is to get these folks struck from the panel during voir dire. If you are not able to remove them from the jury, you should design your case so that your Active Jurors are adequately equipped to do battle with the outliers during deliberations and, hopefully, coax them to your side.

The Characteristics of Successful Persuasion Tools

Even though you will design your Persuasion Tools to appeal to different people, all of this material will share four basic features. (Ill. 4-13) First, highly persuasive tools rely on simple everyday language. By suggesting that you err on the side of simplicity, I am not advocating that you "dumb down" your presentation; I am reminding you that your jurors do not come into court with an existing knowledge and understanding of the issues in your case. Unlike you, they have not spent years—or even months—learning your case. Follow the example of Clarence Darrow, of whom his biographer, Irving Stone,

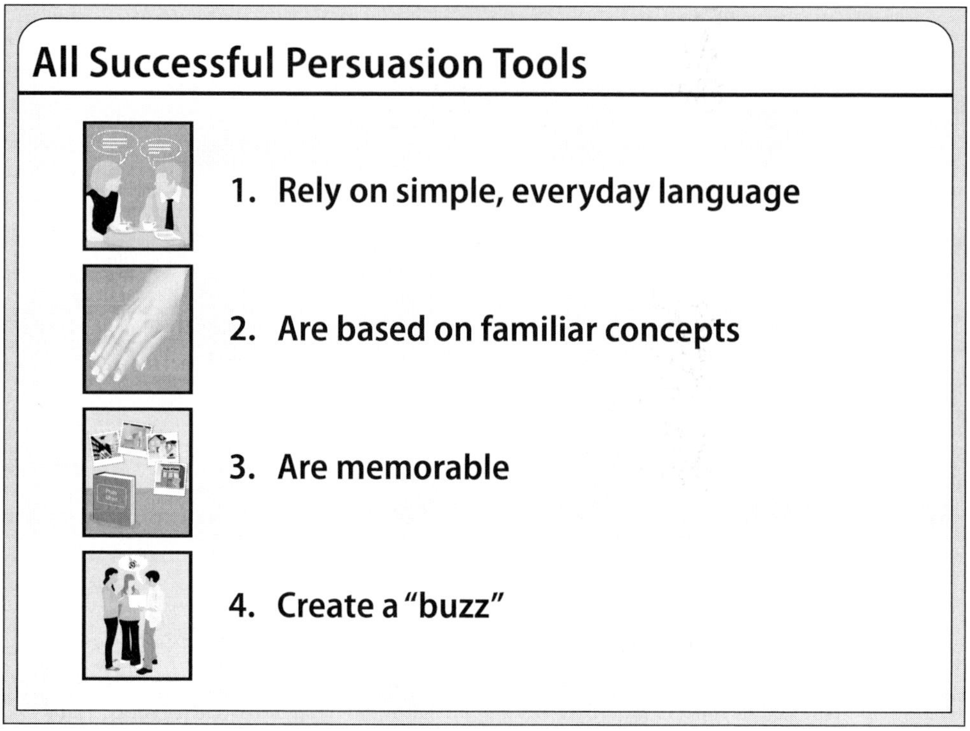

ILLUSTRATION 4-13 Successful Persuasion Tools Have Four Characteristics

wrote: "[Darrow] talked to a plumber as though he, too, were a plumber; to a groceryman as though he, too, were a groceryman."

The second characteristic of all effective Persuasion Tools is that they are created based on concepts and ideas that are already familiar to the jurors. Jurors can understand new or complex topics only if they can first compare these topics to something with which they are already familiar. You need to relate important facts and arguments to the jurors by comparing the new facts to things that the jurors already understand.

This is one of the reasons that analogies are often so powerful in persuading jurors. Analogies increase understanding by tying together two seemingly disparate concepts—one familiar and one unfamiliar—and using the characteristics of the familiar one to make sense of the latter. If there is such a thing as "guilt by association," analogies promote "understanding by association."

Rhetoricians occasionally remind us that using analogies is traditionally considered to be a weak form of argument. The fact that something is similar to something else, or that two concepts have commonalities, means that, by definition, the two objects are *not* the same. As such, analogies inevitably fall apart if taken too far. While this is true, it misses the point. Analogies are powerful ways to introduce subjects; their strength lies in their ability to provide effective toeholds to concepts and to give jurors an orienting view of the subject at hand. Use them for this purpose and then move on.

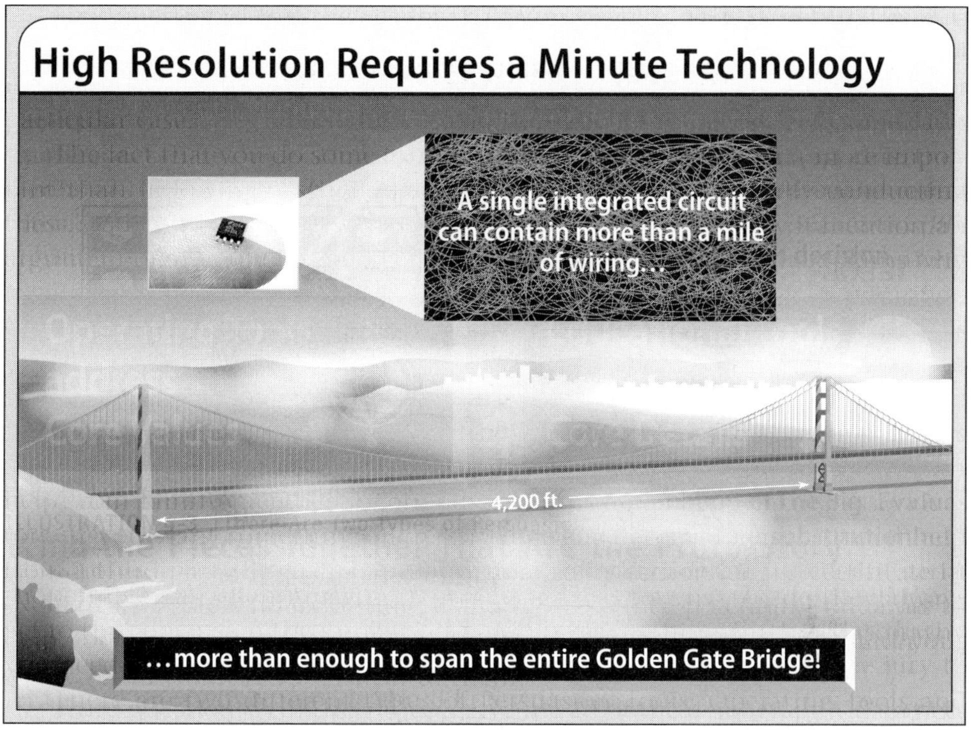

ILLUSTRATION 4-14 This Persuasion Tool Provides a Memorable Fact to the Jury

Let me also remind you that an analogy's ultimate success depends on your ability to supplement the analogy with appropriate factual support. At trial, an analogy without the backup that comes from substantiating evidence is, at best, a humorous sideshow (and, more likely, a complete waste of time).

The third characteristic of all highly effective Persuasion Tools is that they are memorable. This sounds obvious, yet you would be amazed how much information jurors forget during a trial unless you have taken steps to help them remember. I have read scores of post-trial interviews where jurors cannot remember a single thing a witness said about a very important event. Ideally, you will provide the jurors with tools that will help them remember your key points long after you adjourn. Through careful preparation, your facts (or series of facts) will not only be remembered and used to your advantage during deliberations, but they will be repeated at cocktail parties and other gatherings for years to come. Consider the wonders of an integrated circuit as shown in the graphic. (Ill. 4-14)

The fourth and final characteristic of highly effective Persuasion Tools is that they create what I call a "buzz." This term is difficult to define, but is very easy to recognize when you come across it. You know you have caused a buzz when you see your jurors lean forward and pay attention. Occasionally, you will see these same jurors chuckle to themselves, as if to indicate, "Oh, I get it!"

ILLUSTRATION 4-15 This Persuasion Tool Creates a Buzz
You can dryly describe an eighteen percent distortion, or you can create a buzz by showing this amount of distortion using a familiar image. An eighteen percent distortion would convert a Da Vinci into a Picasso.

For example, we once created a trial graphic to explain the term "percentage of distortion" to a jury. You would typically expect such an explanation to be made using numerical equations and detailed diagrams. Think how much more of a buzz we created by showing this distortion using an image that everyone knows. (Ill. 4-15)

CHAPTER 5 The Five-Step Process for Creating Your Proto-Story and Persuasion Tools

Chapter Introduction

Your Proto-Story and your Persuasion Tools are end products. They are created and recreated, formed and reformed as you prepare your case. In some instances, this process of reworking the Proto-Story and Persuasion Tools doesn't stop until you finally sit down at the end of trial. This chapter describes the Five-Step Process that my colleagues at The Focal Point and I have developed to help our clients assemble the materials necessary to create and shape Proto-Stories and Persuasion Tools.

As will be discussed below in greater detail, we recommend the following a Five-Step Process:

1. Develop *Understanding*—of both detail and overall context—about your case.
2. Go through a process of brainstorming (or, as we prefer to call it, *Mental Mining*) to develop concepts that help your jurors understand.
3. *Simplify* your case to make sure that what you are teaching is easy for your jurors to follow.
4. Emphasize what really matters in your case, using the principles of *Information Architecture.*
5. Use appropriate technology to enhance, rather than constrain, how you *Present* your message.

Overview of the Five-Step Process

In my mind's eye, I see the Five-Step Process as a series of three rings, two of which are joined together and located squarely in the foreground. The third ring sits alone in the background. The two connected rings partially overlap to form four connecting parts, labeled "Understand," "Mentally Mine," "Simplify," and "Architect"—representing the first four steps in the process. The third ring, the one that is not connected to the other two and sits alone, is labeled "Present"—representing the final step. (Ill. 5-1)

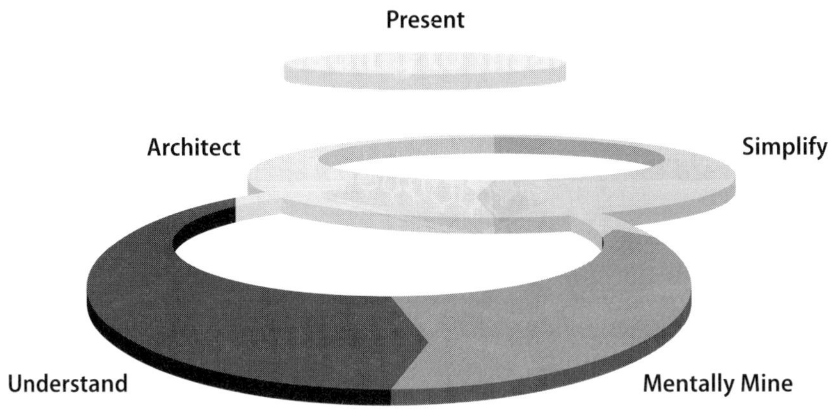

ILLUSTRATION 5-1 The Five-Step Process Looks Like Three Rings

Observation One: The First Four Steps Are Connected

At the outset, let me point out four important characteristics of this diagram. First, as represented by the two interlocking rings, the first four steps are all connected to each other and, as we shall discuss, must always stay connected. (Ill. 5-2) There are three reasons for this.

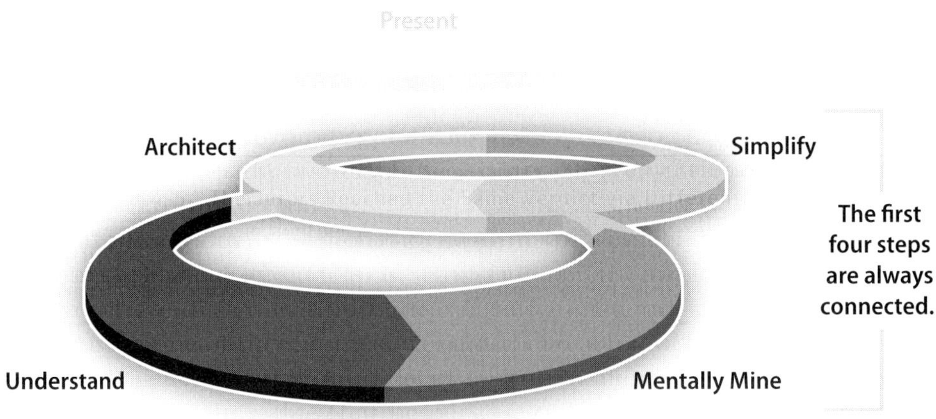

ILLUSTRATION 5-2 The First Four Steps Are Always Connected

First, each step is dependent upon the other. It is not possible to Mentally Mine unless you Understand. At the same time, your ability to Understand is substantially increased by your efforts at Mental Mining. Likewise, using Information Architecture improves your ability to Simplify—just as Simplification improves your Information Architecture. Thus, a reciprocal relationship exists among each of the subparts between these two rings.

Second, there is not always a clear boundary separating each step. For example, an image or a concept that radically Simplifies your case is often a result of Mental Mining. Likewise, the tools used to Understand are equally helpful for Mental Mining. In short, the actual boundary between any two steps is somewhat porous and not rigidly defined.

Third, you cannot skip any one of these steps; you must make a conscious and deliberate effort to go through each and every one. While you may spend more time on one step than another and (as we will see) the order may shift, you need to spend some time with each. Do not skip any part of this process.

Observation Two: The Process Is Nonlinear

The second observation that you should take away from the illustration is that the process of going through the first four steps is never linear. You do not start at "A" and work your way straight though the alphabet to "Z." (Ill. 5-3)

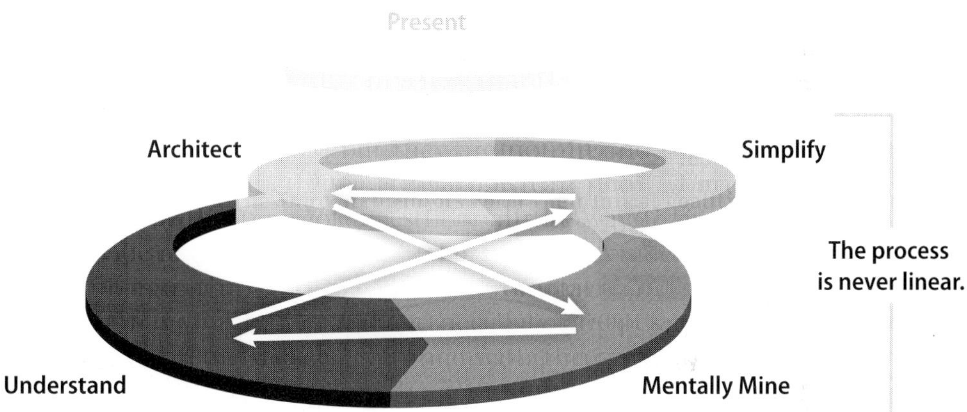

ILLUSTRATION 5-3 The Process Is Never Linear

Progressing through the first four steps involves a fair amount of forward and backward motion. For example, you may start moving forward, from Understanding to Mental Mining, and realize you do not have all the information you need to complete the step. So, you temporarily go back to Understanding and discover that your backward move is propelling you rapidly into Simplifying.

There is nothing wrong with this nonlinear (some would say "convoluted") way of proceeding. Unless you are a genius like Mozart, who reportedly composed much of his work without bothering with drafts and rewrites, the nonlinear process reflected by these two interlocking rings is both inevitable and advantageous, because it is precisely this way of thinking and creating that makes your end product effective and well conceived.

But be warned: This lack of linear movement can drive some people nuts. If you are one of those people, I strongly urge you to follow Elvis's advice and "Just hang loose for a minute." Relax and go with the flow—at least for now.

Your progress through the steps will naturally become more fluid as you work your way through the process, and your case will be stronger and easier to present as a result.

Observation Three: Deciding How to Present Your Material Must Always Be the Last Step

The third thing you should notice from the illustration is that the final step—Presenting—is a ring in and of itself, disconnected from the first two and pushed to the back of the diagram. This deliberate design choice is intended to emphasize a very important point: Choosing the media to display your message must always be *the final step* in the process. (Ill. 5-4)

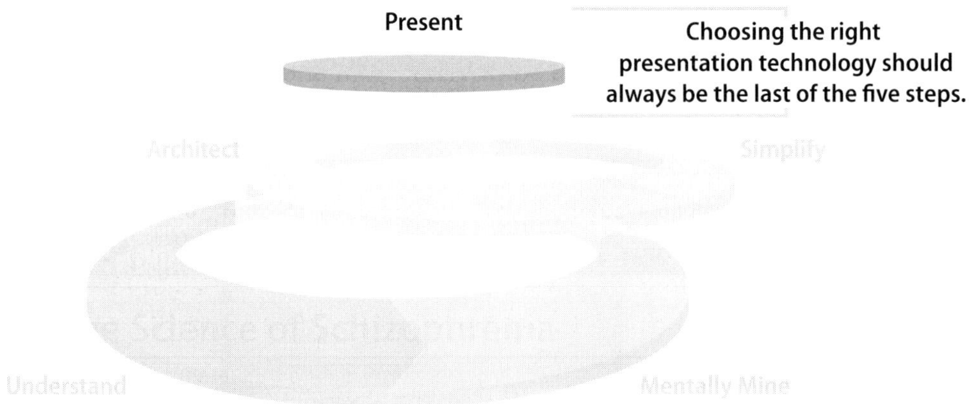

ILLUSTRATION 5-4 The Final Step Is Presenting
Choosing the right media must always be the final step in the process.

While the method by which you present your material in court—whether you do it orally, electronically, by way of pictures, or through animation—is an important part of the Five-Step Process, the decision associated with this step must always be made *after* you have sufficiently navigated your way through the first four steps represented by the two interconnected front rings.

Why is this the case? The answer is simple, but I will repeat it several times throughout this chapter: The media (i.e., how you display material) should never drive the message (i.e., what you have to say). In other words, what you tell the jury is always more important than the technology you choose to convey that message to them.

While this intuitively makes sense, many trial lawyers forget this key point and, as a result, they start thinking about how to display or use the material rather than focusing on refining the message itself.

For example, some lawyers decide early on that they are going to display all of their Persuasion Tools using PowerPoint. By making this decision, these lawyers prematurely limit their creative options. PowerPoint is a wonderful and powerful tool, but it is best used with certain material presented in a certain way. These limitations naturally affect the message. By prematurely choosing *any* media, you limit your own creativity.

Let me be clear that I am not picking on just PowerPoint. My warning that you not prematurely pick the media is equally applicable to everything from chalkboards to the latest three-dimensional animations. By illustrating Presentation as a fifth step, in its own circle, alone, unconnected to the first four, and at the end of the process, I hope you will remember this crucial point—*Never let the media drive the message!*

Observation Four: The Five-Step Process Takes Time; Give Yourself That Luxury

Occasionally, when people first see the illustration of the Five-Step Process, they comment that it seems like it takes a lot of time to implement all five steps. When they say this, they typically imply that taking up so much time is a bad thing. I acknowledge that, yes, it does take time. But it is not a waste of time; it is time exceedingly well spent.

Why do the Five Steps take so much time? I have three answers for this. First, this is a composting process. The product itself needs time to mentally ferment. Ideas that are useless need time to be identified, filtered out, and discarded; those that are valuable need time to evolve, ripen, and be effectively incorporated into your case.

Second, most of us are unable to turn our creativity on and off at will. Our brains need time to quietly ponder, and much of this pondering takes place subconsciously, while we are doing other things. This phenomenon is what I call "Passive Mental Mining." It is the kind of creativity that emerges from the subconscious while taking a walk or a shower, doing yard work, or doing nothing at all. If you wait until the last minute to begin the Five Steps, you won't have enough time to let your creative juices percolate. After all, how many walks and showers can you realistically take when your trial is set to open the next morning? Allow yourself the luxury of spreading this process out. Start early.

The final reason the process takes time is that you cannot effectively do it alone. You need to recruit others to help you evaluate your Proto-Story and Persuasion Tools. Whether this support group is formal (as in a Feedback Forum or consultant-assembled mock trial) or informal (as in talking to family members, a group of friends, or a colleague in your law firm), you need sufficient time to assemble an audience, present your case to them, and get their honest impressions and suggestions.

There is no such a thing as starting your preparation too early. You get a lot of information about your case right from the beginning and you can use it to immediately start the Five-Step Process. Formal discovery is an important period for preserving material that you will need for trial, but I strongly believe that most lawyers know (or suspect) the vast majority of necessary information to start this process long before depositions are taken and interrogatories are completed.

In addition to basic, specific information from your client about your new case, there is considerable material available to you by virtue of the fact that you come to the process as an adult, with knowledge of how the world works and what motivates people to behave the way they do. These two sources of information, that is, your client's initial case-specific details and your intuitive general understanding, give you sufficient material to get started with the process right away. Starting early means you need to keep an open mind and, if things change and your perspective shifts, there is nothing in this process that prohibits you from changing your approach as well. You will undoubtedly have some false starts, but the end cost is usually the same (or even less), because you are able to focus earlier on those issues that ultimately matter.

The Five Steps

Step One: You Need to Understand Your Case

You need to understand—*really* understand—your case. In order to do so, you need to be able to see what happened at and around the Big Bang from two different vantage points. First, you must understand the details. Second, you need to develop perspective based on those details.

Fortunately, most lawyers are generally pretty good at learning the details of their case. They know they need to identify who the parties are, what is in the documents, and the general chronology of events. This is a lot of information. So much so that, unfortunately, many lawyers stop their analysis after they have mastered just these details alone. The fact is that there is a big difference between learning the facts of a case and being able to use those facts effectively. Merely "knowing" the details is not enough to piece together a powerful Proto-Story and develop effective Persuasion Tools. In order to accomplish these goals, you need to develop a second level of understanding. You need to develop perspective.

Perspective is the tool that helps you identify which parts of your case are important, how these parts are interconnected, why these parts matter, and why your jurors should care.

You need *both* of these views; you need to know the details *and* have perspective as to what they mean. You cannot have perspective without first learning and digesting the basic facts. Likewise, you cannot expect to develop either an effective Proto-Story or powerful Persuasion Tools unless you first develop sufficient perspective.

You must be able to see the trees *and* the forest. Or as my colleagues and I like to say, "You need to have two views—one *under* and one *over*. Specifically,

Maintain Two Views: One Under and One Over

You must maintain an <u>under</u>standing of the <u>under</u>lying facts...

...and an <u>over</u>view of the <u>over</u>all case.

ILLUSTRATION 5-5 You Need to Have Two Views—One Under and One Over
You must maintain an understanding of the underlying facts and an overview of the overall case. This allows you an up-close view of the details while maintaining perspective of what is really important to your case.

you must have an *under*standing of the *under*lying facts and an *over*view of the *over*all case." (Ill. 5-5)

So, how do you do this? The short answer is that there are different techniques for each of the two perspectives. Understanding the underlying facts is generally a mechanical process involving organizing, conscious thought, and memorization. It is the process of learning facts and figures.

Specifically, with respect to understanding the underlying facts, I have three suggestions. (Ill. 5-6) The first is that the person ultimately responsible for the case must do this work. It is not a task that can be delegated to someone else. If the case is your responsibility, you need to reach down in the case file and not be afraid to dig.

Second, one of the most effective ways to gather this information is to use what I call a "master chronology." Specifically, I am referring to an itemized collection of written materials that lists and summarizes the main events, key documents, and other relevant information in chronological order. There is no specific or universal format for this master chronology; use what works best for you. Creating and updating this tool takes time; make the commitment to revise the chronology as the facts unfold. If you skimp, the value of your master chronology will diminish.

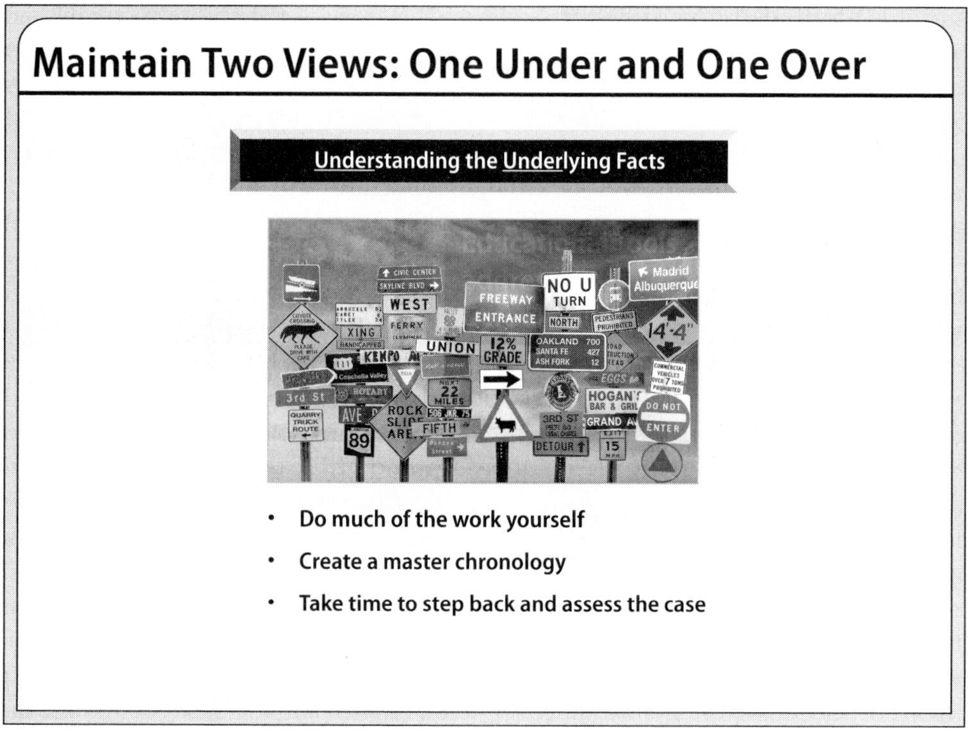

ILLUSTRATION 5-6 Three Suggestions for Understanding the Underlying Facts

The third suggestion is perhaps the most important. Before you get too far into developing all of this detail, take the time to step back and begin anatlyzing the case from the "inside-out." That is, determine what really matters. Assess what the case is about. Start putting together an overall story. How do you do this? You need to engage in Mental Mining, the second step of the Five-Step Process.

STEP TWO: YOU NEED TO MENTALLY MINE YOUR CASE

What Is Mental Mining?

When a person is inundated with new data, his mind does two things simultaneously. On a conscious level, he begins to memorize the details. At the same time, the subconscious does its best to put all these details into some kind of understandable order. The most obvious way the subconscious does this is by associating as much of the new material as possible with items already stored there. (Ill. 5-7)

By placing these facts into categories, or "buckets," as I like to call them, the subconscious mind begins the process of connecting the unfamiliar with something familiar. As we have previously discussed, this link provides a toehold that is the first crucial step in the learning process.

These subconscious buckets are more than just a collection of random facts. The buckets are the result of a sorting process that says, "while these

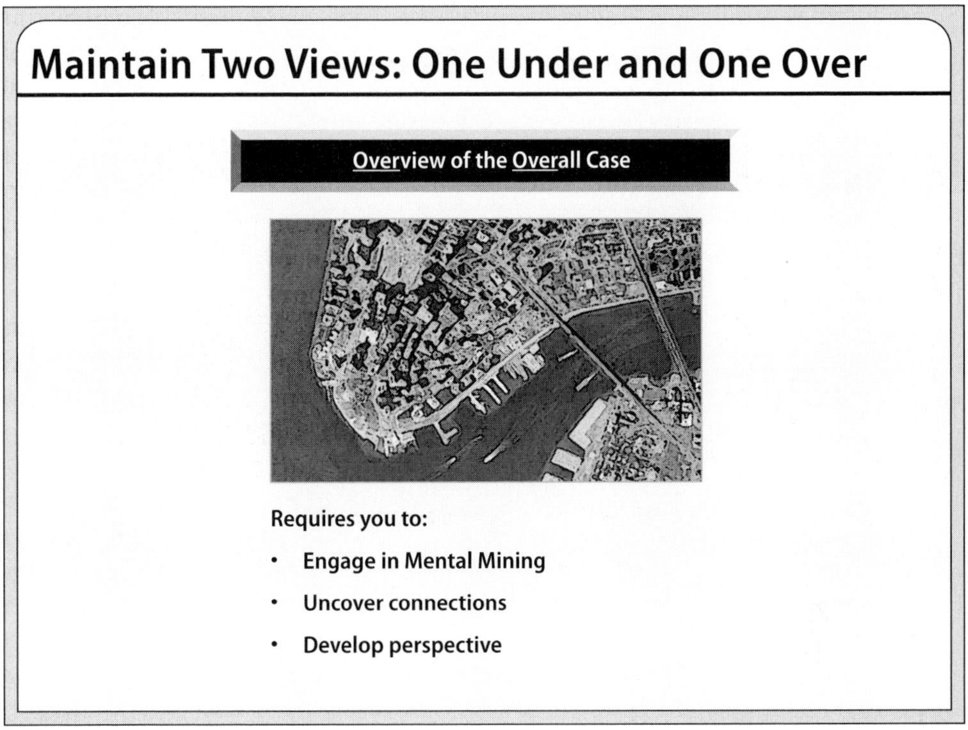

ILLUSTRATION 5-7 Developing an Overview of the Overall Case Means Finding Perspective

two facts appear to have very little in common, they both illustrate the same general principle of what happens when [fill in the blank]" or "this fact reminds me of that earlier time when [fill in the blank]" or "this fact reminds me of the story about the [fill in the blank]." Based on these types of associations or links, the subconscious mind sorts the new facts into the appropriate buckets.

This sorting mechanism—or more specifically, the link between the new fact and the familiar bucket into which that fact is placed—is very important and should be carefully examined. These basic links often include important, universal organizing principles, which have the convenient effect of delegating new facts into the same respective buckets in each of our subconscious receptacles. In fact, one link can easily have applicability across your entire jury pool!

Mental Mining is the process of consciously finding those links, dislodging (or Mentally Mining) them from the subconscious, and bringing them into the conscious mind, where they can be examined to see if they provide the toeholds necessary for the jurors to understand the new and potentially complex facts of your case.

Once the information has been dislodged from the subconscious, it can be used by the conscious mind to better explain (often in a broadly accepted manner) the events of a case. Without making this conscious effort, the material would remain submerged and inaccessible.

How to Engage in Mental Mining

In the broadest sense, there are two forms of Mental Mining: Passive Mental Mining and Active Mental Mining. We have already discussed Passive Mental Mining, which is the process of letting your ideas percolate while you focus on other things, typically unrelated to the case.

Active Mental Mining involves at least two people: you and a "Critical Listener." The objective of the exercise is to spend a few uninterrupted hours during which you and the Critical Listener can examine what your case is really about. (Ill. 5-8)

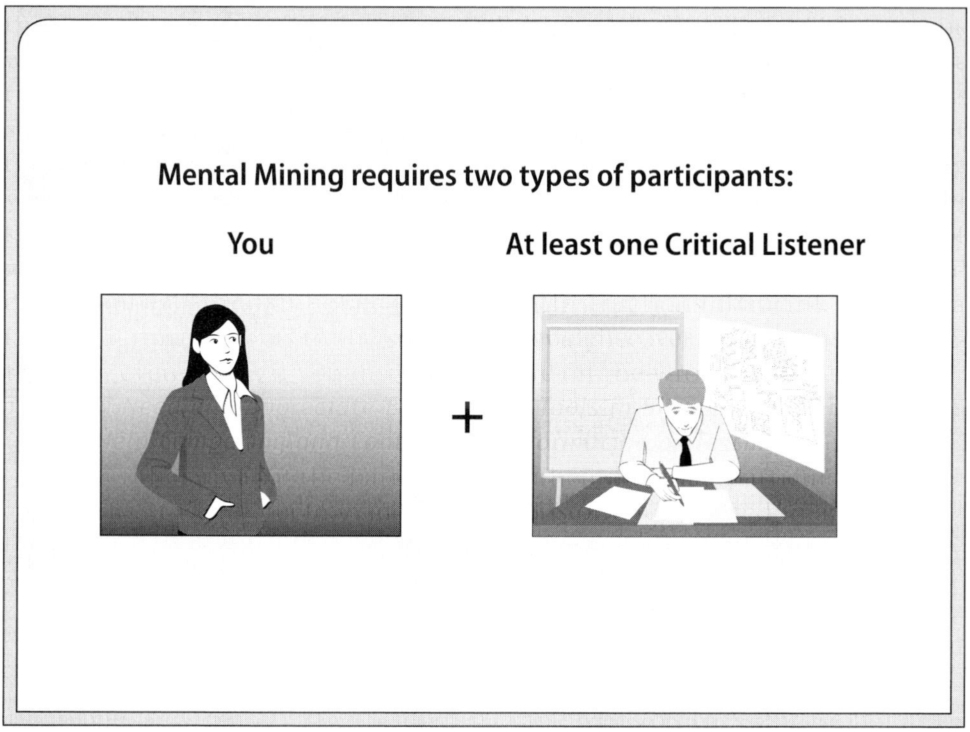

ILLUSTRATION 5-8 Mental Mining Requires Two Types of Participants
In addition to the lawyer, Mental Mining requires at least one Critical Listener.

Usually, what emerges from this spirited discussion are a variety of very important *tools* that commonly include: (Ill. 5-9)

- A better-articulated understanding of what is really in dispute, which often forms the Case Themes
- A better understanding of what really motivated the key players, which is a necessary element of the Factual Strand
- Insights that often help you better understand the likely Core Values and Core Details
- Various concepts that evolve into key Persuasion Tools
- A list of analogies, expressions, metaphors, and other tools that will eventually serve as key toeholds for many of the jurors

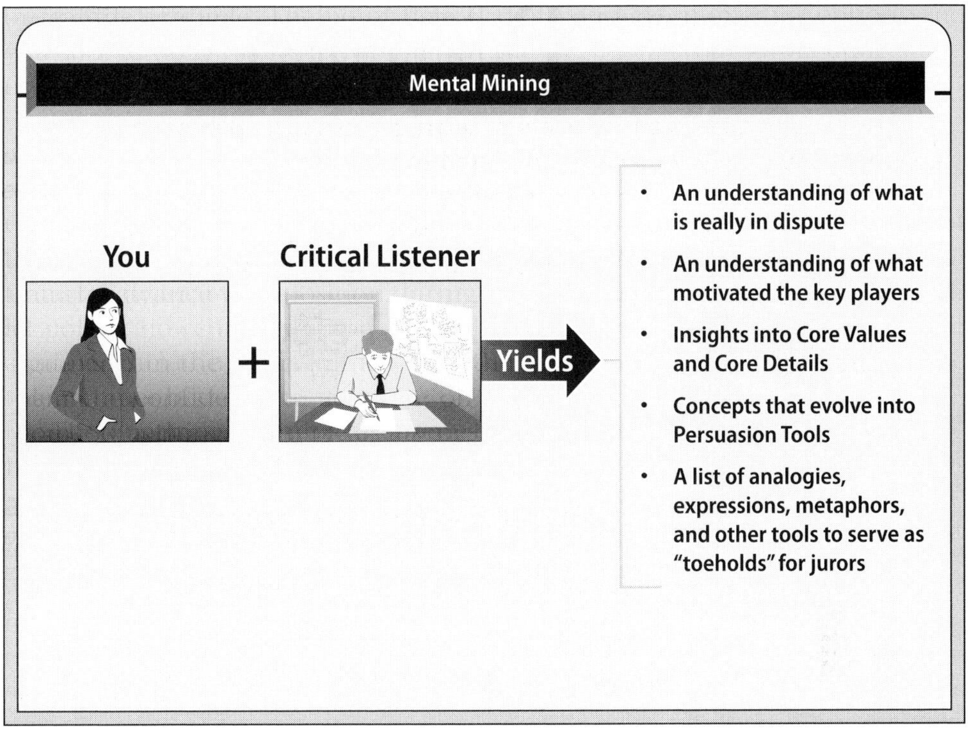

ILLUSTRATION 5-9 The Benefits of Mental Mining

Another important benefit gleaned from Mental Mining is that the lawyer often experiences what I call "The Click." The Click is that "a-ha moment" when the lawyer seems to suddenly understand what her case is really about and how she is going to try it. It is the moment when the lawyer gets her first glance at the "coherent whole" of her case.

Many people who experience The Click perceive it as something that happens spontaneously—and it often feels that way when, all of a sudden, an idea hits you that seems to have come fully formed from nowhere. Because such moments are so breathtaking, it is easy to forget that this burst of creativity is generally preceded by a fair amount of rather mundane (but absolutely essential) hard work and preparation.

These preparatory tools, the tools that "get you to" or help trigger The Click, are often the bread and butter of trial preparation.[1] They include:

- A variety of different chronologically based devices, including a carefully assembled master chronology, an action/reaction timeline, and a topical timeline
- Annotated instructions that link key elements of the law with supporting facts

1. Examples of these tools can be found in Ritter, G. Christopher, *Creating Winning Trial Strategies and Graphics,* American Bar Association, 2004.

- Motive maps that help explain why key players behaved the way they did
- Sketch maps that track the overall case and key witness testimony

While there is no single format or absolute way to conduct Mental Mining sessions, they generally proceed in five phases. (Ill. 5-10)

Mental Mining Usually Proceeds in Five Phases

Phase one:	**Prior to meeting, provide the Critical Listener with a limited amount of information.**
Phase two:	**Tell the Critical Listener the story of what happened.**
Phase three:	**Engage in a no-holds-barred discussion.**
Phase four:	**Go back and restructure the story.**
Phase five:	**Repeat phases two, three, and four.**

ILLUSTRATION 5-10 The Five Phases of Mental Mining

Phase One: You Need to Provide Your Critical Listener with a Limited Amount of Information Prior to the Mental Mining Session

The first phase begins a few days before the Mental Mining session, when the lawyer provides the Critical Listener with a limited amount of background material related to the case. The idea is not to bury the Critical Listener in documents, but to provide him with the basic facts. As a rule of thumb, the Critical Listener should be able to read and digest this written material in one hour or less. Do not burden the Critical Listener with minutia, unless there are specific details crucial to your version of the case. Provide the Critical Listener with the same kind of material that you might prepare for a settlement judge or as part of a trial brief. You want the material to summarize your position, but not be so partisan as to be unduly biased or inaccurate. By reviewing the materials and thinking about the case a few days in advance of your session, the Critical Listener will start to consciously process the materials and subconsciously assign the details to mental buckets.

Phase Two: Tell the Critical Listener What Happened in Your Case by Way of a Story

The second phase of the process involves forcing yourself (with the assistance of the Critical Listener) to explain what happened in your case in the form of a story. For some lawyers, this is not easy. Instead of telling a story, some automatically slip into a boring account of facts, told in chronological order. Others hide the story behind excessive legal mumbo jumbo. A good Critical Listener will not let this happen and will stop you and demand that you go back and explain what happened by way of a story.

While you are telling the story, your Critical Listener needs to be doing four things. He needs to pay close attention to what you are saying, both directly and indirectly; he needs to feel free to interrupt you for clarification as often as necessary; he needs to jot down any images that come to mind as he hears the story; and he needs to monitor his own thinking and note any strong feelings or associations that come to him.

Once you get involved in the Mental Mining process, you will often spontaneously begin to offer analogies, stories within the story, examples, and other verbal pictures that help explain particular parts of the case. Many lawyers are actually surprised when they start coming up with these examples, since they had not previously thought of them during their ordinary case preparation.

Generally, I think that these images are examples of the links I previously described that exist between the conscious learning of detail (which is where the lawyer has probably focused much of his earlier efforts) and the subconscious buckets that help make sense of the new information. As is often the case, these links already exist in the lawyer's subconscious, but they have never been forced to the surface for conscious examination and possible future use at trial. Again, these are examples of links between the details that the Critical Listener is hearing and the subconscious buckets with which he is making sense of this new material.

Phase Three: You and the Critical Listener Need To Engage in a No-Holds-Barred Discussion

I find the final phase of a Mental Mining session to be the most enjoyable part of the process. At this point, the Critical Listener and the attorney engage in a no-holds-barred discussion of what the case is really about, what is important, and the best possible way to explain it to the jury. During this discussion, no one holds back or self-edits and no idea or suggestion is too silly to be raised.

It is generally incumbent upon the Critical Listener to begin this discussion. When I am the Critical Listener, I typically begin by walking up to a whiteboard or flipchart with a marking pen and outlining what I think the case is about, based on the story that the lawyer has just told me. I start this process by literally saying (as much to myself as to the lawyer), "Here is what

I heard you say. . . ." Usually, this comment and the resulting list is enough to get a very spirited discussion going.

Whatever comes out of this discussion needs to be preserved for future use in some format, whether it be written notes, drawings on butcher paper, or a digital photo of a whiteboard capturing everything that was outlined.

Phase Four: You Need to Go Back and Restructure the Story

The fourth phase requires that you take what you have uncovered and retell your story. To do this, it is sometimes helpful for you to outline the story on a whiteboard or newsprint while you are (re)telling it. The point of writing the outline is threefold: (1) to incorporate the images from the prior portions of the Mental Mining session into the next version of your story, (2) to stimulate additional ideas during this phase of the exercise, (3) to capture an outline that can serve as a basis for future efforts.

During this phase, the Critical Listener needs to continue to interrupt you if matters don't make sense or if you veer toward simply reiterating the case facts and law instead of telling a story.

Phase Five: Repeat Phases Two, Three, and Four

The more times you repeat the Mental Mining process, the better your end product will be.

STEP THREE: YOU NEED TO SIMPLIFY YOUR CASE

Most trial lawyers know that the art of presenting a case lies in simplifying it enough to make it powerful, palatable, and persuasive. Lawyers are not alone in this knowledge. Writers, philosophers, and marketing professionals have long advised us to "keep it simple." As Henry David Thoreau famously noted, "Simplify, simplify." (Ill. 5-11)

Simplifying is important because it helps you find the "sweet spot" of interest for your audience—the place where comprehension and interest converge and boredom is nowhere in sight. The more time you spend on a topic, the more likely your jurors are to understand it, but also the more likely you are to bore your jurors. And once they are bored—once they have had enough of your chronology, your technical explanations, and your carefully crafted line of reasoning—they stop absorbing your information, they fail to understand your arguments, and they are not very likely to become Active Jurors who will advocate for your position in the jury room.

Merely stopping or quickly wrapping up your case as soon as you see boredom set in is not an effective way to simplify. Such a strategy gives short shrift to the important (even crucial) information that you have yet to present. In short, if you find yourself facing twelve bored people in a jury box, you have missed a valuable opportunity to continue teaching your case to your jurors.

ILLUSTRATION 5-11 Forcing Thoreau to Follow His Own Advice
I recently saw a wonderful piece of graffiti.

Knowing you have to simplify your case is usually not the problem for most lawyers. The difficulty lies in figuring out which of four methods of simplification will work best for you.

When I tell clients that there are at least four different ways to simplify, some of them are perplexed. Most believe that there is only one way; they think of "simplifying" an argument as "subtracting" elements—i.e., taking out the information that masks, convolutes, or otherwise distracts from the main thesis. Simplification by subtraction is certainly the most common technique, but it is not the only one. There are at least three other significant ways to simplify: simplification by addition, simplification by division, and simplification by multiplication.

While simplification by subtraction is the most common way to simplify a message, it is often harder to implement than you might think. It is in our nature to get attached to our favorite facts and ideas—particularly those that took a long time to collect and develop or those you think of as especially inspired. This attachment sometimes makes it difficult for a lawyer to give up or discard such material, so he holds on to it, like the old ratty security blanket toted around far beyond childhood.

The other factor that makes it difficult to subtract material is that it often takes considerable courage and confidence to do so. Just as the traditional marriage vow requires that you "forsake all others," simplification by subtraction requires that you forsake all material that does not support your central Case Theory or is not consistent with your Case Themes.

As I often tell my clients, you need "to pass up the good for the great." In other words, if you want people to focus on your great facts and ideas, you need to eliminate some good (but perhaps extraneous) facts and ideas from your presentation. Too much material confuses the jurors and buries the crucially important facts that you want your jury to retain and use during their deliberations.

Most people simplify the same way that I do my spring cleaning. I start with a mound of stuff that I cannot decide what to do with and, item by item, I decide what I want to donate to charity and what I need to keep. Unfortunately, at the end of this process I have very few things in the donation box and a huge pile of things I "need" to save.

My problem is that I have adopted the wrong perspective. Instead of asking myself what I should get rid of, I should be asking myself what I should keep. In other words, unless I consciously decide to discard something, that item will most likely remain in the pile in the middle of my room. But if I approach my mound of stuff from the other angle, that is, by asking myself what items I should *keep,* my process automatically defaults to throwing everything away unless I make a deliberate exception. A good way to start this process with your case material is to consult your jury instructions and make a list of the minimum points you need to prove in order to establish your claim or defense. Once you have this information, determine how to make your prima facie case with as few witnesses and exhibits as possible. Then, add only those facts that help capture or keep the jurors' interest, help the jury understand your case, or provide you with the material you will need for your closing argument.

About eighty percent of the simplifying we do is accomplished via subtraction. But there are other ways to simplify, too, including *adding* information. To some people, adding information in order to simplify seems counterintuitive, but it does makes sense. Think of your worst, most nightmarish expert testimony—the one in which the expert begins talking about the Governmental Accounting Standards Board and ends on the not-so-high note of a description of post-employment retirement benefits in school districts. Such trial presentations often drive jurors to boredom not because there is too *much* information, but because there is too *little* information. Such testimony is better received and made easier to understand (which is the essence of simplicity) when information has been added that might, for example, help put the expert opinions in a real-world context or explain certain underlying basic concepts. In those instances, additions actually serve to simplify by increasing understanding and, thereby, eliminating confusion.

Sometimes, expert testimony gets so complicated, so fast, that the "Yikes!" alarm goes off in the jurors' heads and they are compelled to cover their ears, lest they become completely overwhelmed. The "Yikes!" alarm sounds when jurors think, "Yikes! There is no way I can understand this stuff!" Make no mistake: the "Yikes!" alarm signals danger, because once the jurors tune out, they are no longer thinking about you, your witness, or your case. They are more likely to be counting the hours until lunch. This type of scenario is the perfect place to use the third form of simplification—simplification by division.

Simplifying by division uses the strategy of "divide and conquer" and is implemented in three steps. First, you break that big chunk of technical material into small, easily digestible units. Next, you keep only those units that are needed to make your point. Finally, you figure out how best to present this reduced number of small units to the jury.

Conversely, sometimes the best way to simplify large numbers is to use simplification by multiplication. That is, starting with small units and then extrapolating to large numbers.

In one of our cases, 3,000 plaintiffs were seeking $90 million for unpaid overtime they had earned over the course of four years. Ninety million dollars is a lot of money—so much so that during mock jury trials, the jurors balked at awarding such a large amount, despite the large number of plaintiffs.

In our first attempt to persuade the jurors, we used simplification by division. We started with $90 million, divided that amount by the number of class members, and then divided that quotient by four years, to show that the average amount per year per plaintiff totaled $7,500. But even with that breakdown, the mock jurors still felt that $90 million was too much to award.

So we decided to take the opposite approach. Rather than starting with the big number and dividing it up into smaller, more palatable numbers, we had one plaintiff tell the jurors her story: how she routinely worked sixty to seventy hours per week, but was only paid for forty hours of work; how she even had to work—without pay—on the morning of her wedding day.

We then presented a handful of other plaintiffs, each of whom had equally poignant stories of the egregious employment conditions they suffered. In the wake of this testimony, the jury had no problem understanding why each plaintiff was entitled to $7,500 per year for four years—even though that dollar amount, multiplied by the number of class defendants, reached the $90 million figure we sought. In the end, the judge and jury awarded them $210 million in damages, attorneys' fees, costs, and interest.

You need to try more than one approach to simplifying your material. That's because the more that trial lawyers understand a case, the harder it is to remember how complicated the material is for lay people hearing it for the first time. Having several simplification tools in your toolbox gives you a range of options for reaching your goal. If you can simplify by cutting back, do it. If you decide your jurors need more information, give it to them. Break it down. Extrapolate. Do whatever you need to do. The process of simplifying will help both you *and* your audience understand your case more fully.

STEP FOUR: YOU NEED TO SHAPE YOUR CASE USING INFORMATION ARCHITECTURE

While it is often difficult to form a well-structured argument, it is easy to spot one: The argument is structured in a logical order; similar topics are linked;

dissimilar ones are not forced together; an appropriate amount of time and space is allocated to what really matters. Such arguments are an intellectual delight.

Some people, known as information architects, make their livings by *explaining how to explain* in a way that is accurate, simple, and persuasive. They have developed certain principles that lawyers should be aware of before they attempt to persuade, whether it be in a brief or at trial.

At trial, two of the scarcest resources are time and space. Jurors will give you only so much time before they start ignoring you, and the judge will order you to move on to the next subject if she thinks you have spent too much time on it. Space is scarce because, at least with respect to visual Persuasion Tools, you can include only a limited amount of information before the graphics become unusable.

Because time and space are such precious commodities at trial, you want to make sure that you allocate these resources appropriately. Consistent with this, I have developed three rules, which I call the Three Rules of Time and Space. (Ill. 5-12)

The Three Rules of Time and Space

The First Rule:	**Not all information is of equal value; pass up the good for the great.**
The Second Rule:	**Allocate time and space in direct proportion to the value of the information.**
The Third Rule:	**Allocate the time and space necessary to make the points that matter.**

ILLUSTRATION 5-12 The Three Rules of Time and Space

The First Rule of Time and Space: Not All Information Is of Equal Value; Do Not Hesitate to Pass Up the Good for the Great

Some bits of information carry more weight than others. Some will, as we described above, go directly to Core Details—details that the average person needs resolved in order to comfortably make an important decision. Other bits of information will be nothing more than fluff. Be willing to pass up any number of good facts in favor of the great facts.

The Second Rule of Time and Space: Allocate Time and Space In Direct Proportion to the Value of the Information

Because time and space are scarce, you must be careful how you use them. As a general rule, there should be a direct relationship between the value of the information and how much time and space you are willing to allocate to it. Do not bother wasting time and space on information that is of only marginal value.

The Third Rule of Time and Space: For the Most Important Matters, When Important Information Requires It, Never Be Afraid to Allocate the Time and Space Necessary to Make Your Point

For those issues that really matter, do not hesitate to allocate the time and space necessary to make your point. Carefully determine what your most important points are, and then use as much time and space as you reasonably need to present them effectively.

STEP FIVE: AFTER YOU COMPLETE THE FIRST FOUR STEPS (AND *ONLY* AFTER YOU HAVE COMPLETED THE FIRST FOUR STEPS), CHOOSE THE RIGHT TECHNOLOGY TO PRESENT YOUR PERSUASION TOOLS

There is an old story that comedians made popular in New York City's Yiddish theaters back around 1900. Like so many jokes in that venue and of that era, the absurdity of the narrative subtly illustrated one of life's most important lessons.

It seems there once was a man who had wanted to buy a custom-made suit his entire life. After years of scrimping, he finally saved enough money and he went to see a tailor. The man carefully explained to the tailor exactly what kind of custom-made suit he wanted. He described what the buttons should look like, the kind of pleats he wanted in the trousers, how much cuff should be created—all of the details of his ideal suit.

Throughout this description, the tailor, who had been reading the newspaper when his customer walked in, never even bothered to look up. When the man had finished his description, the tailor, still reading the newspaper, reached over to a rack of what appeared to be twenty identical black suits, randomly grabbed one, and said to the man, "Here is your custom-made suit. That'll be $2,000."

"Wait a minute," said the shocked customer. "Don't you have to at least measure me or something?" "No," said the tailor, still reading his paper. "Trust me! I have been doing this for forty years. Just put on the suit. You will see."

The man went into the dressing room and tried on the suit. Not surprisingly, he looked terrible in it. There was way too much room in the backside, yet he could barely button the pants at the waist. And the coat? Don't even get me started about the coat! It looked like something that someone twice his size would wear. The right sleeve was too short; the left one was too long.

"This suit looks terrible!" said the man.

The tailor looked up from his newspaper just long enough to say, "The problem is not the suit, it's the way you're wearing it. Twist your body to the left, pull your right arm up a bit, hunch your back over, throw your hips out." The man did just as he was told, distorting his body every which way in order to accommodate the suit. And, guess what? After going through the painful contortions, the suit looked great. So the man bought the suit and, still wearing it, he hobbled—as best he could—out of the shop.

A few blocks down the street, the man saw two good-looking women. Naturally, he wanted to impress them, so he remembered what the tailor had said and he twisted his body to the left, pulled up his right arm a bit, hunched over, and threw out his hips. As the two women walked by, the first whispered, "Oh that poor man! What do you think happened to him?" "Beats me," said the second woman. "But what a nice suit!"

Many lawyers laugh at this story of the unfortunate man without realizing that they are potentially putting themselves in similar positions each time they choose and use technology during trial. That is, these same lawyers twist and otherwise distort the way they present their case in order to make it fit a particular form of high-end technology—regardless of whether that technology is right for the point they are making, the case they are trying, or their personal style.

You can begin to choose and use technology more efficiently in the courtroom if you follow six basic rules. (Ill. 5-13)

Rule One: There Are Two Kinds of Technology

The phrase "courtroom technology" is enough to scare some trial lawyers. Often, these fears are based on the belief that "courtroom technology" is something new and entirely unfamiliar, something that involves computers and screens and projectors and, well, *disks* of some kind or another.

In fact, technology existed long before computers and there are many kinds of technology, other than computers, that can be used in the courtroom. As a rule of thumb, I divide courtroom technology into two categories similar to what you find in the rock and roll world: acoustic and electric.

Acoustic (or non-electric) technology includes blackboards, newsprint, enlargements, exhibit boards, and models—tried-and-true technology that lawyers have used for generations and that can *still* be used to great effect in the courtroom. Electric technology includes overhead projectors, computers, videotapes, animations, and Flash—newer, slicker technology that can be powerful for certain kinds of presentations.

Often, just knowing that not all technology plugs into a socket can eliminate considerable anxiety. (Think of the Molière character who, upon learning the definition of "prose," declares with great relief and with some pride, "For more than forty years I have been speaking prose without knowing it.")

The Six Basic Rules for Successfully Using Technology

Rule One:	**Remember, there are two kinds of technology: electric and acoustic.**
Rule Two:	**Understand that more technology is not necessarily better technology.**
Rule Three:	**Never let the media drive the message.**
Rule Four:	**Choose your technology with care, always considering:** **• Case-specific requirements, including number of exhibits, budget, and judge's preferences** **• The impression you want to make with the jury** **• How many of the graphics need to be displayed at any one time** **• Your personal preference and style**
Rule Five:	**Mix your media—but in a meaningful way.**
Rule Six:	**Practice, practice, practice.**

ILLUSTRATION 5-13 The Six Basic Rules for Using Technology in the Courtroom

Rule Two: More Technology Is Not Necessarily Better Technology

After twenty-five years in the courtroom, I now know that a flipchart presentation can be just as good as—if not better than—a fancy trial graphic. I also know that few lawyers understand this fact. There is a common misperception that the more high-tech your trial technology, the better and more persuasive it will be. I am not sure where this belief came from, except perhaps from the general societal belief that bigger, faster, flashier, and more expensive is always better.

This myth is simply untrue. It is also dangerous, especially for two kinds of lawyers. The first kind are lawyers with unlimited budgets. Such attorneys sometimes think that they can rely on technology to cover their lack of preparation. The second kind are lawyers who, conversely, have no money to pay for expensive trial tools. These lawyers sometimes skip over the process of thinking graphically because they assume they cannot afford to create or present any material to the jury.

Both groups are wrong.

Expensive technology rarely covers for lack of preparation. If anything, it tends to make the lack of preparation even more obvious and less excusable. Likewise, avoiding trial graphics and demonstratives altogether (because you think you cannot afford the necessary technology) completely ignores the fact that some of the most effective trial techniques require nothing more than an old-fashioned blackboard and a piece of chalk.

Let me give you a real-world example of this. We worked as part of the defense team in the rape case against Kobe Bryant. Before the charges were eventually dismissed, one of the most effective graphics we developed for the case was a sketch that Mr. Bryant's lawyer would draw on a blackboard during opening statement. Not only was the information to be illustrated highly persuasive, but when attorneys draw on blackboards, they take on the demeanor of a schoolteacher, which is appealing. A blackboard presentation also tends to capture jurors' interest—after all, most humans like to watch things being created. Blackboards, like newsprint and dry erase boards, allow attorneys to spontaneously change or enhance their graphic, according to what the witness is saying.

If a witness gets confused while on the stand, for instance, the attorney can quickly create a sketch to get both the witness and the jury back on track (e.g., "So you're saying you saw the defendant turn left—which would be west—on 23rd Street, right?" or "This gets confusing, doesn't it? Let's make a quick timeline of which e-mail messages came from whom on which date.").

Rule Three: Don't Let the Media Drive the Message

Despite what Marshall McLuhan once professed, the medium is not the message. Nor is the message the media. The message is *what* you show the jurors and it consists of two elements: (1) the content of what you want the jurors to remember in your case, and (2) the design (including the layout and format) that best conveys that content. (Ill. 5-14)

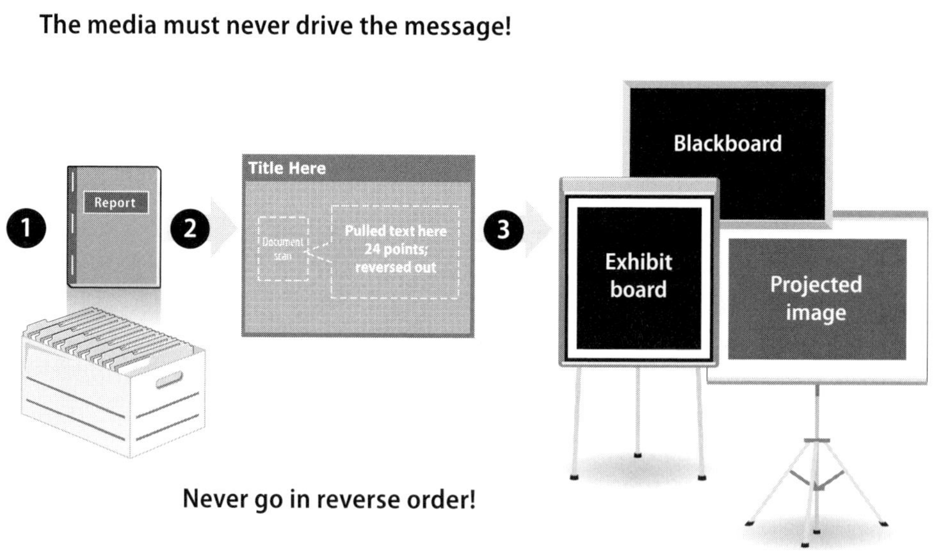

ILLUSTRATION 5-14 Never Let the Media Drive the Message
You must always move through the three-step process in the following order: (1) determine the message, (2) design the format for your message, (3) then, and only then, choose the media that best conveys your message.

The media is the *how* in the technology equation; it is simply the delivery system through which you channel your message. Of the two, the message is always more important than the media, which means you should never use a particular technology for your presentation just because you can. Said slightly differently, "The media should never drive the message."

Of course, keeping trial attorneys away from computerized graphics can be a lot like keeping teenagers away from instant messaging—you can practically hear the choruses of "But everybody's doing it!" The easiest way to avoid making decisions based on this reasoning is to follow a basic three-step, *unidirectional* process for creating demonstrative material.

First Step: Determine the Message

Figure out what you are saying; know what you want the jury to take away. Make sure that your message is consistent with the overall theme of your case. Any message that is inconsistent with your overall theme is unnecessary clutter. (No technology, no matter how impressive, will change this basic fact!)

Second Step: Design the Format for Your Message

"Format" is not technology. "Format" is simply the form your message will take. Will the material work well as an enlargement of the primary source material? Would an excerpt from the deposition work better? Would a checklist be the best way to explain this complex information? Or would a model—or even an animation—be most effective?

Final Step: Choose the Media That Best Conveys Your Message

Only *after* you have determined both the message and the format can you decide what media or technology will work best. For example, if you have decided that a graphic is appropriate, you may want to draw it on a blackboard. You may want to display it on an overhead projector. You may decide that a flipchart with overlays works best, or, conversely, that a magnetic board with removable pieces illustrates your point most clearly. Or, yes, you may want a chart projected on-screen with hyperlinks to PDFs that contain enlargements of important evidence. The point is that there are many, many different ways to create a format that will convey the message you are trying to communicate.

Again, this is a unidirectional process. Following these steps will help you resist the urge to use certain technology just because your firm invested in it or because the winning attorney at your last trial had the bigger trial graphic toys. A crummy graphic does not get better by displaying it using expensive technology; it just becomes a more expensive crummy graphic.

Rule Four: Choose Your Technology With Care

How do you decide which technology is right for your case? I generally consider four broad variables. The first is what I call "case-specific requirements," which include such factors as the number of documents needed at trial, the number of exhibits, the case budget, the courtroom limitations (e.g., Is there a screen? Is there room for a few easels?), and the judge's preferences or limitations (e.g., May lawyers move around the courtroom? Or does the judge insist that lawyers remain at the podium?).

The second consideration is the *impression* you want to make with the jury. As I noted above, some kinds of graphics are more effective when it looks like the lawyer (or witness) is spontaneously creating them during testimony. These graphics carry a certain sense of immediacy that does not exist in a highly coordinated, prepared package.

The third criteria to consider is *quantity:* that is, how many of the graphics need to be displayed at any one time. Certain graphics naturally complement each other, particularly if they are shown simultaneously. For example, I often recommend that a lawyer point to a timeline on a board while a document related to that timeline is displayed electronically.

The final consideration is the *personal preference and style* of the trial lawyer. A traditionalist may be most comfortable (and effective) using a blackboard or dry erase board; a tech-savvy lawyer may be perfectly at ease navigating a Flash platform loaded with animations. What matters is that the chosen medium is a good match for that particular attorney.

Rule Five: Mix Your Media—But in a Meaningful Way

We once had a client who insisted that every demonstrative be printed as an exhibit board. At trial, he ended up with approximately sixty boards. Such monothematic treatment of demonstratives dilutes your message and becomes tedious to your jurors. When you display a graphic on a board (or on a PowerPoint slide or as an animation), you want your jurors to instinctively understand that you are about to make an important point. You want them to sit up and pay attention. If you overuse a medium by putting everything—the important facts and the not-so-important facts—on exhibit boards, for example, your jurors are more likely to feel a sense of dread rather than anticipation.

To keep the jurors interested—and to be sure you are using the right technology for the right information—mix up your use of media. Display some of your graphics electronically, write some on a blackboard or flipchart, and put some on exhibit boards. When done properly, this mixture not only keeps things interesting, it also encourages you to be more creative in the way you explain key facts.

Rule Six: Practice, Practice, Practice

It is amazing how even the simplest presentations can go awry if you do not rehearse them before trial. We were once involved in a case in which opposing counsel decided to use an overhead projector, with very little forethought into his presentation. To his credit, he had a colleague run the equipment while he delivered his closing argument, but he neglected to actually coordinate his presentation with the images projected by the assisting colleague. As a result, while the lawyer talked about one topic, the assistant displayed something completely unrelated. This was, understandably, very confusing for the jurors.

The real low point of the attorney's presentation occurred when he forgot that the overhead projector could display only acetate versions of the docu-ment. He handed his assistant a paper copy and insisted she put the image on the screen. The assistant knew that the image on the paper would not appear on the display screen, but she was so flustered by the lawyer's insistence that she laid the paper on the overhead projector anyway. Of course, the result was a completely blank screen.

To make matters worse, the attorney repeatedly pointed to the document and discussed its content as if there were an image that the jury could see. Finally, the stalwart assistant decided she had to do something, so she bravely took the 8½ by 11 inch document, and, holding it in front of her, approached the jury box and stuck the paper within inches of the jurors' noses. This prompted the judge to interrupt the closing and order the assistant to step away. Needless to say, the net result was a complete and total disaster—especially because the bumbling lawyer's client went on to lose over $200 million.

If this can happen with an overhead projector, imagine what could go wrong with more high-tech equipment! That is why practice is so important. A good presentation needs to run smoothly without any glitches so that the jurors can focus on your message, not on your technology.

In the end, of course, the trial lawyer's primary objective is to persuade. Technology can help, but it can never replace the critical process of uncovering the key points of a case and then carefully structuring—and communicating—them in a way that convinces the jury that your client's position is the correct one. As such, technology should be tailored to your case, rather than being a one-size-fits-all solution to your presentation. One of the worst things that can happen is for your jurors to be more focused on the technology you're using (and the way that you twist, turn, and shorten your evidence to fit that technology) than on who you are, who your client is, and what your case is really about.

Index

Note: Page numbers followed by the letter "i" indicate references to illustrations; page numbers followed by the letter "n" indicate references to footnotes.

D

E